[guns_&_]
[swords_]

CABLE BY GERRY DUGGAN VOL. 2. Contains material originally published in magazine form as CABLE (2020) #7-12. First printing 2021. ISBN 978-1-302-92179-8. Published by MARVEL WORLDWIDE, INC., a subsidiary of MARVEL ENTERTAINMENT, LLC. OFFICE OF PUBLICATION: 1290 Avenue of the Americas, New York, NY 10104. © 2021 MARVEL No similarity between any of the names, characters, persons, and/or institutions in this magazine with those of any living or dead person or institution is intended, and any such similarity which may exist is purely coincidental. **Printed in Canada.** KEVIN FEIGE, Chief Creative Officer; DAN BUCKLEY, President, Marvel Entertainment; JOE QUESADA, EVP & Creative Director; DAVID BOGART, Associate Publisher & SVP of Talent Affairs; TOM BREVOORT, VP, Executive Editor; NICK LOWE, Executive Editor, VP of Content, Digital Publishing; DAVID GABRIEL, VP of Print & Digital Publishing; JEFF YOUNGQUIST, VP of Production & Special Projects; ALEX MORALES, Director of Publishing Operations; DAN EDINGTON, Managing Editor; RICKEY PURDIN, Director of Talent Relations; JENNIFER GRÜNWALD, Senior Editor, Special Projects; SUSAN CRESPI, Production Manager; STAN LEE, Chairman Emeritus. For information regarding advertising in Marvel Comics or on Marvel.com, please contact Vit DeBellis, Custom Solutions & Integrated Advertising Manager, at vdebellis@marvel.com. For Marvel subscription inquiries, please call 888-511-5480. **Manufactured between 8/6/2021 and 9/7/2021 by SOLISCO PRINTERS, SCOTT, QC, CANADA.**

10 9 8 7 6 5 4 3 2 1

CABLE

Writer:	Gerry Duggan
Artist:	Phil Noto
Letterer:	VC's Joe Sabino
Cover Art:	Phil Noto

Head of X:	Jonathan Hickman
Design:	Tom Muller
Assistant Editors:	Annalise Bissa
Editor:	Jordan D. White

Collection Editor:	Jennifer Grünwald
Assistant Editor:	Daniel Kirchhoffer
Assistant Managing Editor:	Maia Loy
Assistant Managing Editor:	Lisa Montalbano
VP Production & Special Projects:	Jeff Youngquist
SVP Print, Sales & Marketing:	David Gabriel
Editor in Chief:	C.B. Cebulski

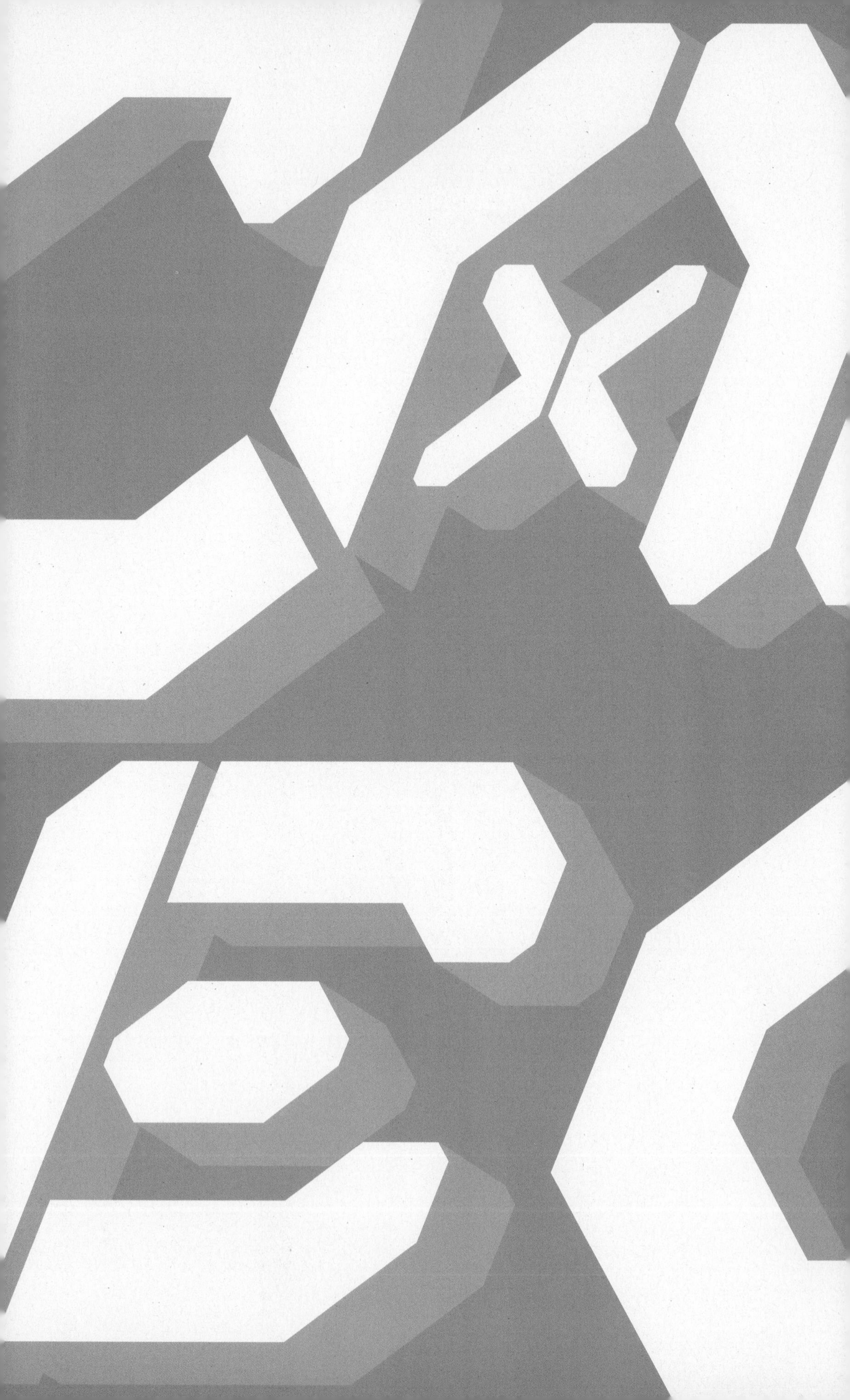

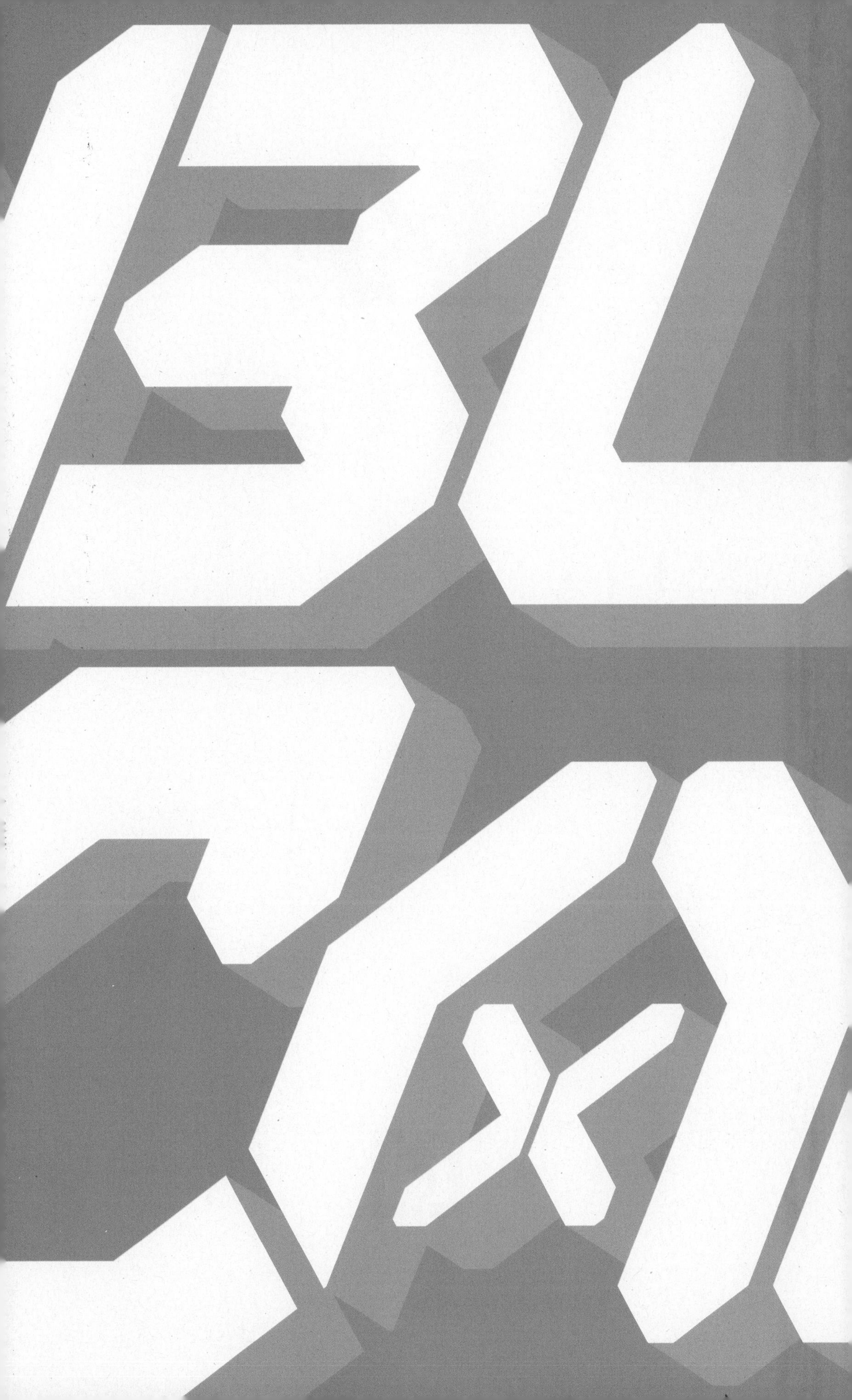

⌜[ca__[0.7]
[ble_[0.7]

It's tough when the past that comes back to haunt you hasn't happened yet.

-- CABLE

⌜[ca__[0.X]
[ble_[0.X]

[ca__[0.7].....]
[ble_[0.7].....]

[Cable_alpha.]

Grasscutter and Godkiller wait on Krakoa for their fallen master.

Some friends gathered to watch the sunset and remember Gorgon...

...but I have to go to work.

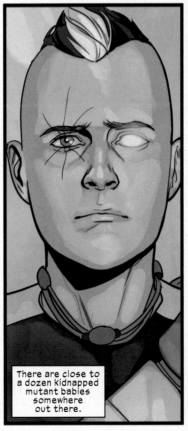

There are close to a dozen kidnapped mutant babies somewhere out there.

I won't fail them.

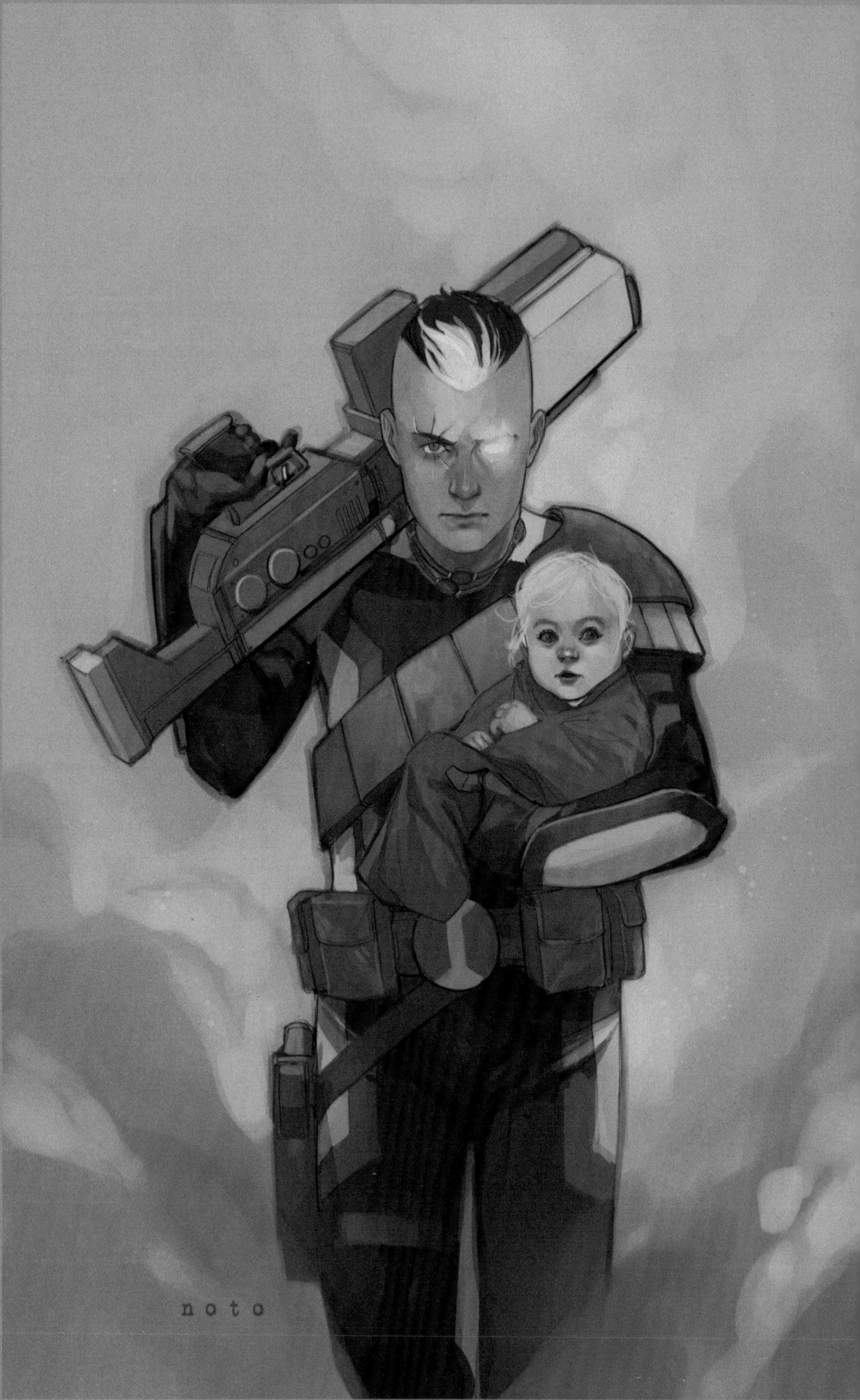
noto

Gritty Days in the City
of Brotherly Love

7

FINISH THE JOB

Following a near-fatal tournament in Otherworld, CABLE is back to right the wrongs of his own world: rescuing kidnapped mutant babies from the Order of X.

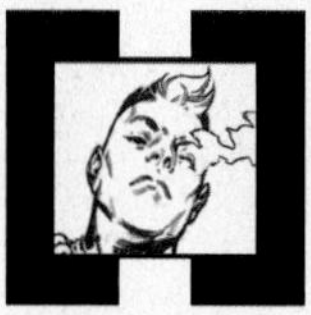
Cable

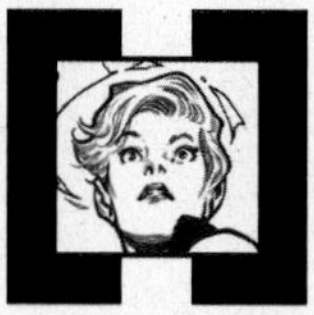
Rachel Summers

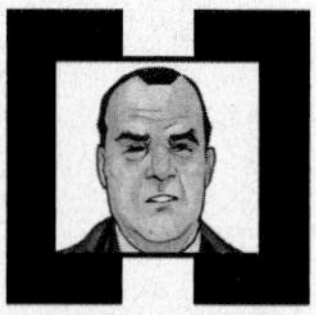
Detective DiStefano

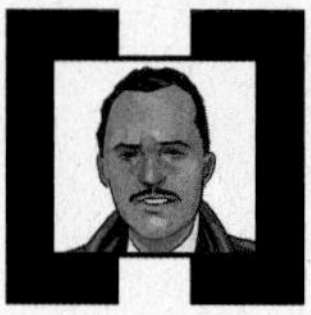
Detective Molina

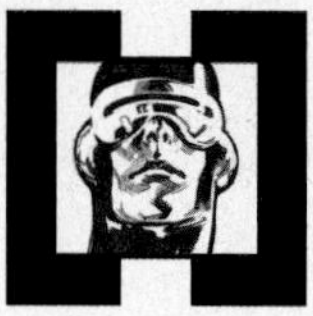
Cyclops

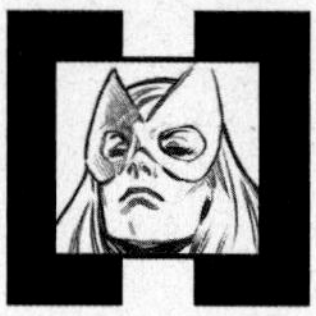
Jean Grey

*Chapters 5-6 can be found in X OF SWORDS.

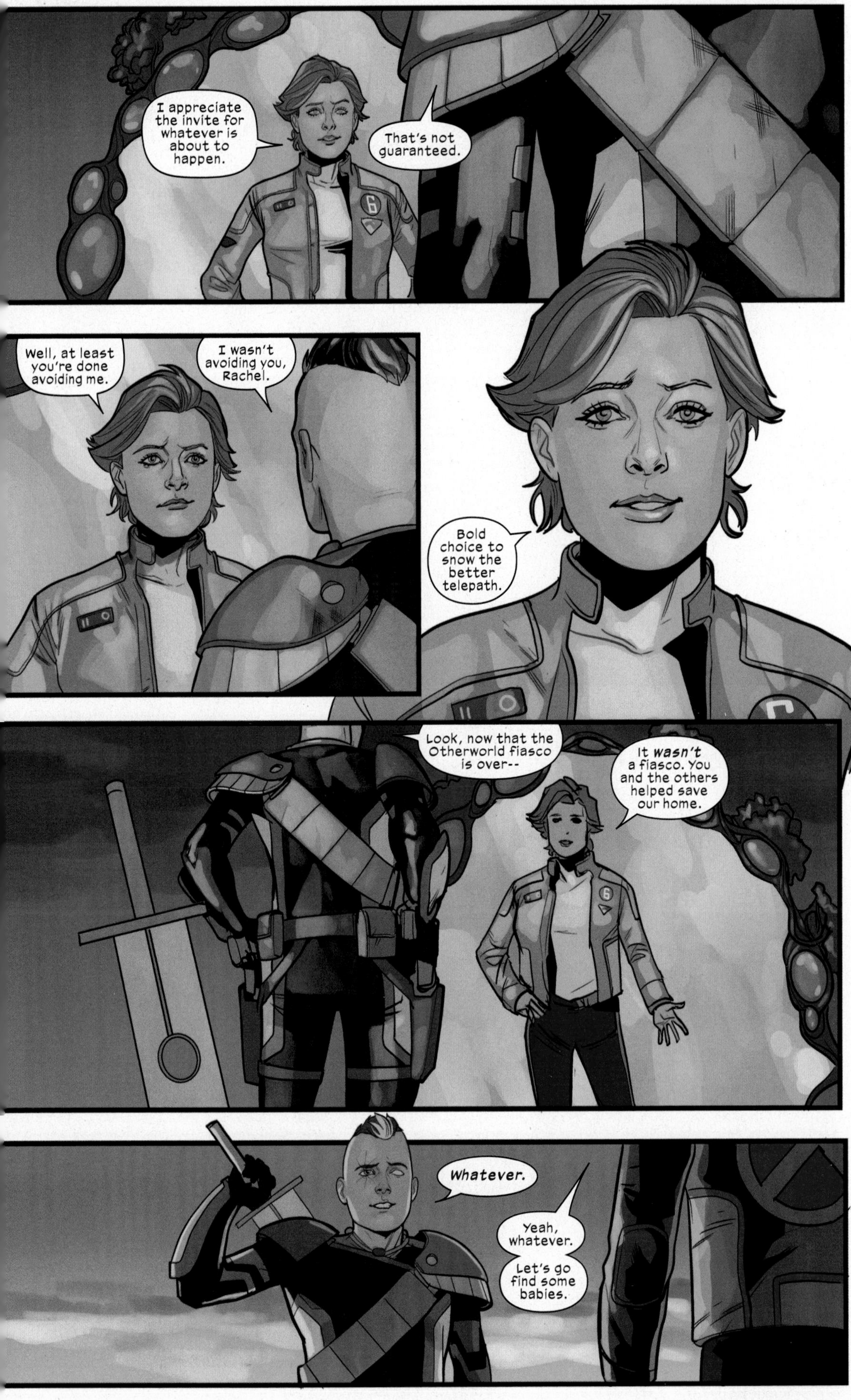

I appreciate the invite for whatever is about to happen.
That's not guaranteed.
Well, at least you're done avoiding me.
I wasn't avoiding you, Rachel.
Bold choice to snow the better telepath.
Look, now that the Otherworld fiasco is over--
It *wasn't* a fiasco. You and the others helped save our home.
Whatever.
Yeah, whatever.
Let's go find some babies.

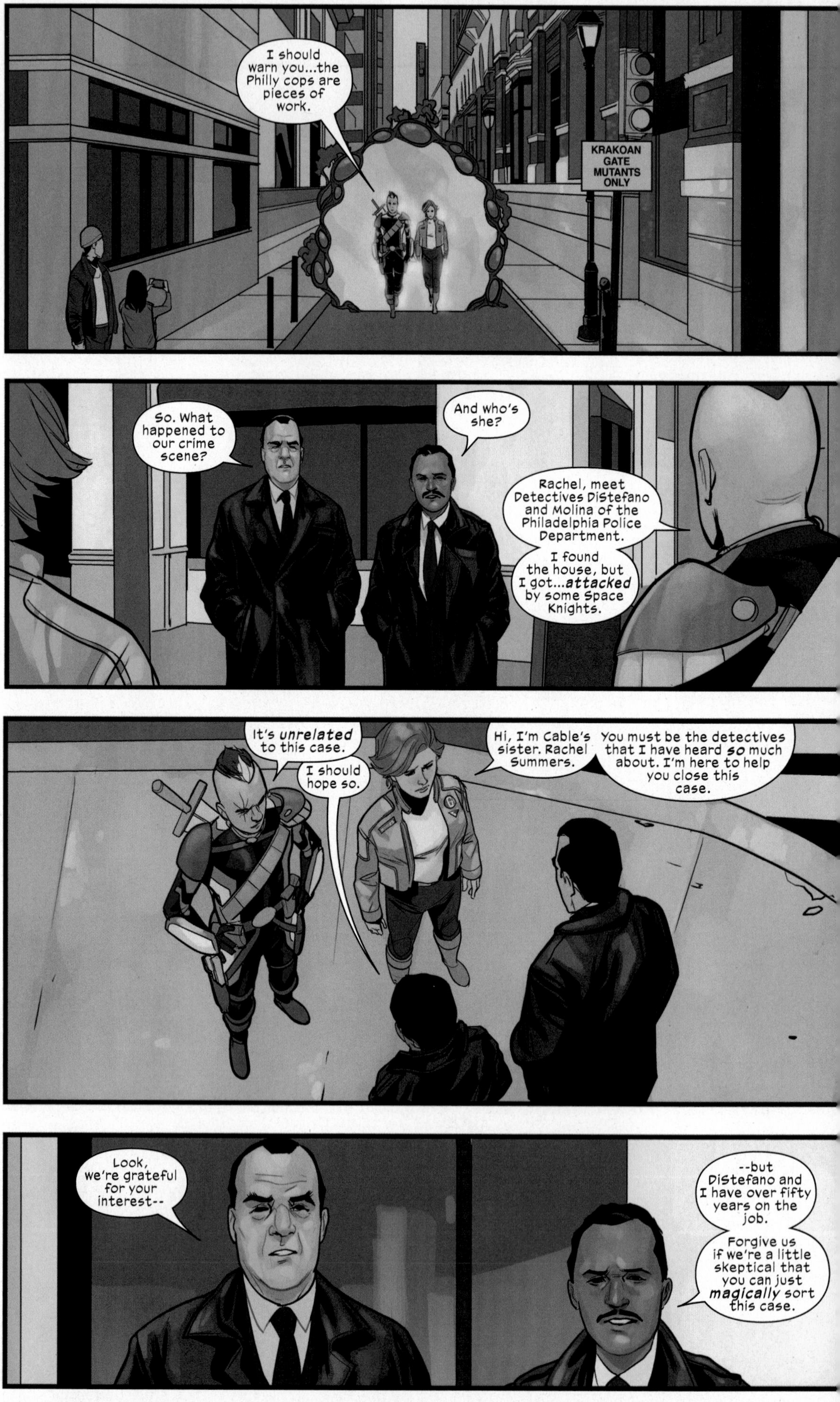
I should warn you...the Philly cops are pieces of work.
KRAKOAN GATE MUTANTS ONLY
So. What happened to our crime scene?
And who's she?
Rachel, meet Detectives DiStefano and Molina of the Philadelphia Police Department.
I found the house, but I got...*attacked* by some Space Knights.
It's *unrelated* to this case.
I should hope so.
Hi, I'm Cable's sister. Rachel Summers.
You must be the detectives that I have heard *so* much about. I'm here to help you close this case.
Look, we're grateful for your interest--
--but DiStefano and I have over fifty years on the job.
Forgive us if we're a little skeptical that you can just *magically* sort this case.

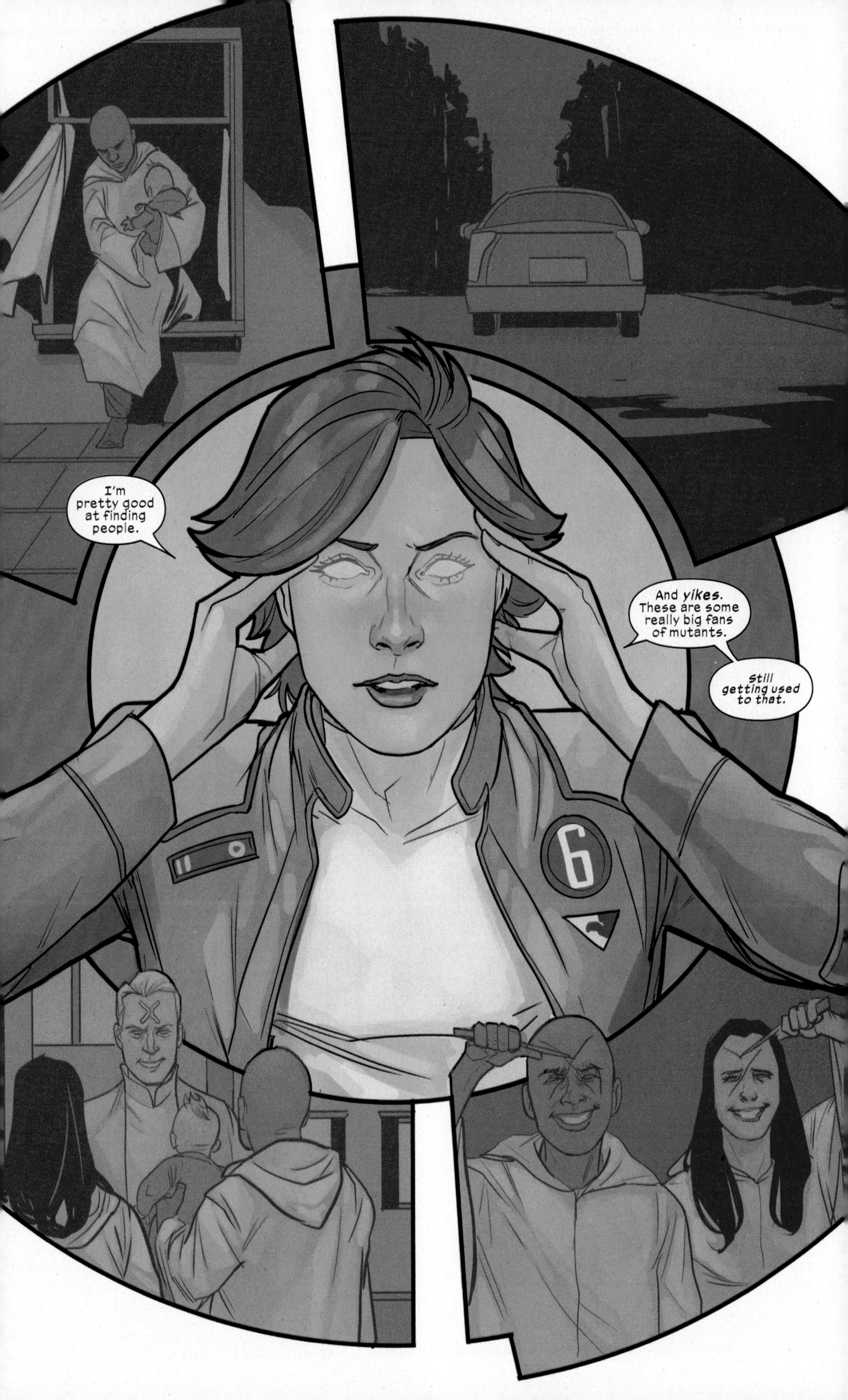
I'm pretty good at finding people.
And *yikes*. These are some really big fans of mutants.
Still getting used to that.

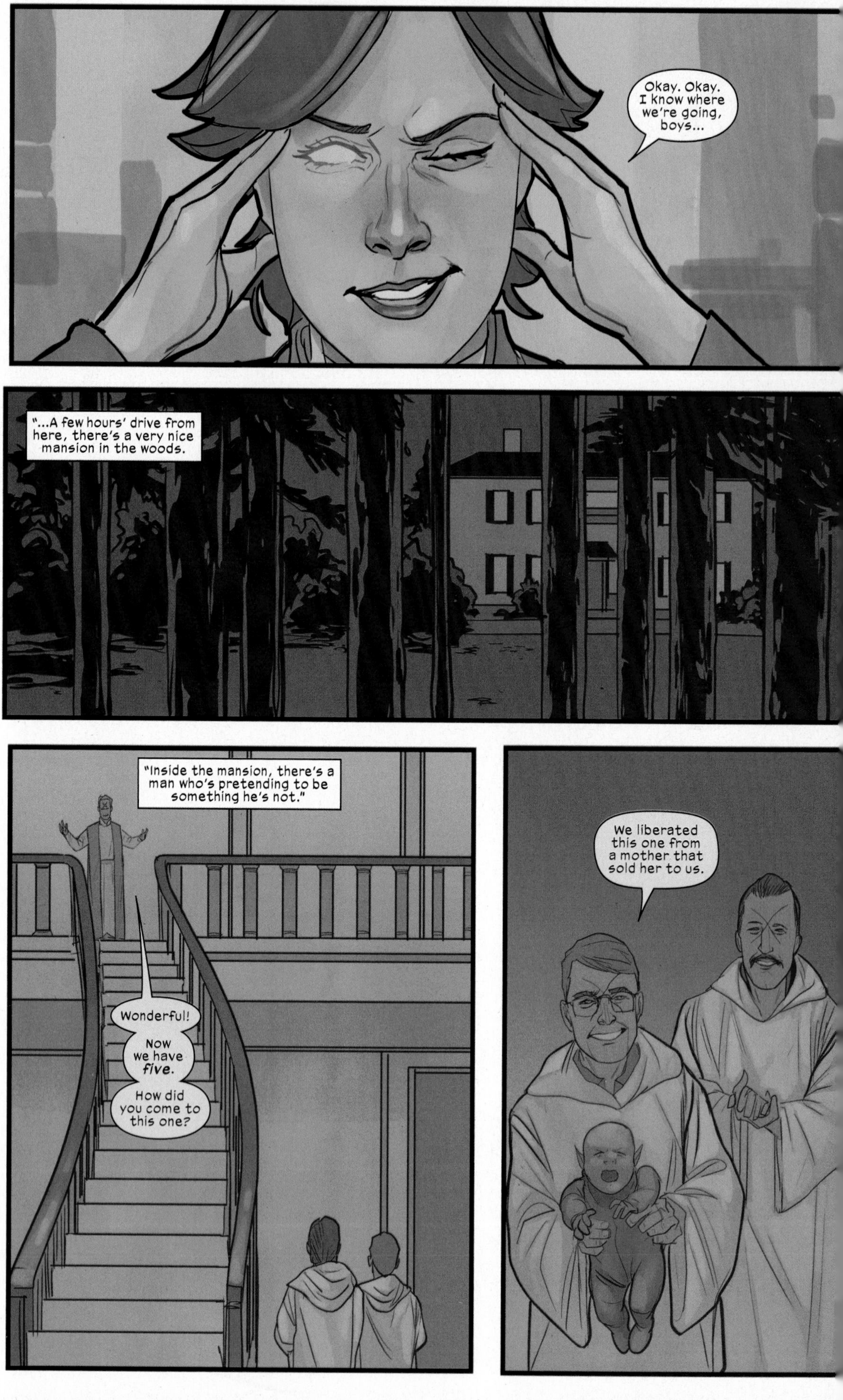
Okay. Okay. I know where we're going, boys...
"...A few hours' drive from here, there's a very nice mansion in the woods.
"Inside the mansion, there's a man who's pretending to be something he's not."
Wonderful!
Now we have *five*.
How did you come to this one?
We liberated this one from a mother that sold her to us.

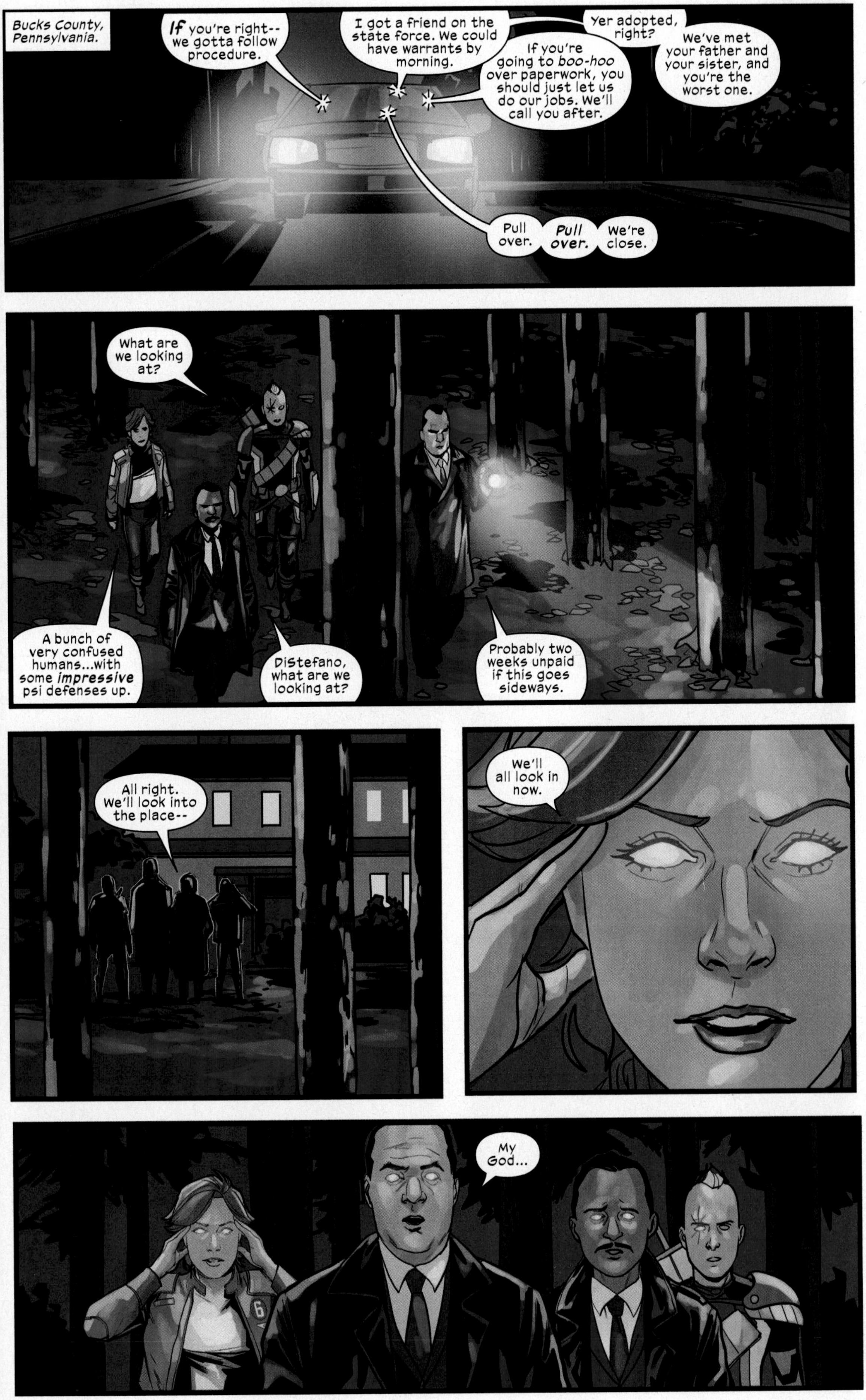
Bucks County, Pennsylvania.
If you're right-- we gotta follow procedure.
I got a friend on the state force. We could have warrants by morning.
Yer adopted, right?
We've met your father and your sister, and you're the worst one.
If you're going to boo-hoo over paperwork, you should just let us do our jobs. We'll call you after.
Pull over.
Pull over.
We're close.
What are we looking at?
A bunch of very confused humans...with some impressive psi defenses up.
Distefano, what are we looking at?
Probably two weeks unpaid if this goes sideways.
All right. We'll look into the place--
We'll all look in now.
My God...

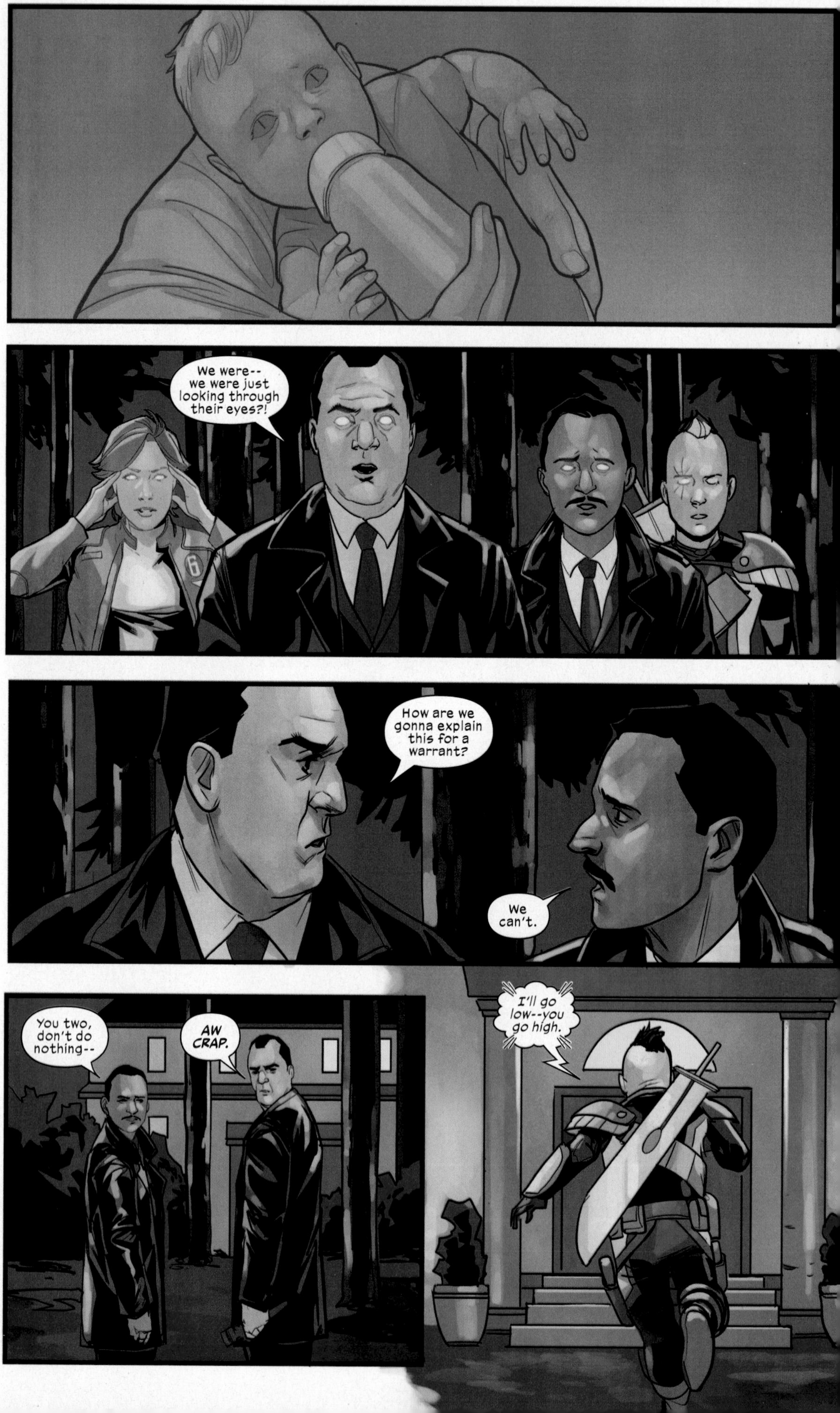
We were--
we were just looking through their eyes?!
How are we gonna explain this for a warrant?
We can't.
You two, don't do nothing--
AW CRAP.
I'll go low--you go high.

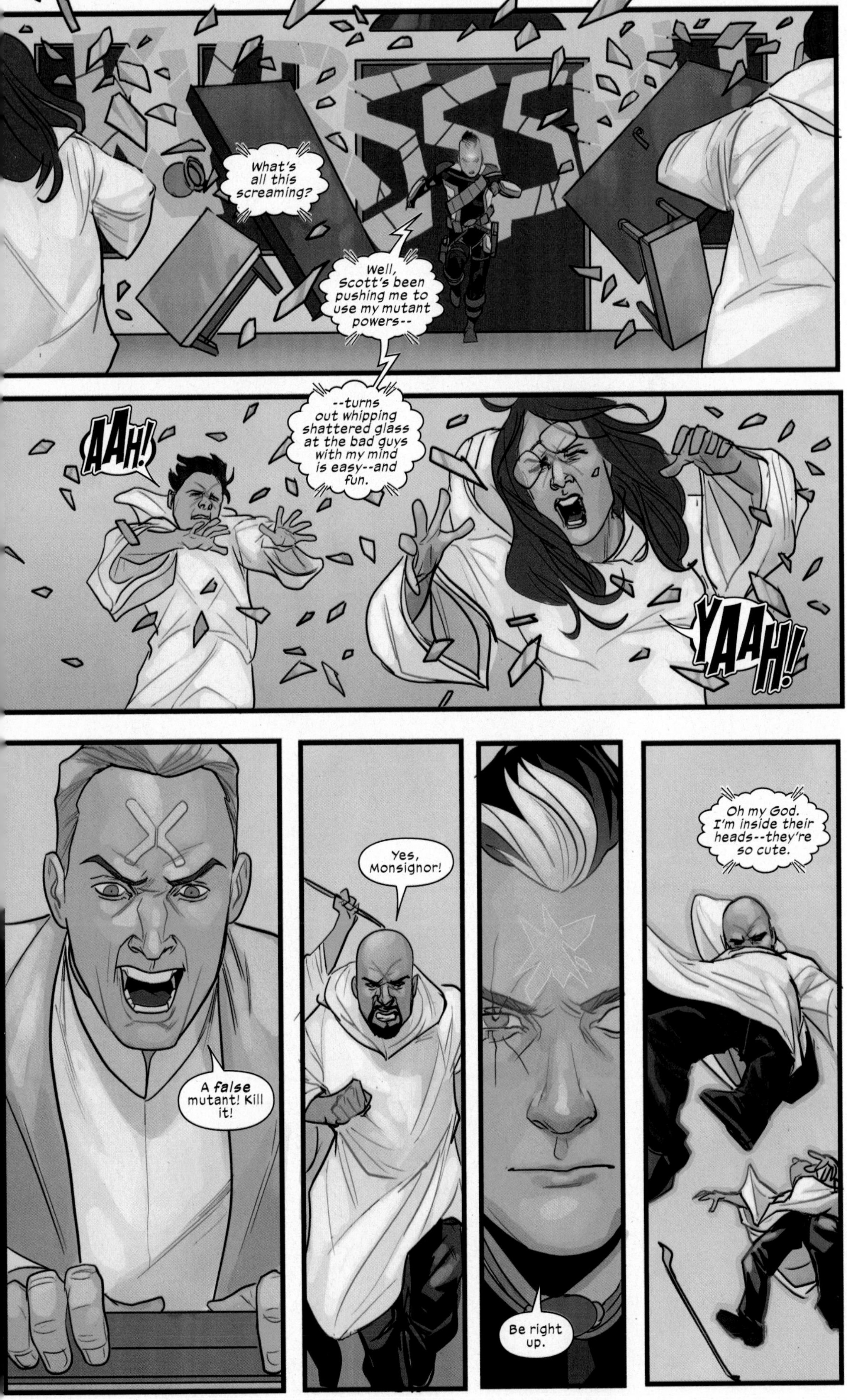
What's all this screaming?
Well, Scott's been pushing me to use my mutant powers--
--turns out whipping shattered glass at the bad guys with my mind is easy--and fun.
AAH!
YAAH!
A *false* mutant! Kill it!
Yes, Monsignor!
Be right up.
Oh my God. I'm inside their heads--they're so cute.

You asked about Otherworld and what happened... That's where I learned...

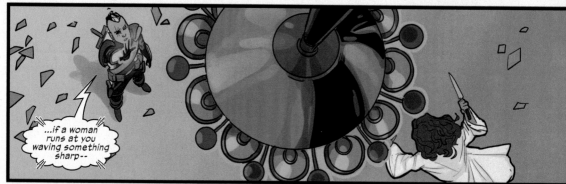

...if a woman runs at you waving something sharp--

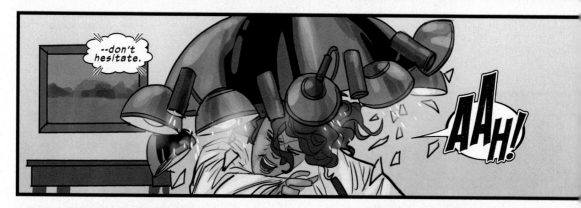

--don't hesitate.

AAH!

There are a few more heading your way. Want me to--

Nah. I got this.

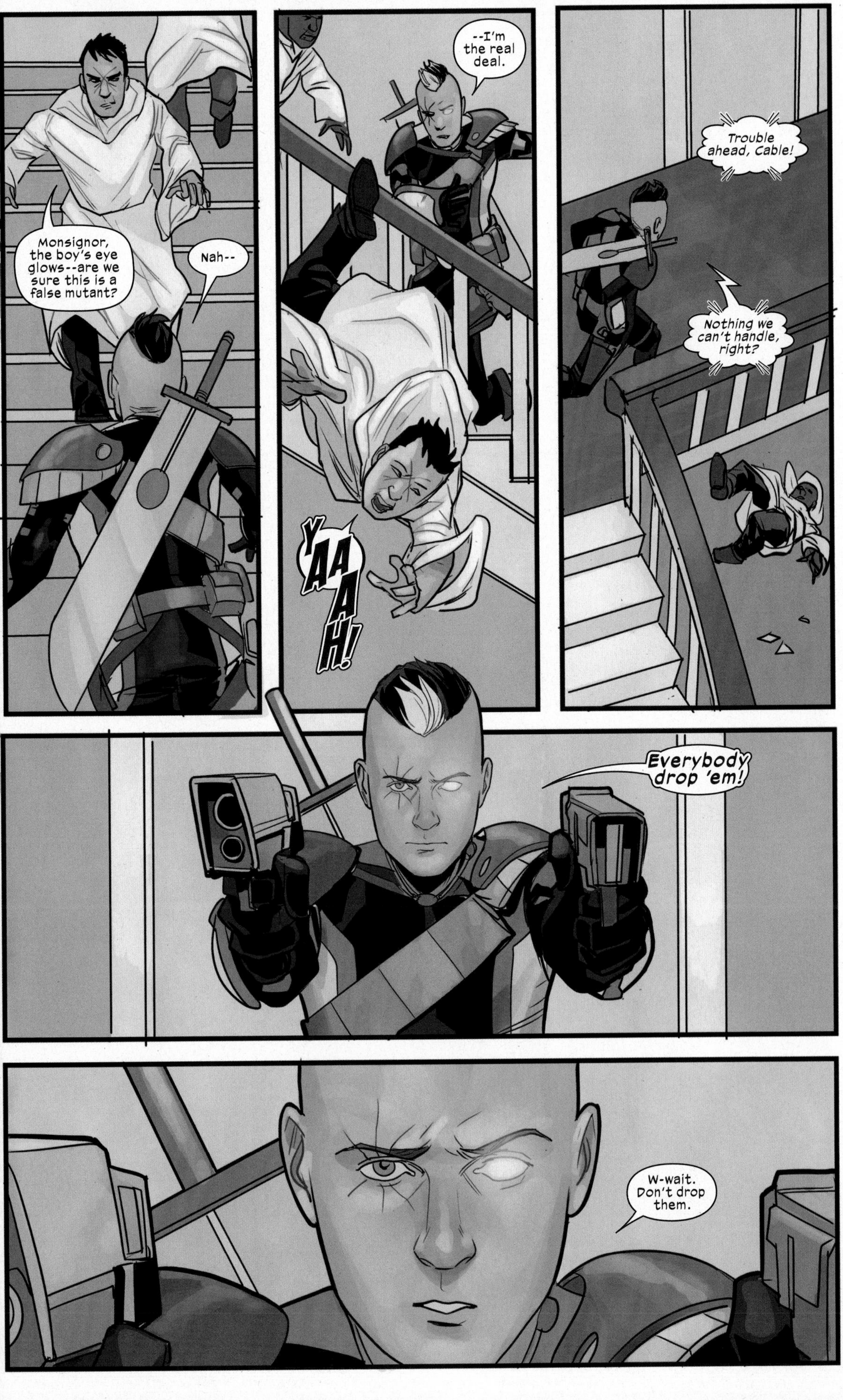
Monsignor, the boy's eye glows--are we sure this is a false mutant?
Nah--
--I'm the real deal.
YAAAH!
Trouble ahead, Cable!
Nothing we can't handle, right?
Everybody drop 'em!
W-wait. Don't drop them.

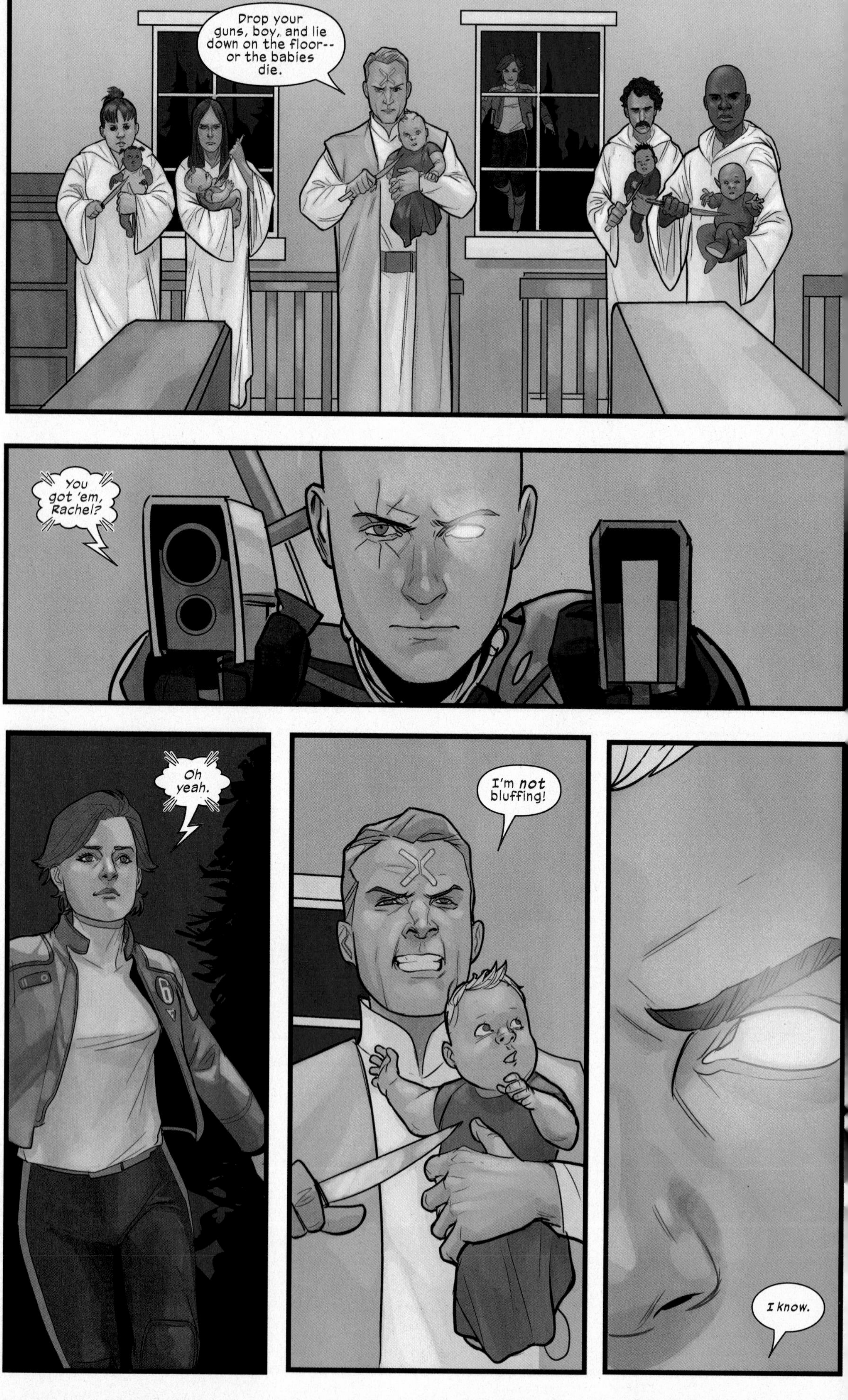
Drop your guns, boy, and lie down on the floor-- or the babies die.
You got 'em, Rachel?
Oh yeah.
I'm *not* bluffing!
I know.

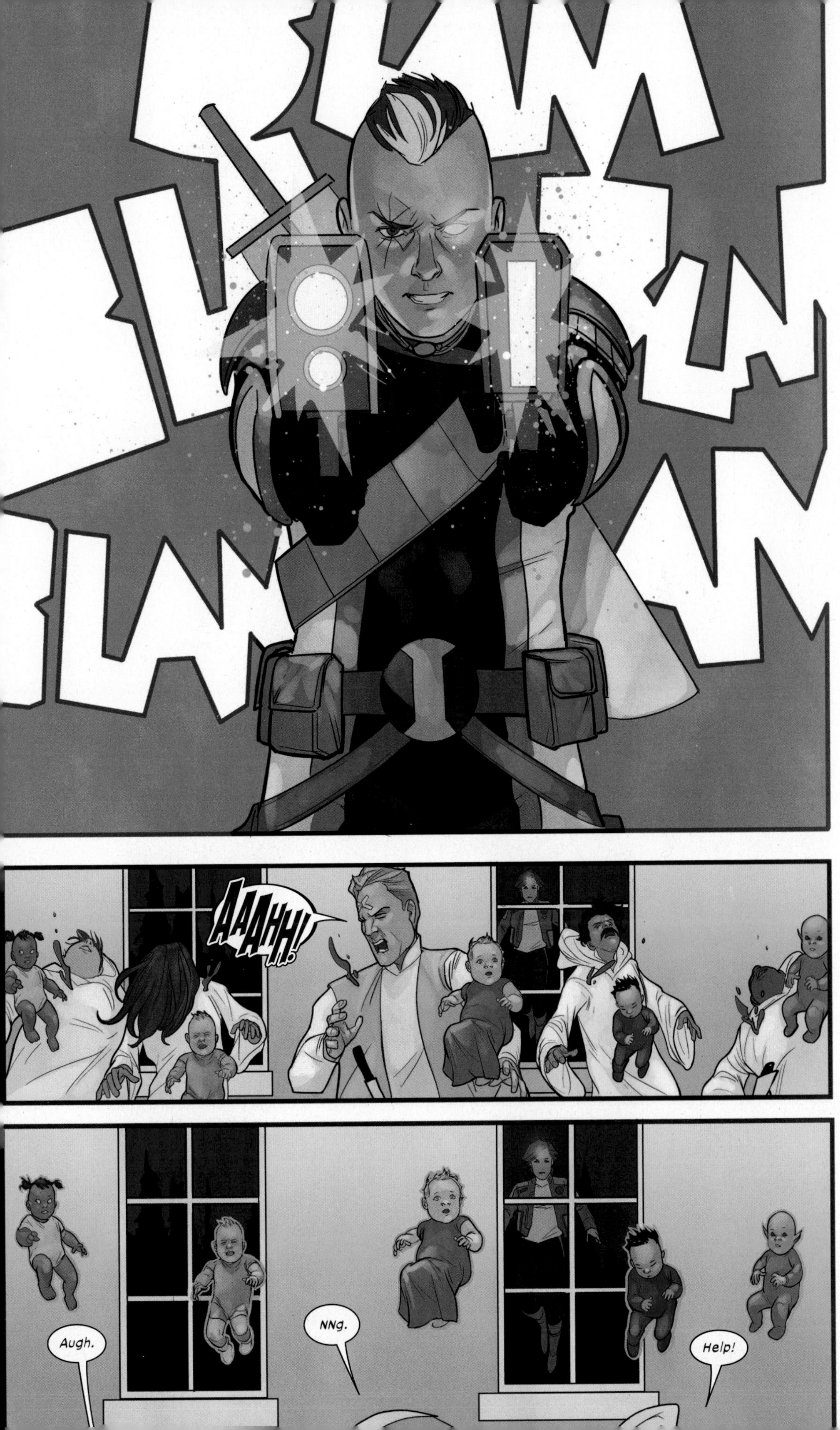
AAAHH!
Augh.
NNg.
Help!

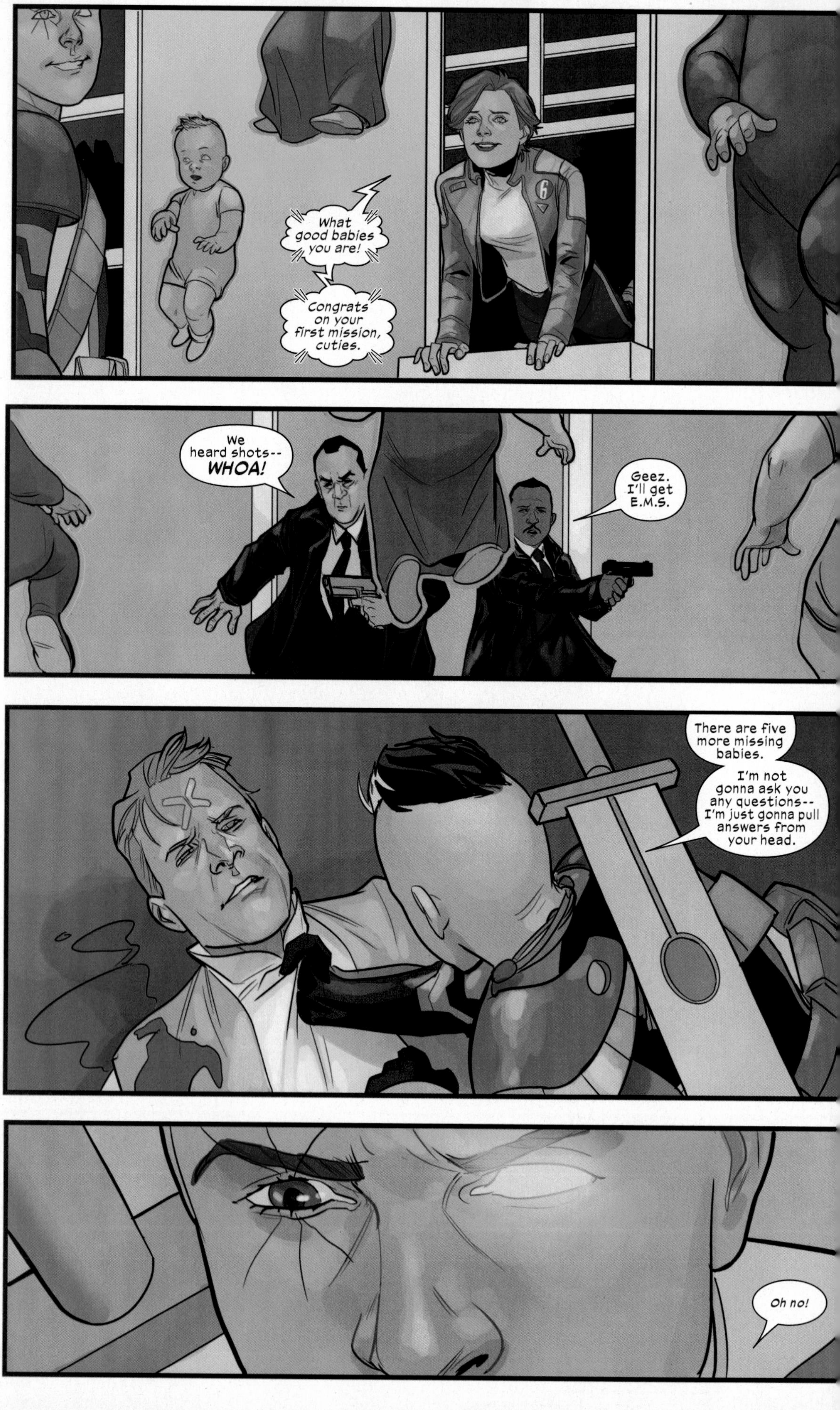
What good babies you are!
Congrats on your first mission, cuties.
We heard shots-- **WHOA!**
Geez. I'll get E.M.S.
There are five more missing babies.
I'm not gonna ask you any questions-- I'm just gonna pull answers from your head.
Oh no!

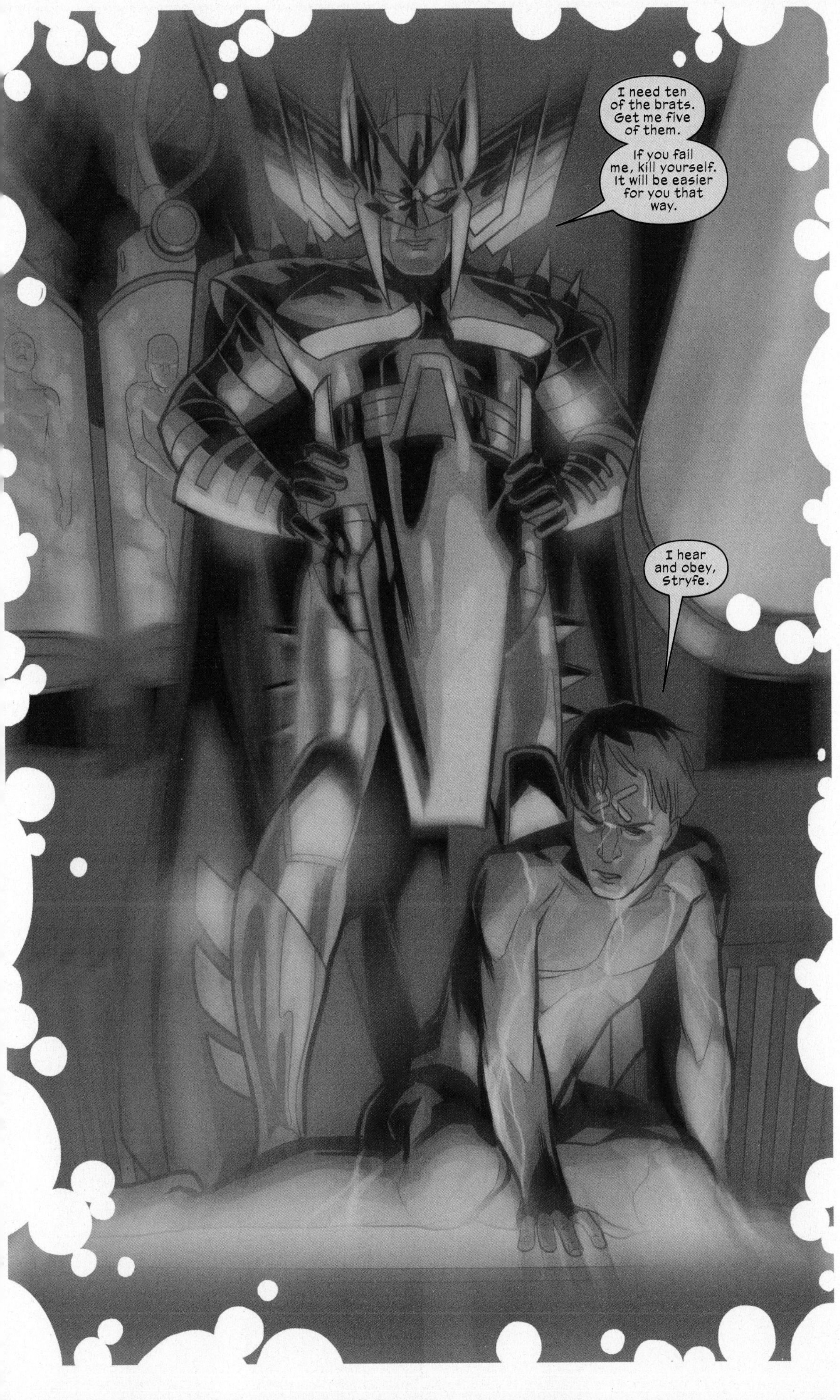
I need ten of the brats. Get me five of them.
If you fail me, kill yourself. It will be easier for you that way.
I hear and obey, Stryfe.

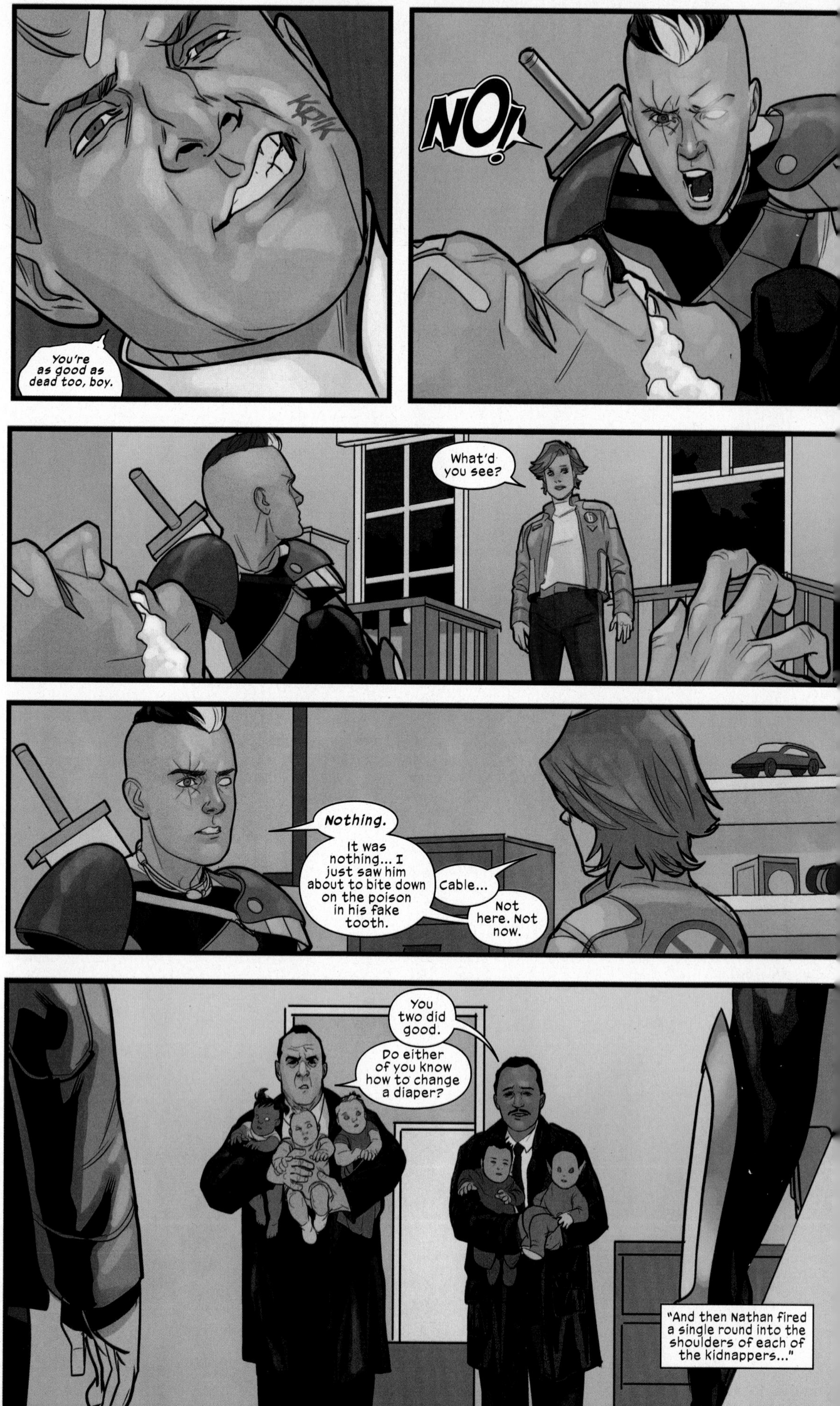

KRIK
You're as good as dead too, boy.
NO!
What'd you see?
Nothing.
It was nothing... I just saw him about to bite down on the poison in his fake tooth.
Cable...
Not here. Not now.
You two did good.
Do either of you know how to change a diaper?
"And then Nathan fired a single round into the shoulders of each of the kidnappers..."

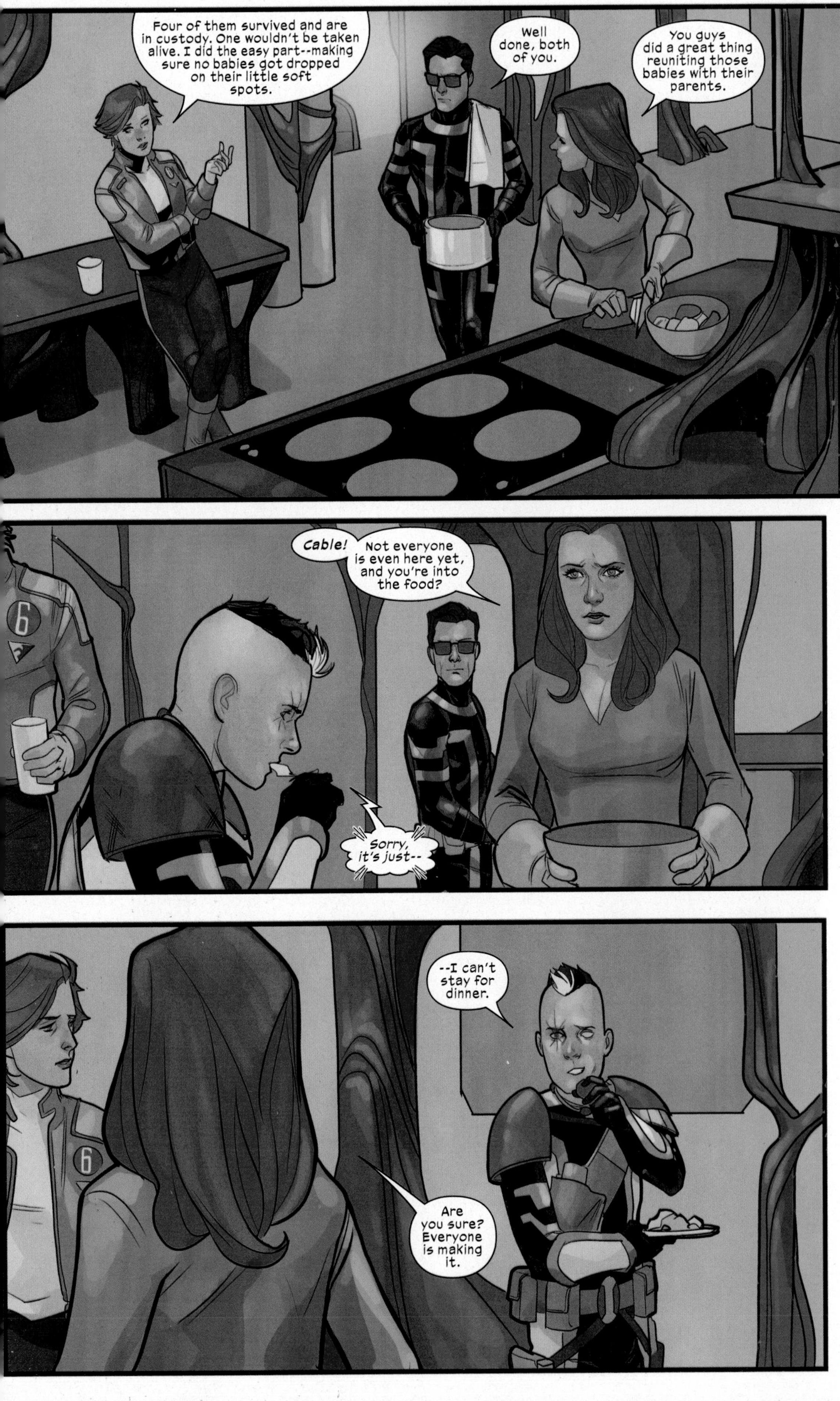
Four of them survived and are in custody. One wouldn't be taken alive. I did the easy part--making sure no babies got dropped on their little soft spots.
Well done, both of you.
You guys did a great thing reuniting those babies with their parents.
Cable!
Not everyone is even here yet, and you're into the food?
Sorry, it's just--
--I can't stay for dinner.
Are you sure? Everyone is making it.

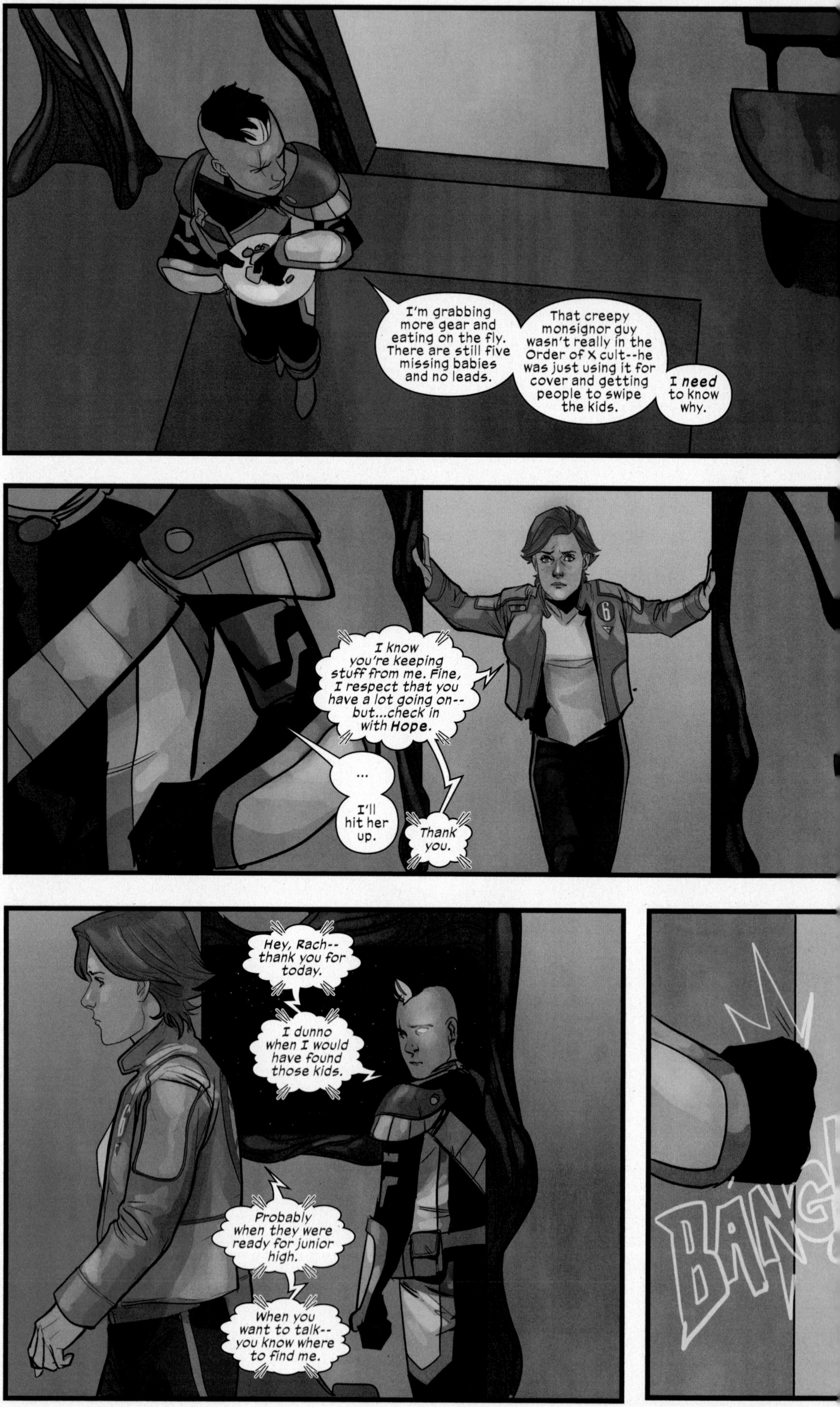
I'm grabbing more gear and eating on the fly. There are still five missing babies and no leads.
That creepy monsignor guy wasn't really in the Order of X cult--he was just using it for cover and getting people to swipe the kids.
I *need* to know why.
I know you're keeping stuff from me. Fine, I respect that you have a lot going on--but...check in with **Hope**.
...
I'll hit her up.
Thank you.
Hey, Rach--thank you for today.
I dunno when I would have found those kids.
Probably when they were ready for junior high.
When you want to talk--you know where to find me.
BANG

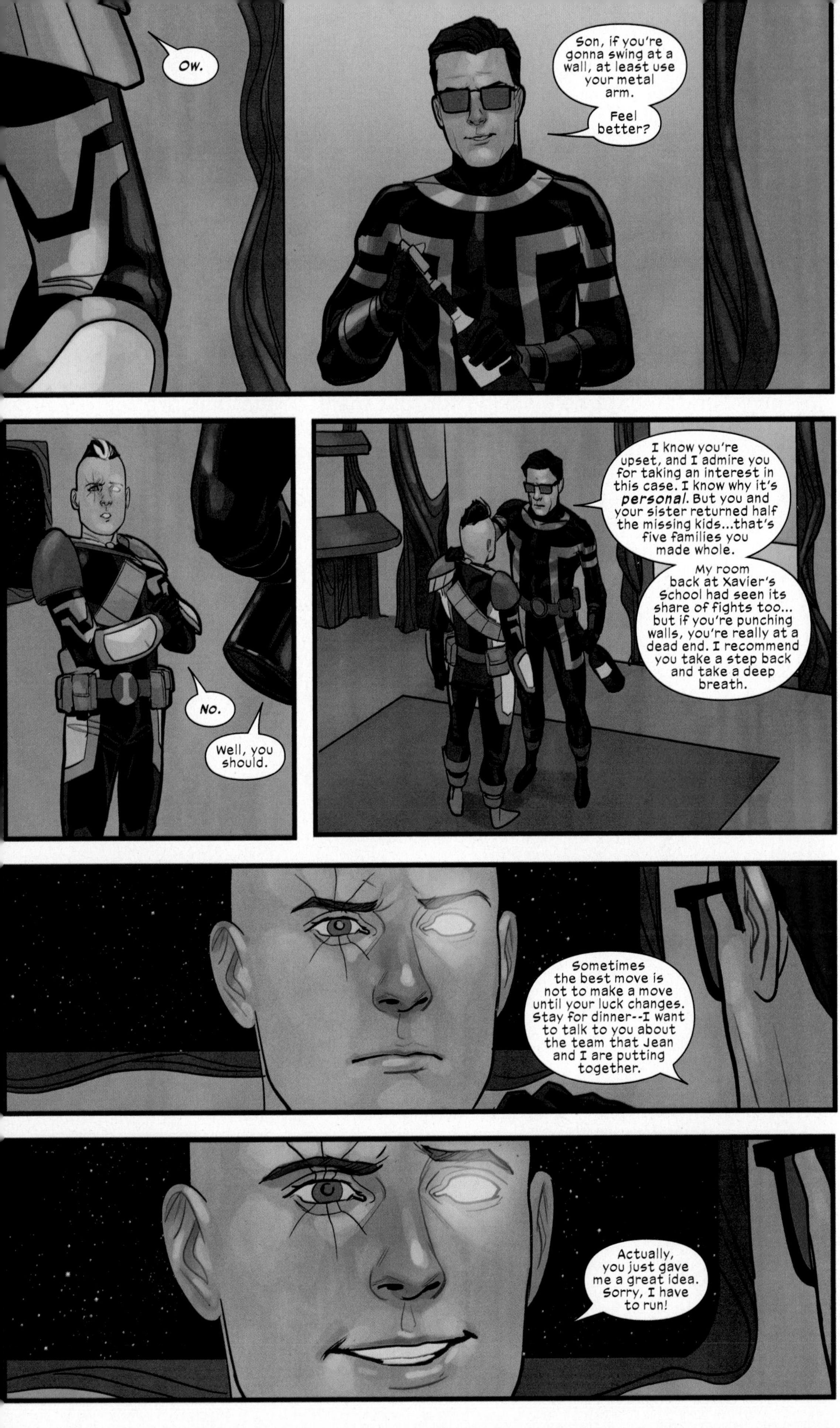
OW.
Son, if you're gonna swing at a wall, at least use your metal arm.
Feel better?
NO.
Well, you should.
I know you're upset, and I admire you for taking an interest in this case. I know why it's *personal*. But you and your sister returned half the missing kids...that's five families you made whole.
My room back at Xavier's School had seen its share of fights too... but if you're punching walls, you're really at a dead end. I recommend you take a step back and take a deep breath.
Sometimes the best move is not to make a move until your luck changes. Stay for dinner--I want to talk to you about the team that Jean and I are putting together.
Actually, you just gave me a great idea. Sorry, I have to run!

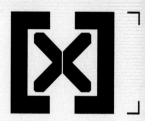

Beast,

Cable is requesting access to all files on Stryfe. Ordinarily I would just give him the data he's asking for, but many of the files are restricted because they are filled with knowledge of future events, and because most files dealing with Apocalypse's former activities remain classified.

The kid doesn't strike me as a big reader, so how worried are we that we might have a Stryfe problem?

Should we bring him in for a little chat? And let me know if you want to give him access to our files.

— Sage

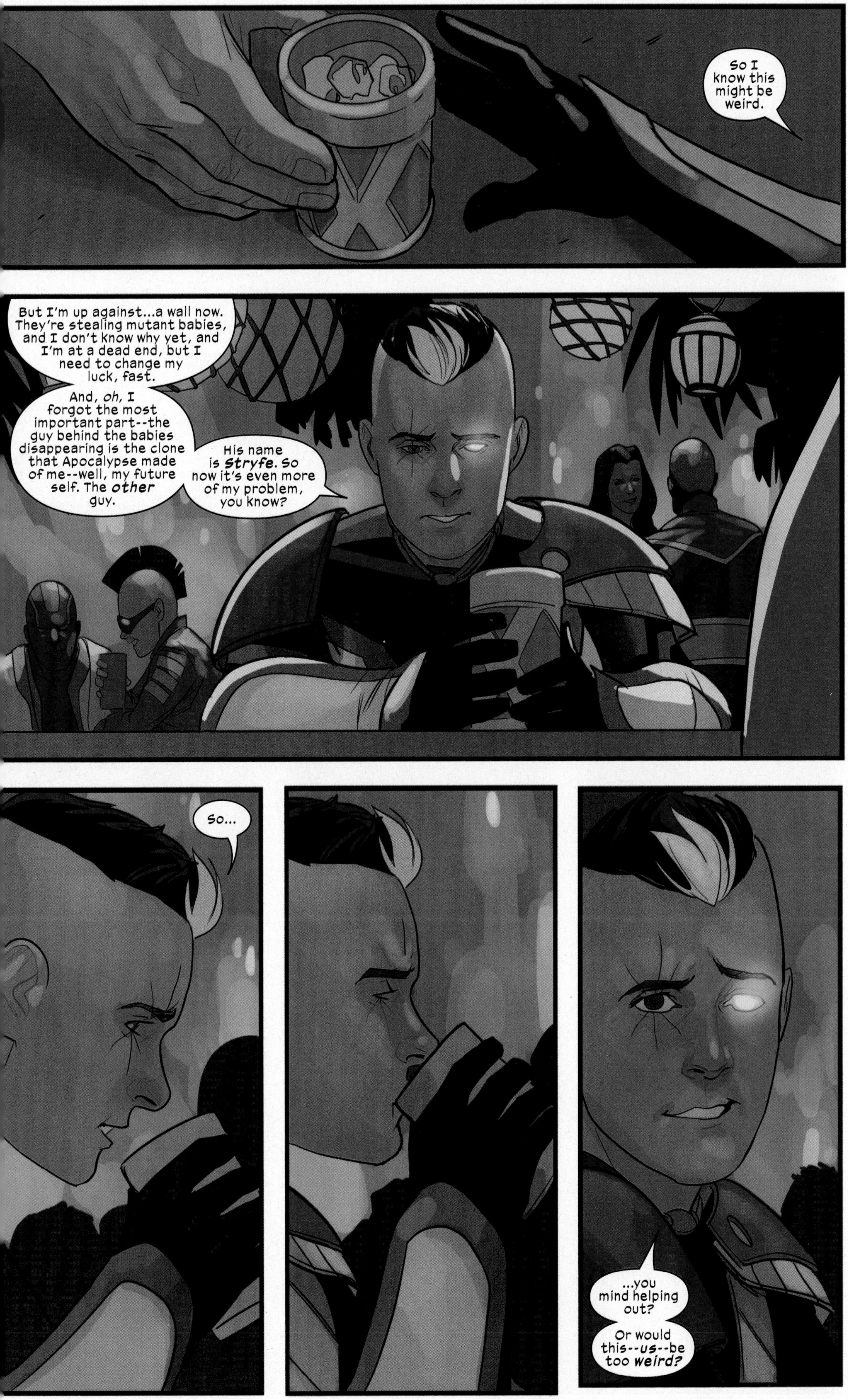
So I know this might be weird.
But I'm up against...a wall now. They're stealing mutant babies, and I don't know why yet, and I'm at a dead end, but I need to change my luck, fast.
And, oh, I forgot the most important part--the guy behind the babies disappearing is the clone that Apocalypse made of me--well, my future self. The other guy.
His name is Stryfe. So now it's even more of my problem, you know?
So...
...you mind helping out?
Or would this--us--be too weird?

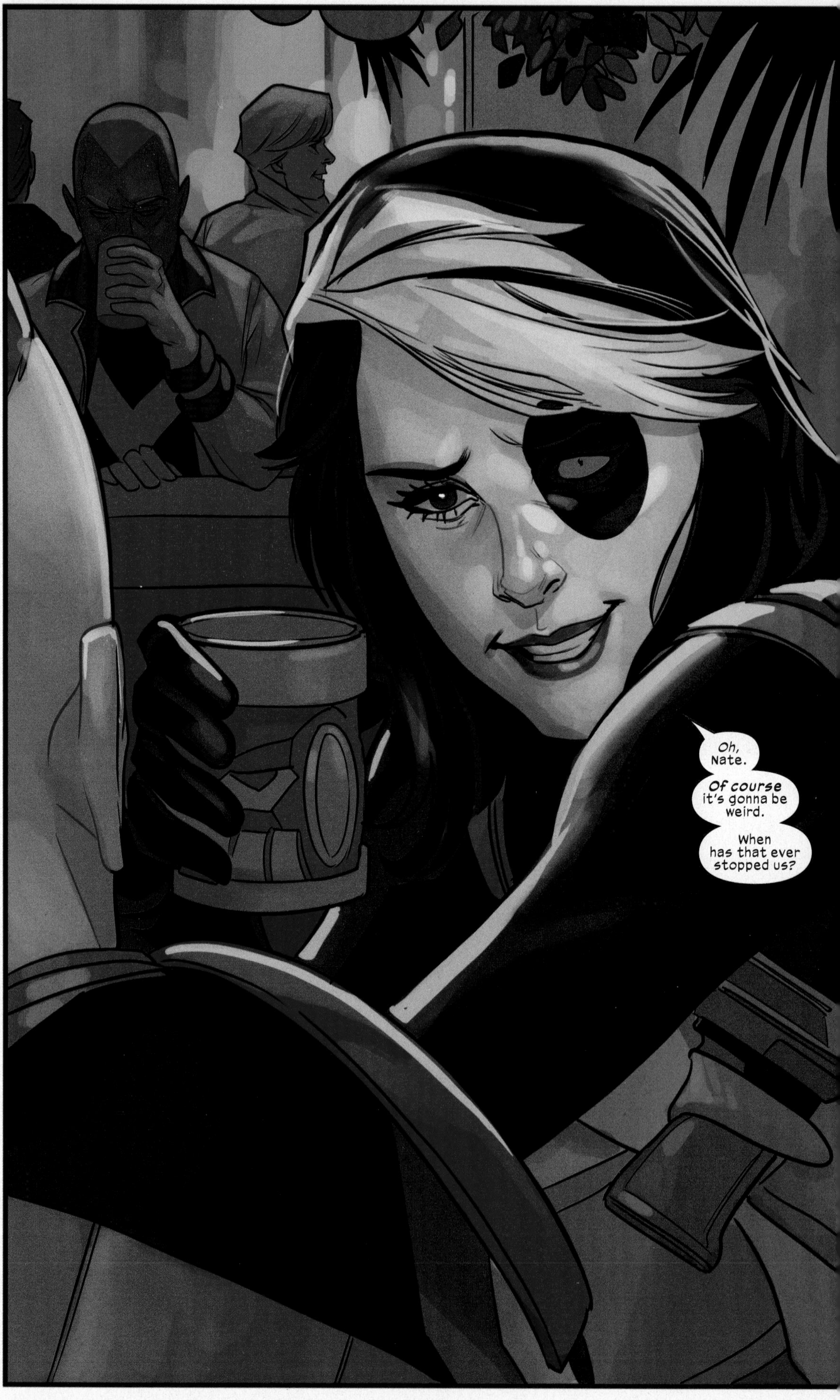

Oh, Nate.
Of course it's gonna be weird.
When has that ever stopped us?

[reign_of_x]

[guns_&_]
[swords_]

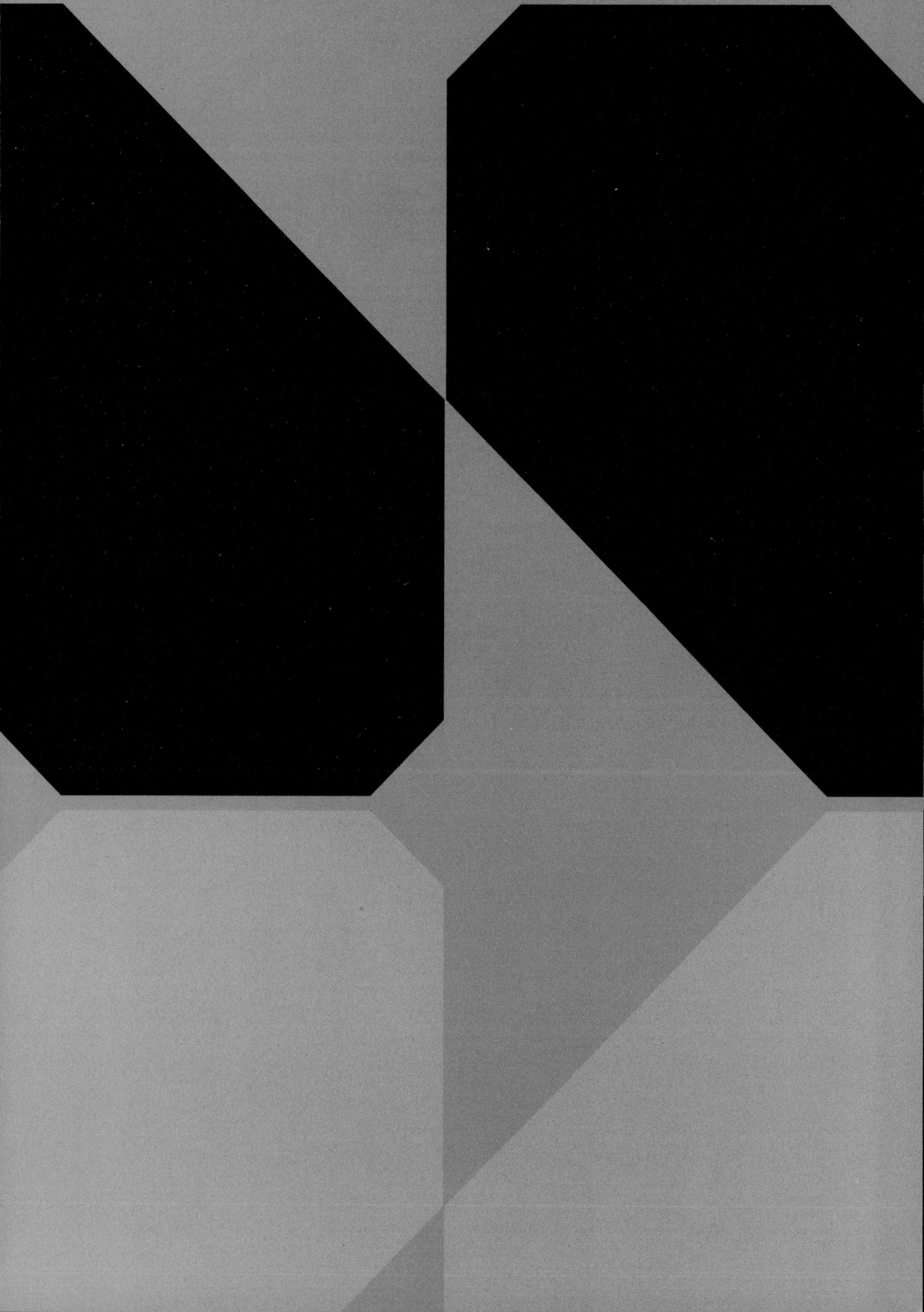

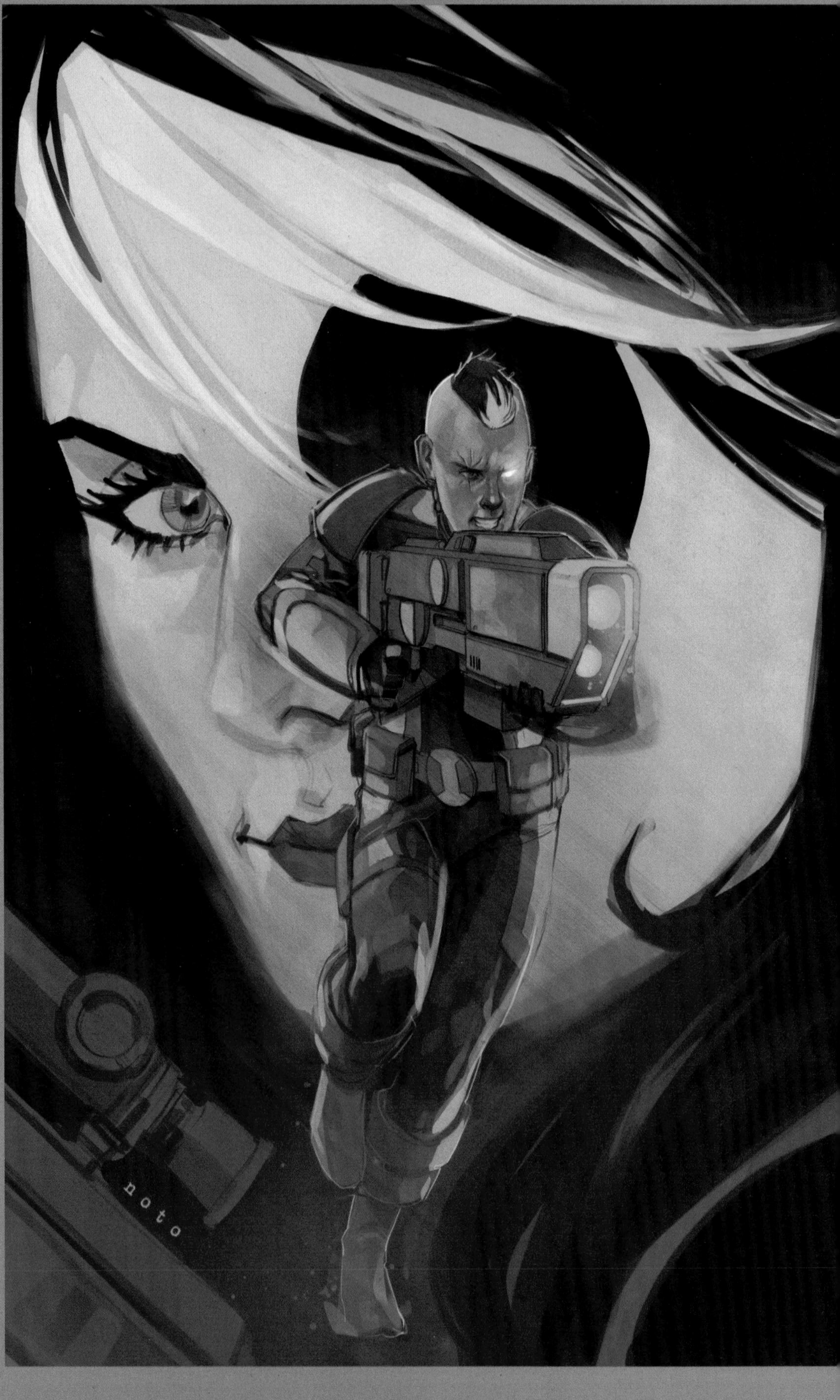
noto

My Dinner with Domino

[ca__[0.8]
[ble_[0.8]

There is only hate in Stryfe's
heart, and I hate that he looks
like me. It puts me off my game.
Causes me to make mistakes.

-- NATE SUMMERS

[ca__[0.X]
[ble_[0.X]

[ca__[0.8].....]
[ble_[0.8].....]

[Cable_alpha.]

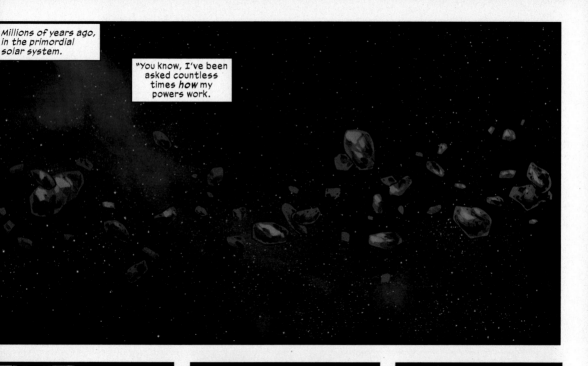

Millions of years ago, in the primordial solar system.

"You know, I've been asked countless times *how* my powers work.

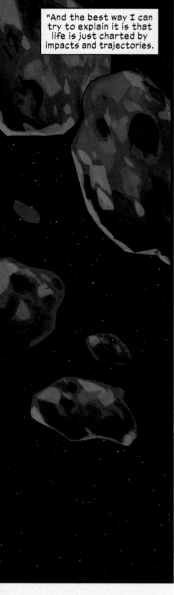

"And the best way I can try to explain it is that life is just charted by impacts and trajectories.

"A new impact leads to a new trajectory...

"...and then another and another--and *that's life*."

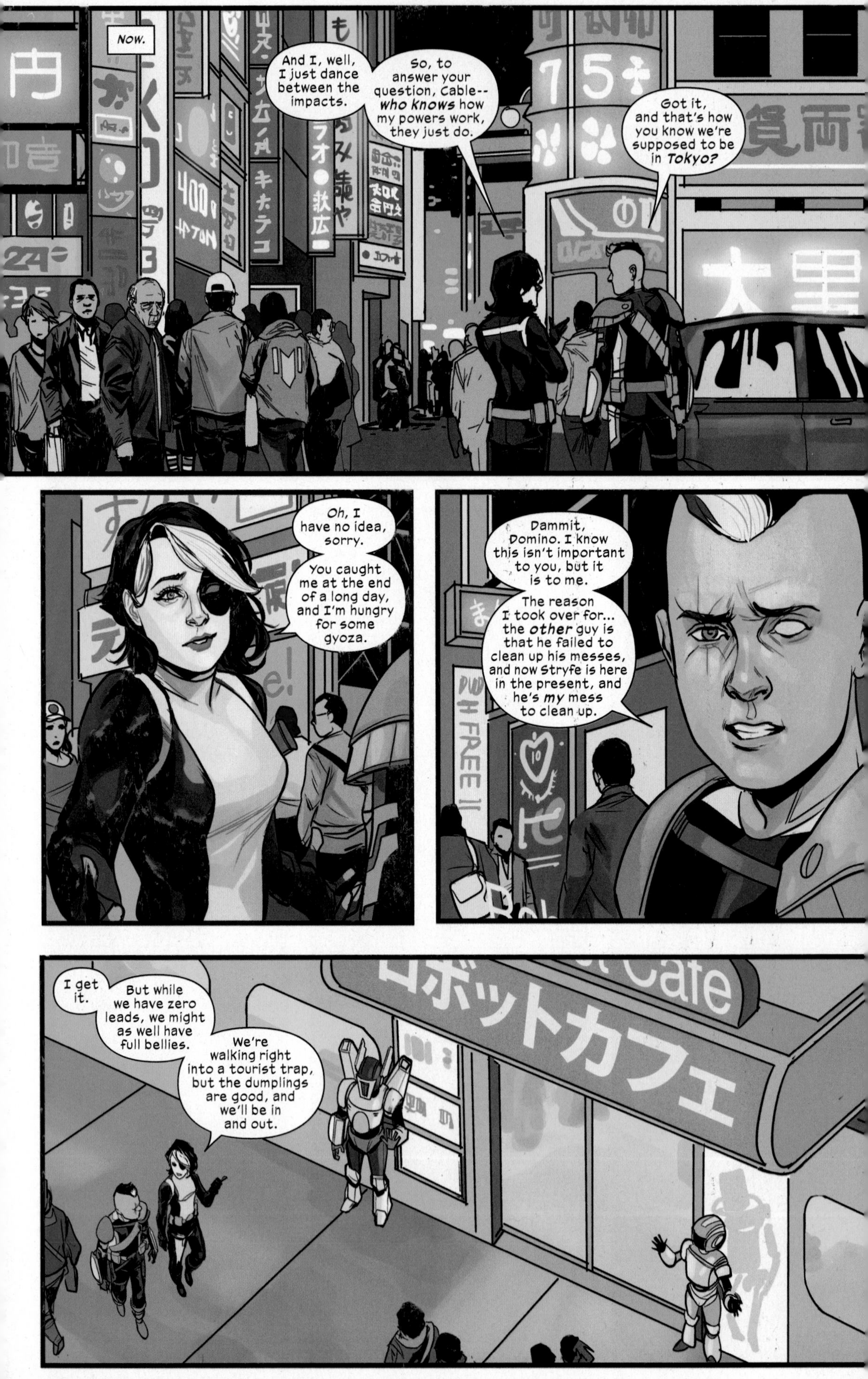

NOW.
And I, well, I just dance between the impacts.
So, to answer your question, Cable-- *who knows* how my powers work, they just do.
Got it, and that's how you know we're supposed to be in *Tokyo?*
Oh, I have no idea, sorry.
You caught me at the end of a long day, and I'm hungry for some gyoza.
Dammit, Domino. I know this isn't important to you, but it is to me.
The reason I took over for... the *other* guy is that he failed to clean up his messes, and now Stryfe is here in the present, and he's *my* mess to clean up.
I get it.
But while we have zero leads, we might as well have full bellies.
We're walking right into a tourist trap, but the dumplings are good, and we'll be in and out.
ロボットカフェ

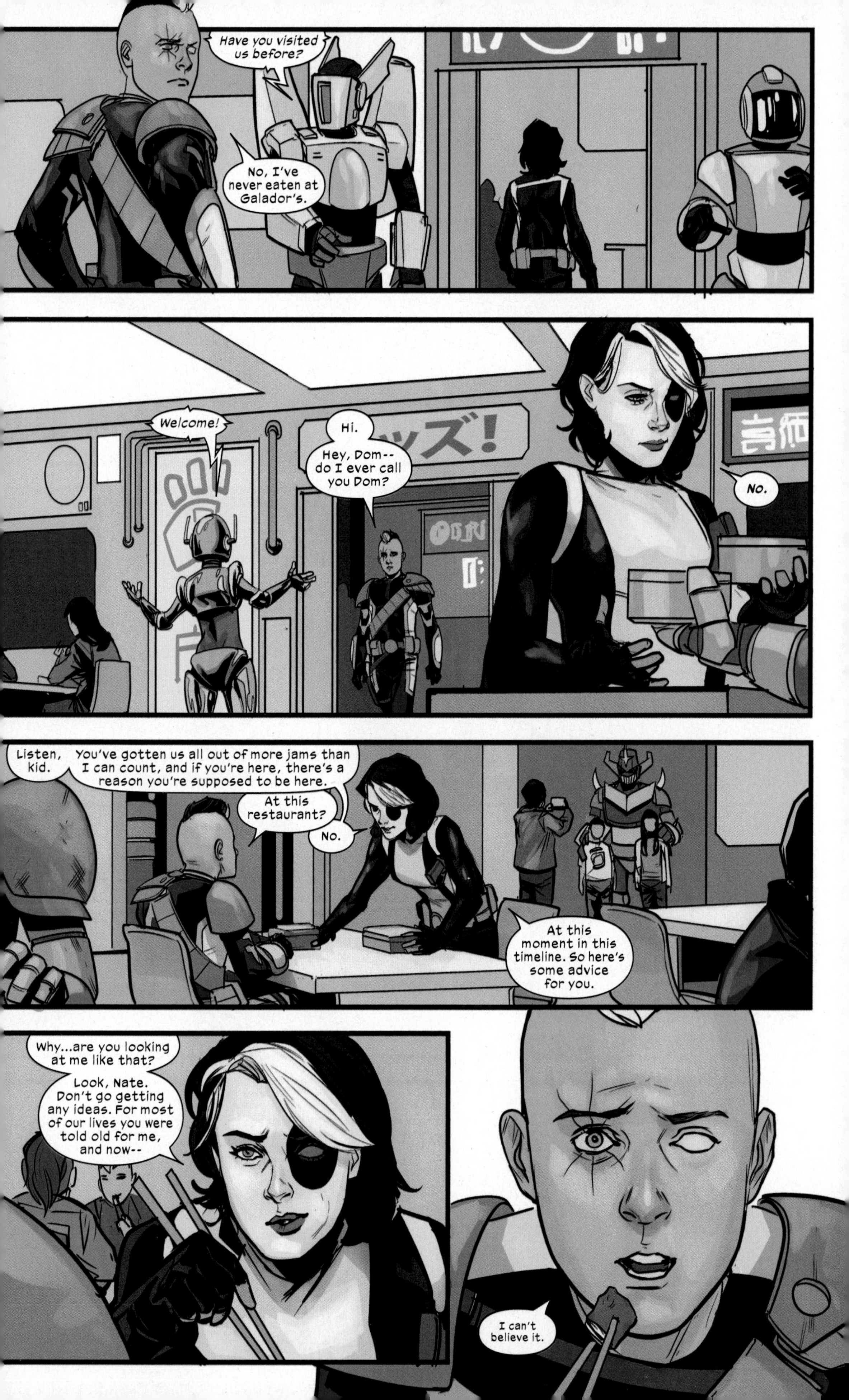
Have you visited us before?
No, I've never eaten at Galador's.
Welcome!
Hi.
Hey, Dom-- do I ever call you Dom?
No.
Listen, kid.
You've gotten us all out of more jams than I can count, and if you're here, there's a reason you're supposed to be here.
At this restaurant?
No.
At this moment in this timeline. So here's some advice for you.
Why...are you looking at me like that?
Look, Nate. Don't go getting any ideas. For most of our lives you were told old for me, and now--
I can't believe it.

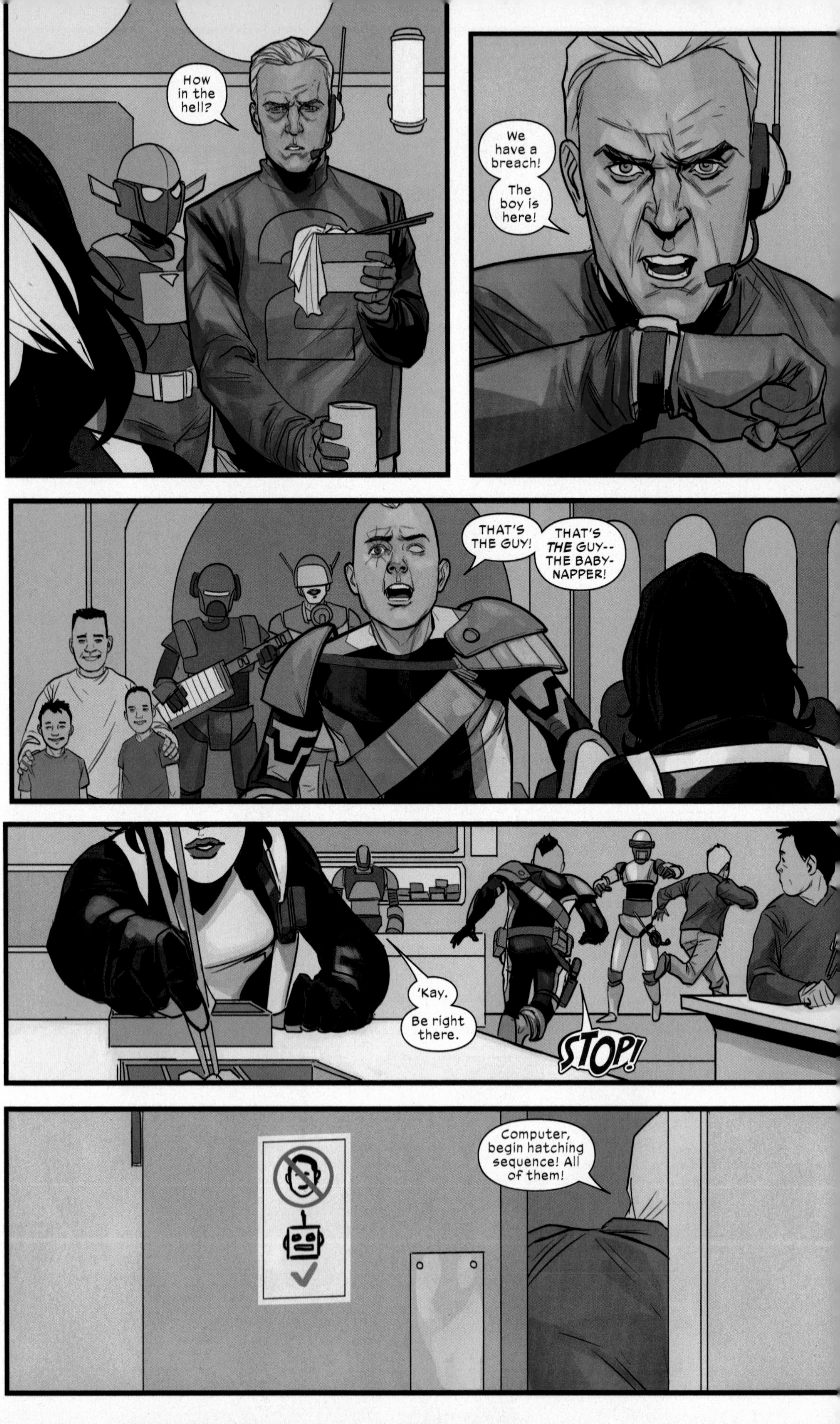

How in the hell?
We have a breach!
The boy is here!
THAT'S THE GUY!
THAT'S *THE* GUY-- THE BABY-NAPPER!
'Kay.
Be right there.
STOP!
Computer, begin hatching sequence! All of them!

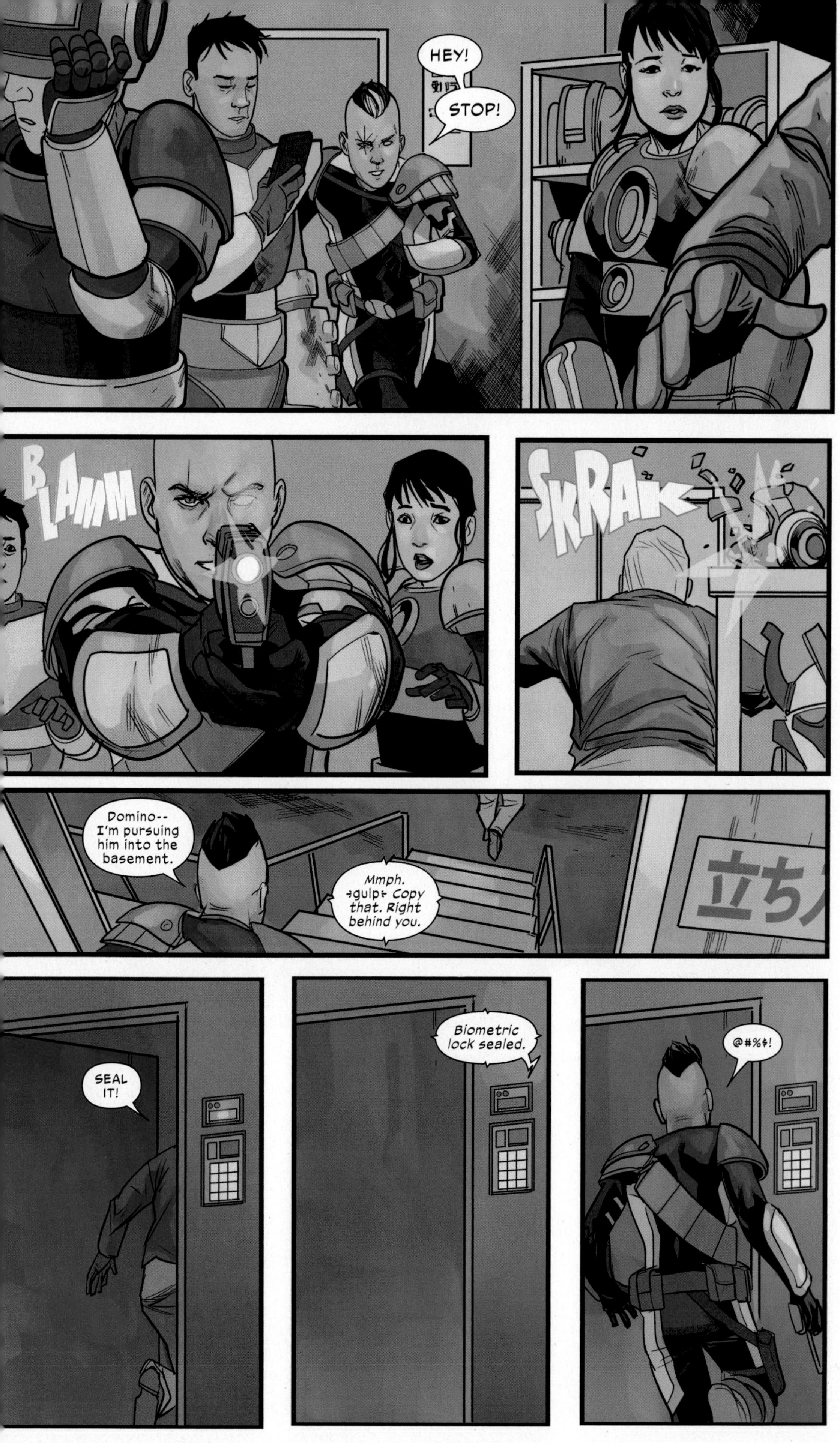
HEY!
STOP!
BLAMM
SKRAK
Domino-- I'm pursuing him into the basement.
Mmph. ‡gulp‡ Copy that. Right behind you.
立ち
SEAL IT!
Biometric lock sealed.
@#%$!

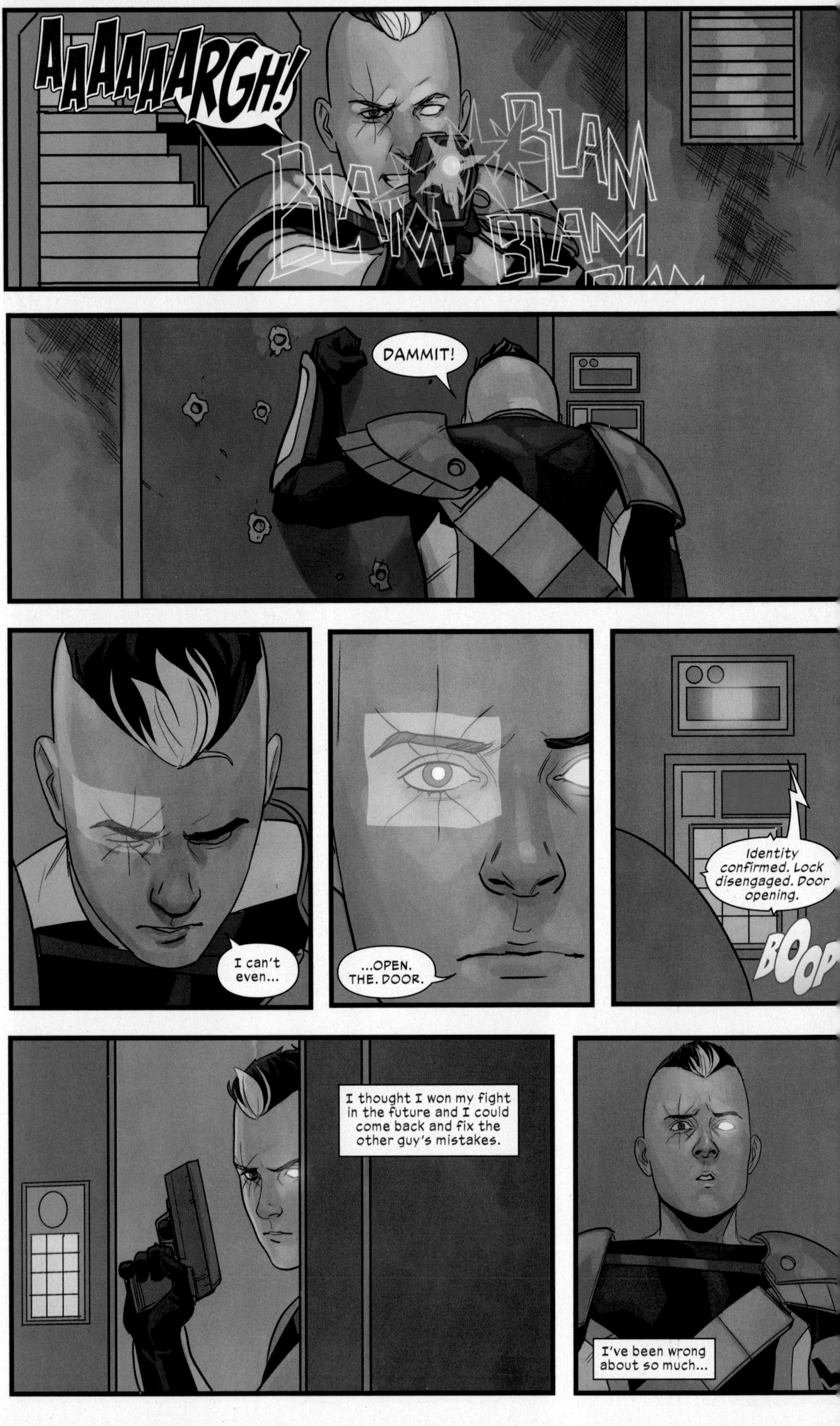

AAAAAARGH!
BLAM BLAM BLAM BLAM
DAMMIT!
I can't even...
...OPEN. THE. DOOR.
Identity confirmed. Lock disengaged. Door opening.
BOOP
I thought I won my fight in the future and I could come back and fix the other guy's mistakes.
I've been wrong about so much...

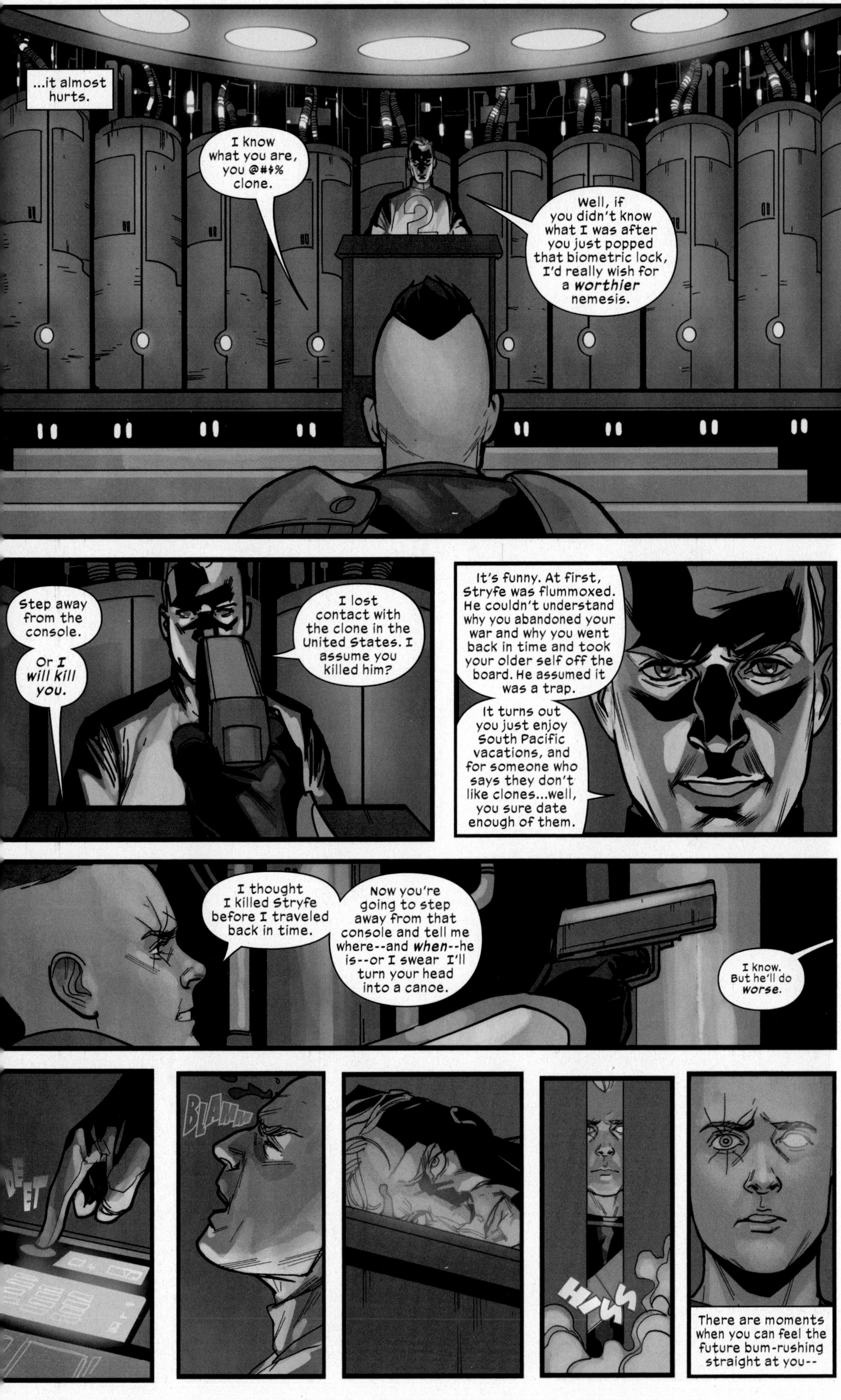
...it almost hurts.
I know what you are, you @#$% clone.
Well, if you didn't know what I was after you just popped that biometric lock, I'd really wish for a worthier nemesis.
Step away from the console.
Or I will kill you.
I lost contact with the clone in the United States. I assume you killed him?
It's funny. At first, Stryfe was flummoxed. He couldn't understand why you abandoned your war and why you went back in time and took your older self off the board. He assumed it was a trap.
It turns out you just enjoy South Pacific vacations, and for someone who says they don't like clones...well, you sure date enough of them.
I thought I killed Stryfe before I traveled back in time.
Now you're going to step away from that console and tell me where--and when--he is--or I swear I'll turn your head into a canoe.
I know. But he'll do worse.
BEET
BLAM
HISS
There are moments when you can feel the future bum-rushing straight at you--

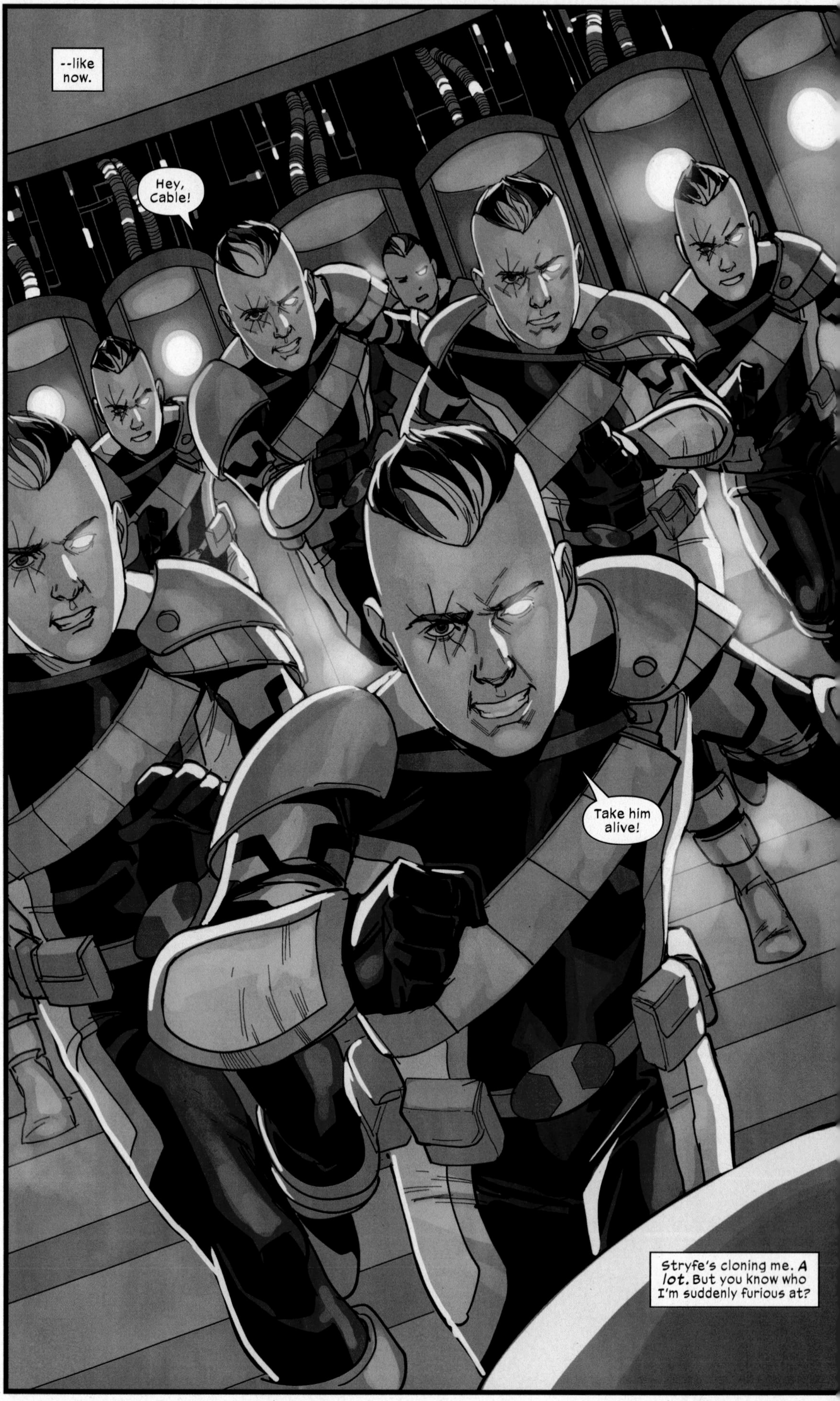
--like now.
Hey, Cable!
Take him alive!
Stryfe's cloning me. *A lot.* But you know who I'm suddenly furious at?

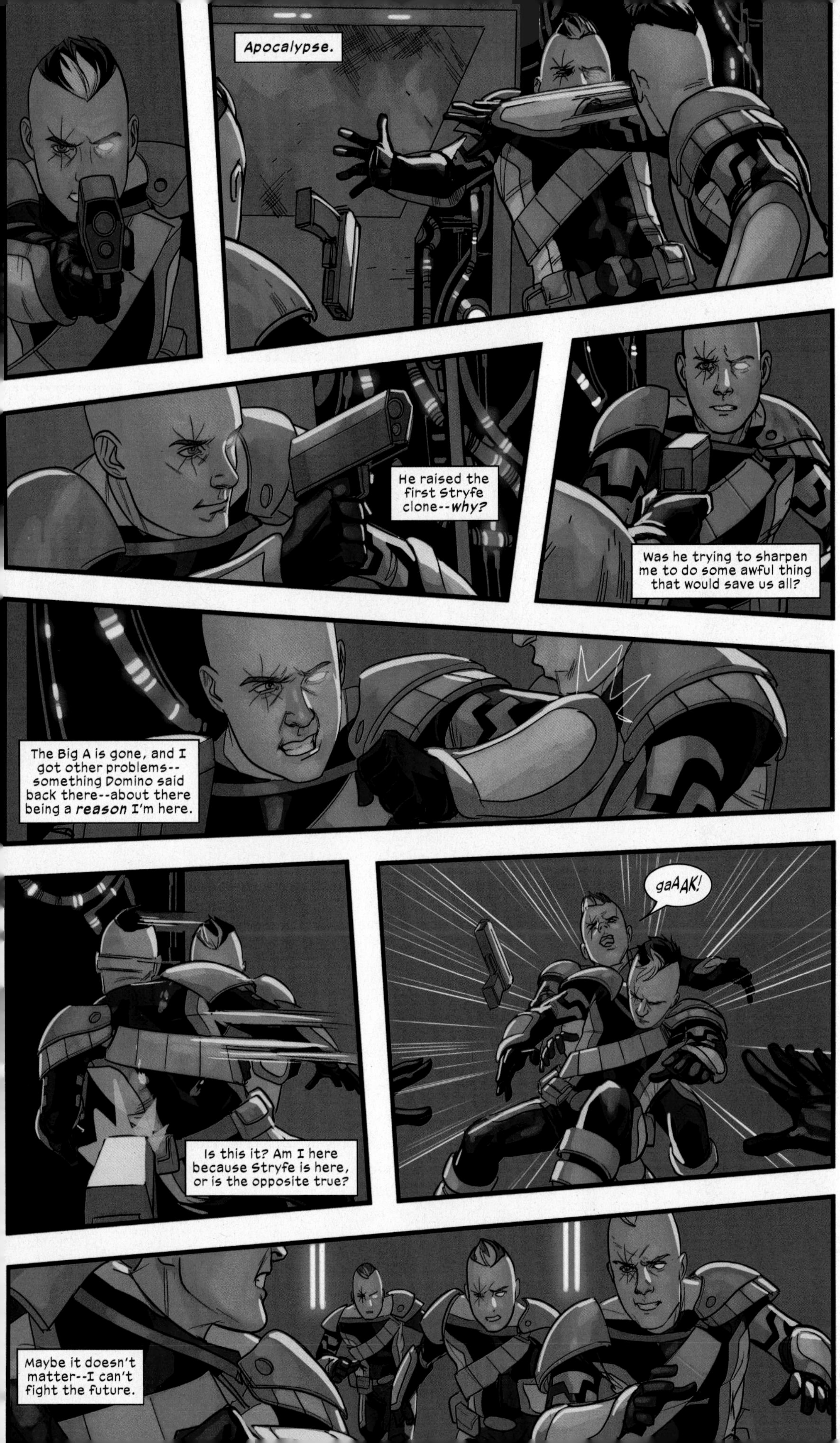
Apocalypse.
He raised the first Stryfe clone--why?
Was he trying to sharpen me to do some awful thing that would save us all?
The Big A is gone, and I got other problems--something Domino said back there--about there being a reason I'm here.
Is this it? Am I here because Stryfe is here, or is the opposite true?
gaAAK!
Maybe it doesn't matter--I can't fight the future.

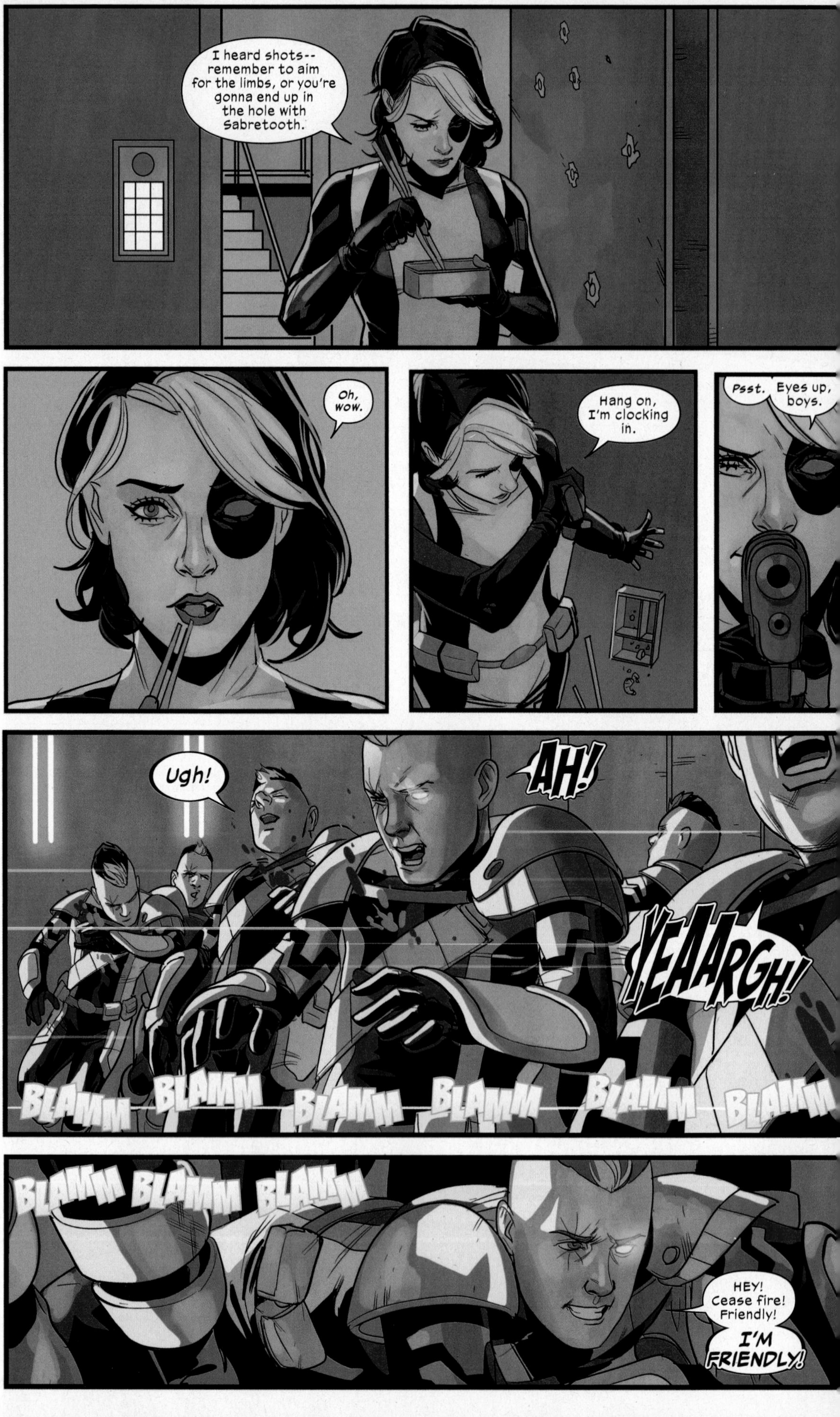
I heard shots--remember to aim for the limbs, or you're gonna end up in the hole with Sabretooth.
Oh, wow.
Hang on, I'm clocking in.
Psst.
Eyes up, boys.
Ugh!
AH!
YEAARGH!
BLAMM BLAMM BLAMM BLAMM BLAMM BLAMM
BLAMM BLAMM BLAMM
HEY! Cease fire! Friendly!
I'M FRIENDLY!

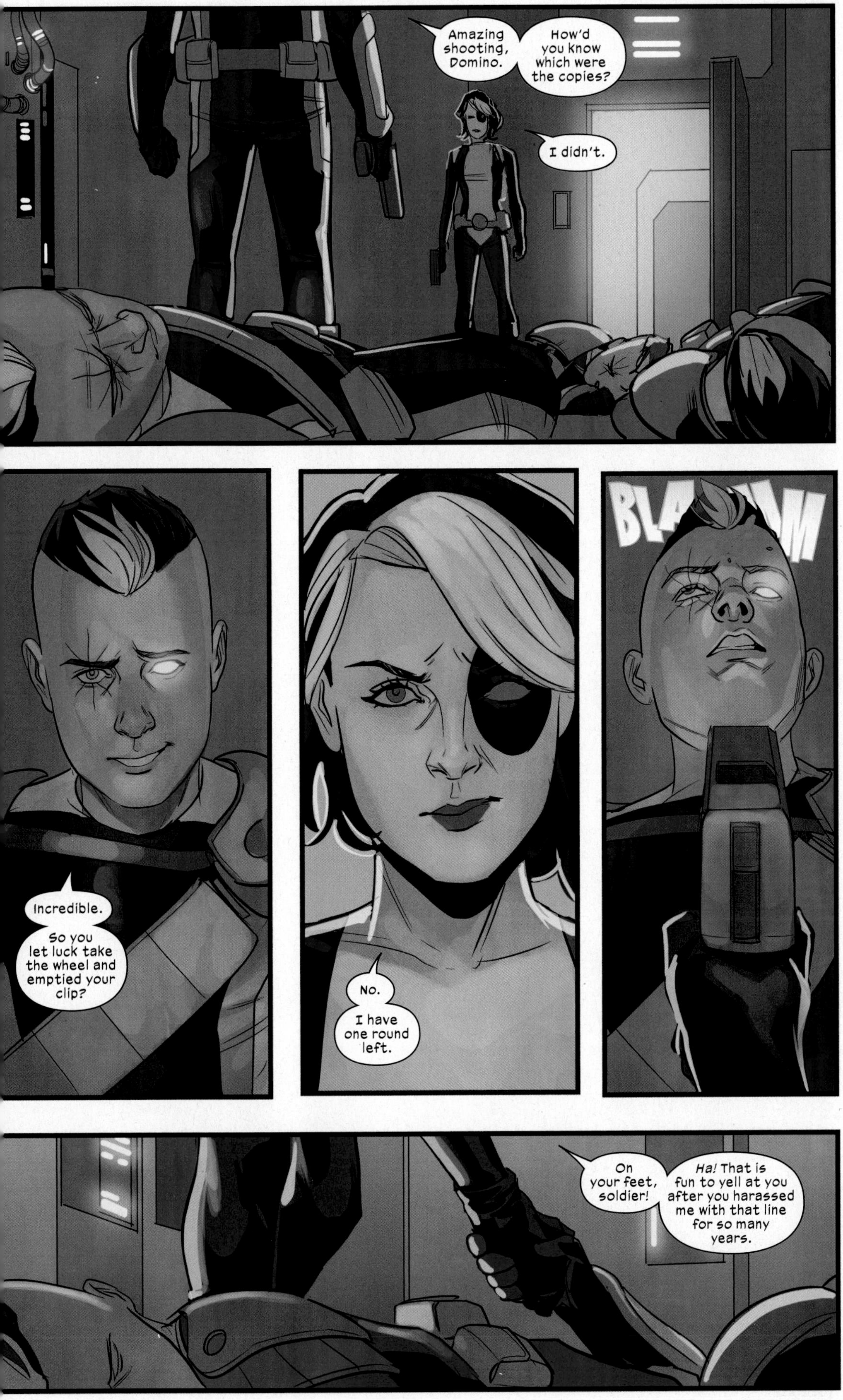
Amazing shooting, Domino.
How'd you know which were the copies?
I didn't.
Incredible.
So you let luck take the wheel and emptied your clip?
No.
I have one round left.
On your feet, soldier!
Ha! That is fun to yell at you after you harassed me with that line for so many years.

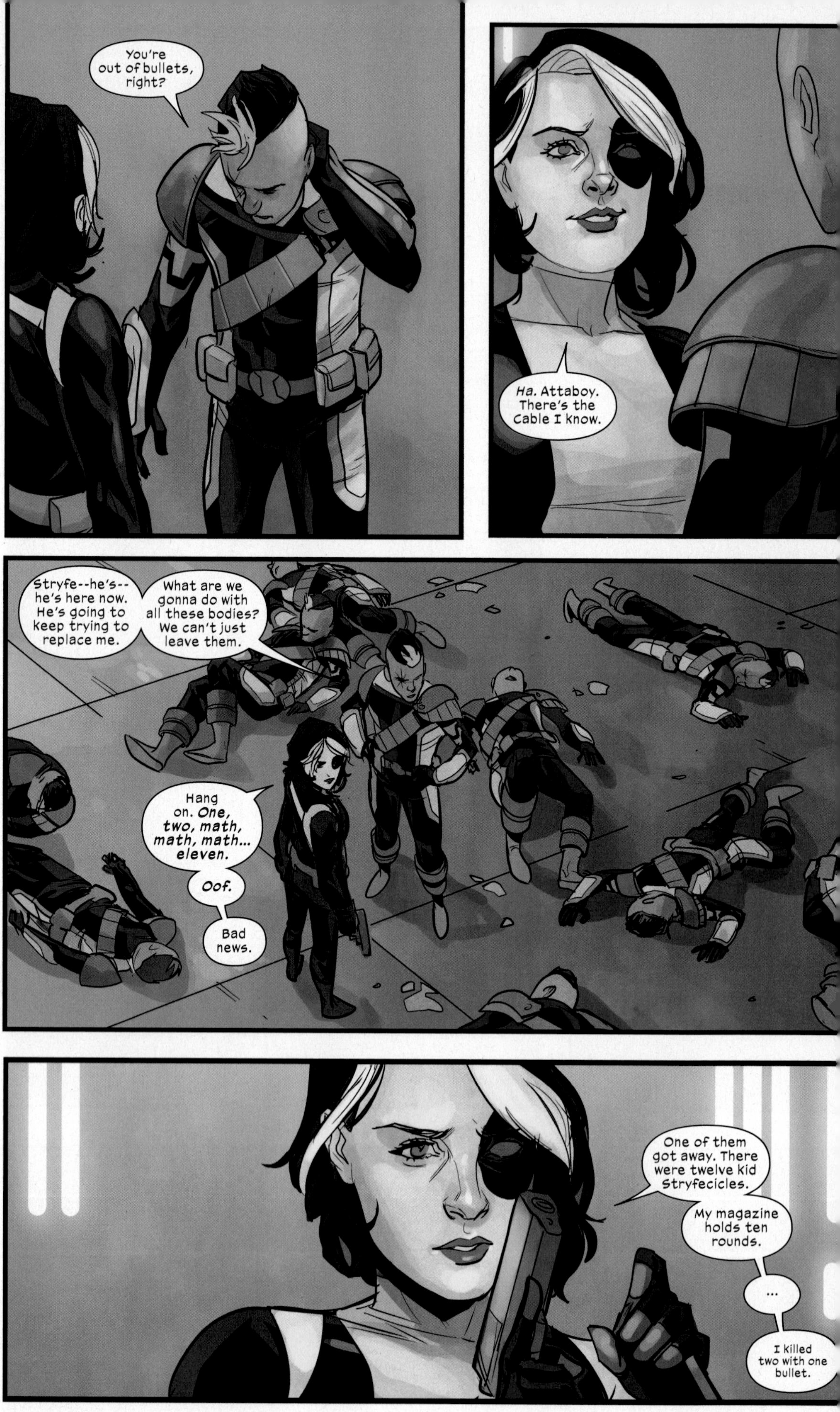
You're out of bullets, right?
Ha. Attaboy. There's the Cable I know.
Stryfe--he's--he's here now. He's going to keep trying to replace me.
What are we gonna do with all these bodies? We can't just leave them.
Hang on. *One, two, math, math, math... eleven.*
Oof.
Bad news.
One of them got away. There were twelve kid Stryfecicles.
My magazine holds ten rounds.
...
I killed two with one bullet.

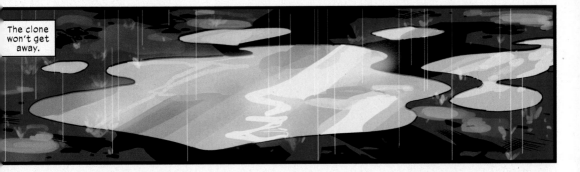

The clone won't get away.

Even with his psi-defenses up--I'll pry the answers I need from his head.

I know I won't like what I find.

Remember-- he's our only lead.

I won't kill him if you don't.

You won't find them, you know. The other babies are already gone.

Drop the gun.

Slow.

Sure.

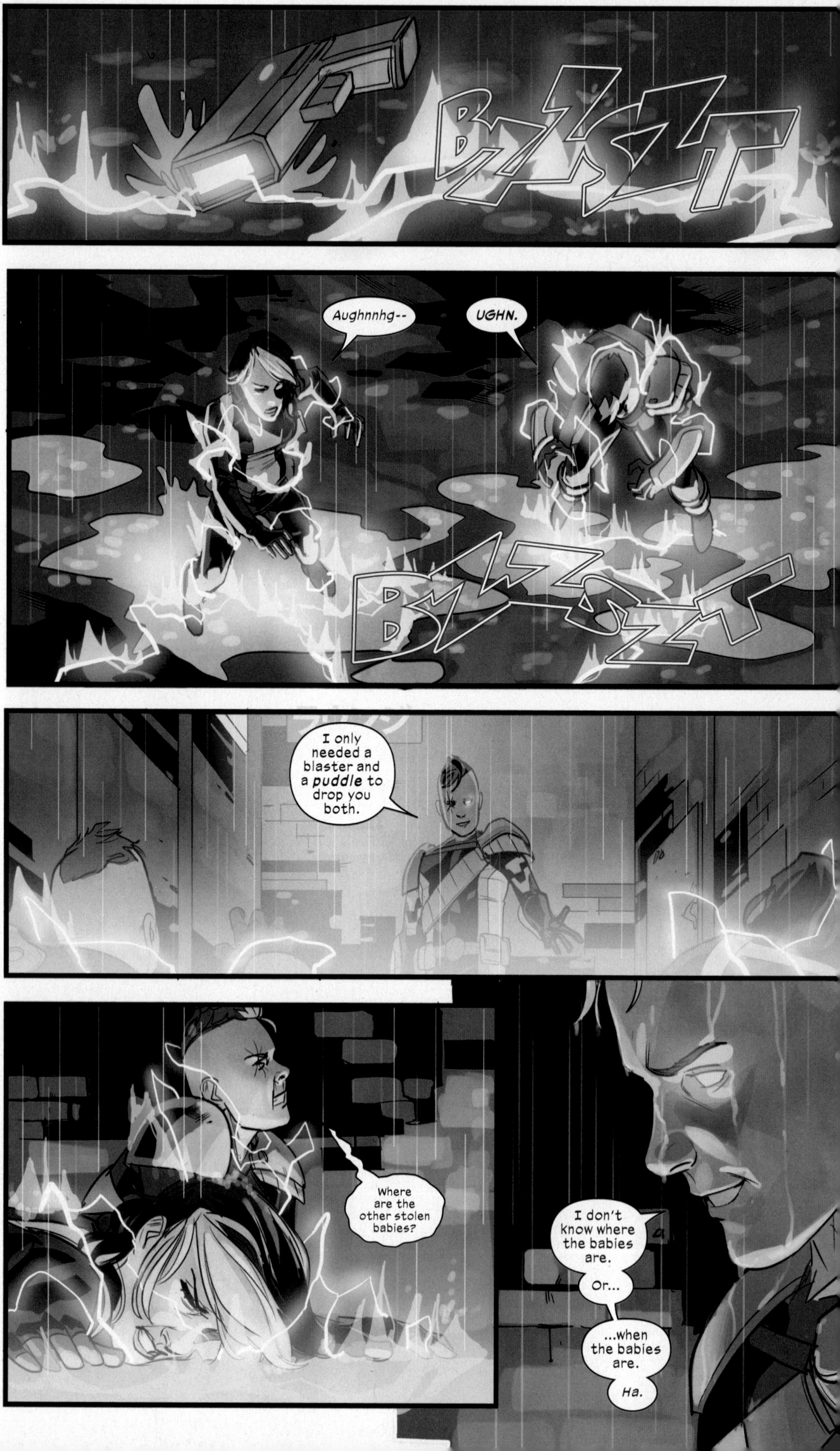
BZZSZT
Aughnnhg--
UGHN.
BZZSZT
I only needed a blaster and a *puddle* to drop you both.
Where are the other stolen babies?
I don't know where the babies are.
Or...
...when the babies are.
Ha.

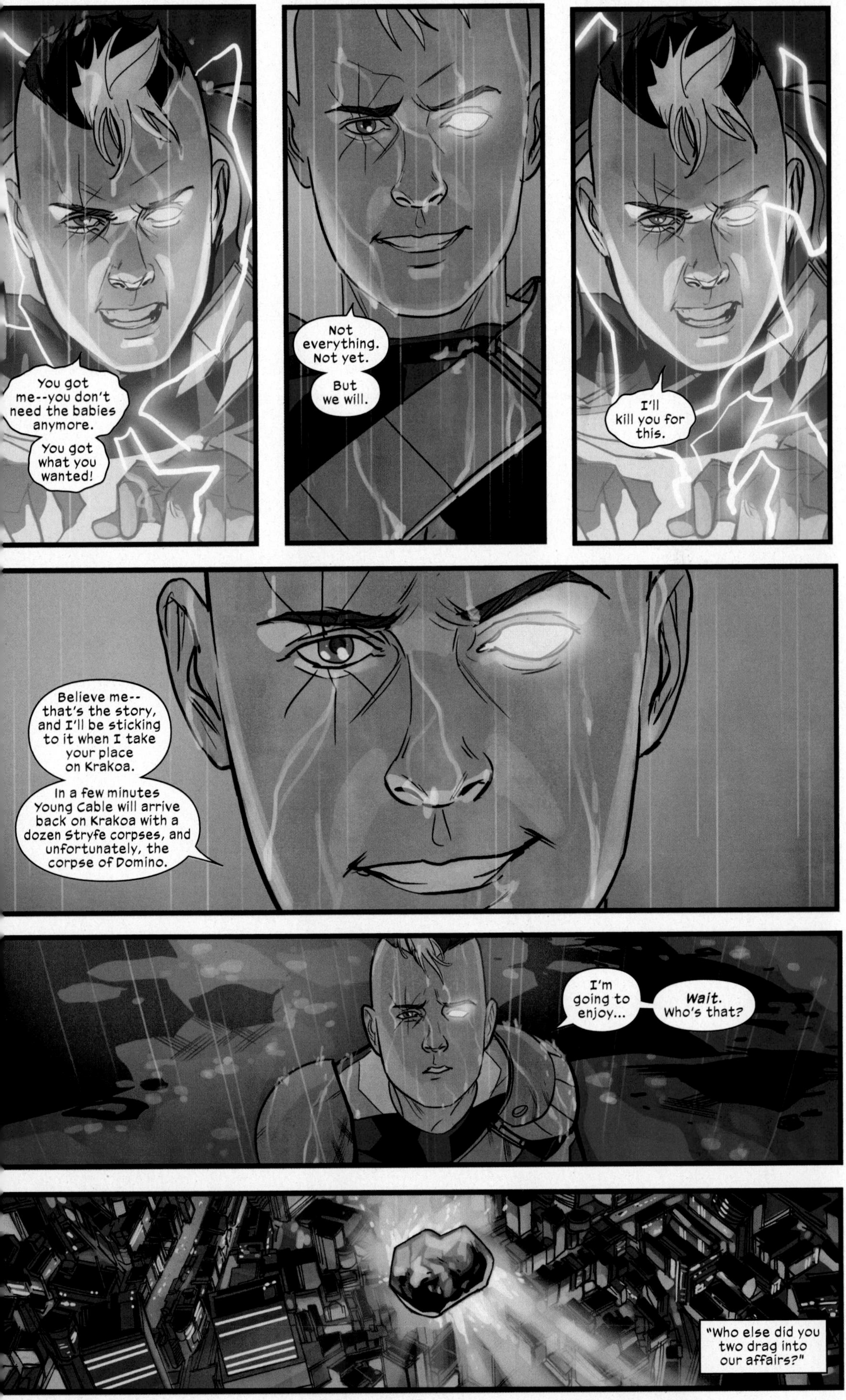
You got me--you don't need the babies anymore.
You got what you wanted!
Not everything. Not yet.
But we will.
I'll kill you for this.
Believe me--that's the story, and I'll be sticking to it when I take your place on Krakoa.
In a few minutes Young Cable will arrive back on Krakoa with a dozen Stryfe corpses, and unfortunately, the corpse of Domino.
I'm going to enjoy...
Wait. Who's that?
"Who else did you two drag into our affairs?"

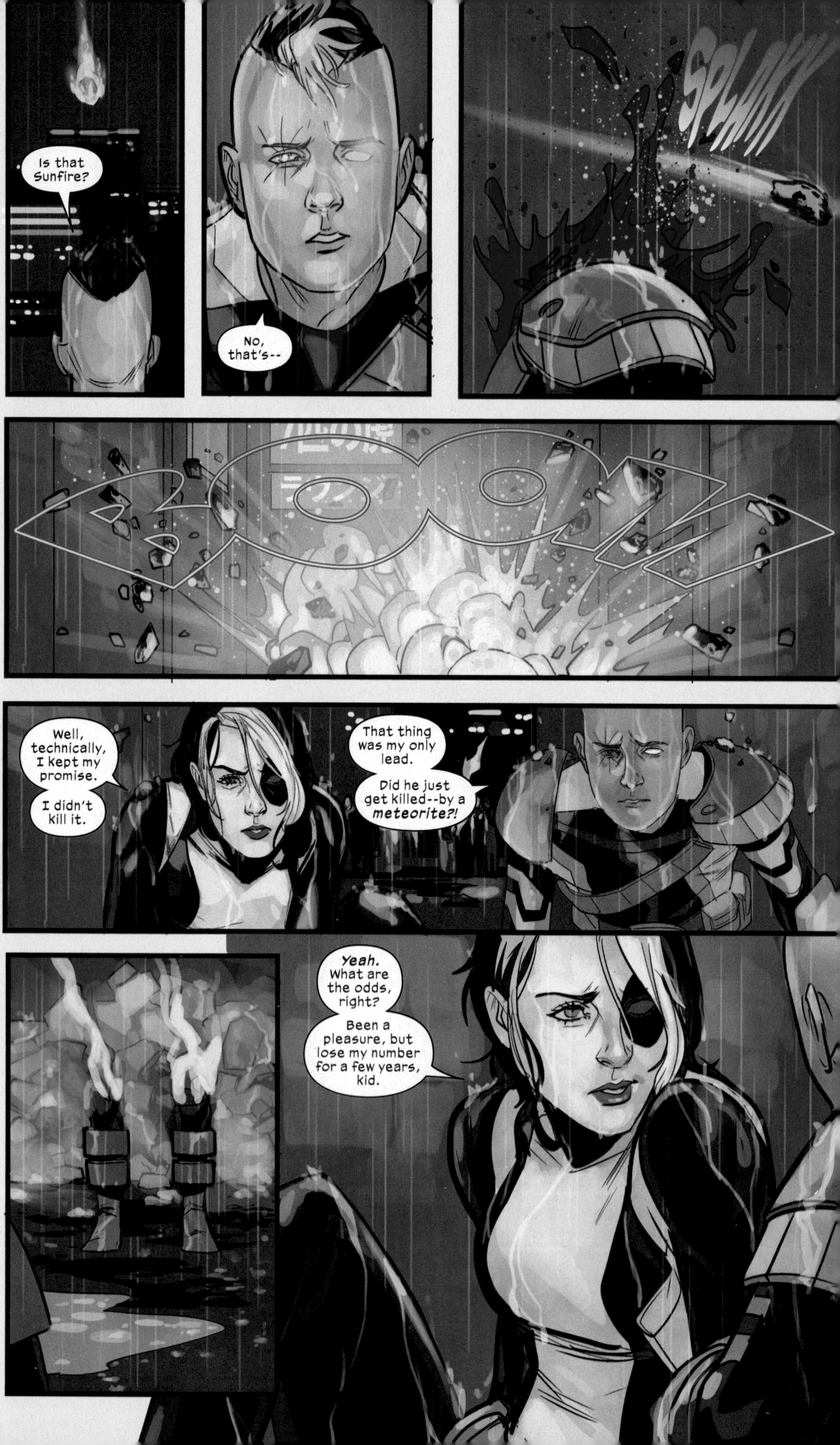

Is that Sunfire?
No, that's--
BOOM
Well, technically, I kept my promise.
I didn't kill it.
That thing was my only lead.
Did he just get killed--by a *meteorite?!*
Yeah. What are the odds, right?
Been a pleasure, but lose my number for a few years, kid.

Beast — Good news/bad news: Cable and I went to Tokyo for gyoza and ended up causing a mess. Decent size. A Logan-sized mess. Need a cleaning crew. — Domino

That's not the business we're in. Will any of the "mess" be missed?

No. It's 12 Stryfe clones -- well, 11 and change. They're in the body of young Nate. Send someone to puke some acid onto them? Tempest?

Oh, there is one clone of middle-aged Nate -- another copy of the one that was stealing babies in Philly. Nobody will miss him, though. Is Sunfire around? He could just wiggle his fingers and sort this,

Hello?

Stand by.

What's the hold-up? Will Maggot's worm guys eat clones? Do you have Deadpool's number? Maybe he'll want them?

X-Factor is inbound.

Thank you.

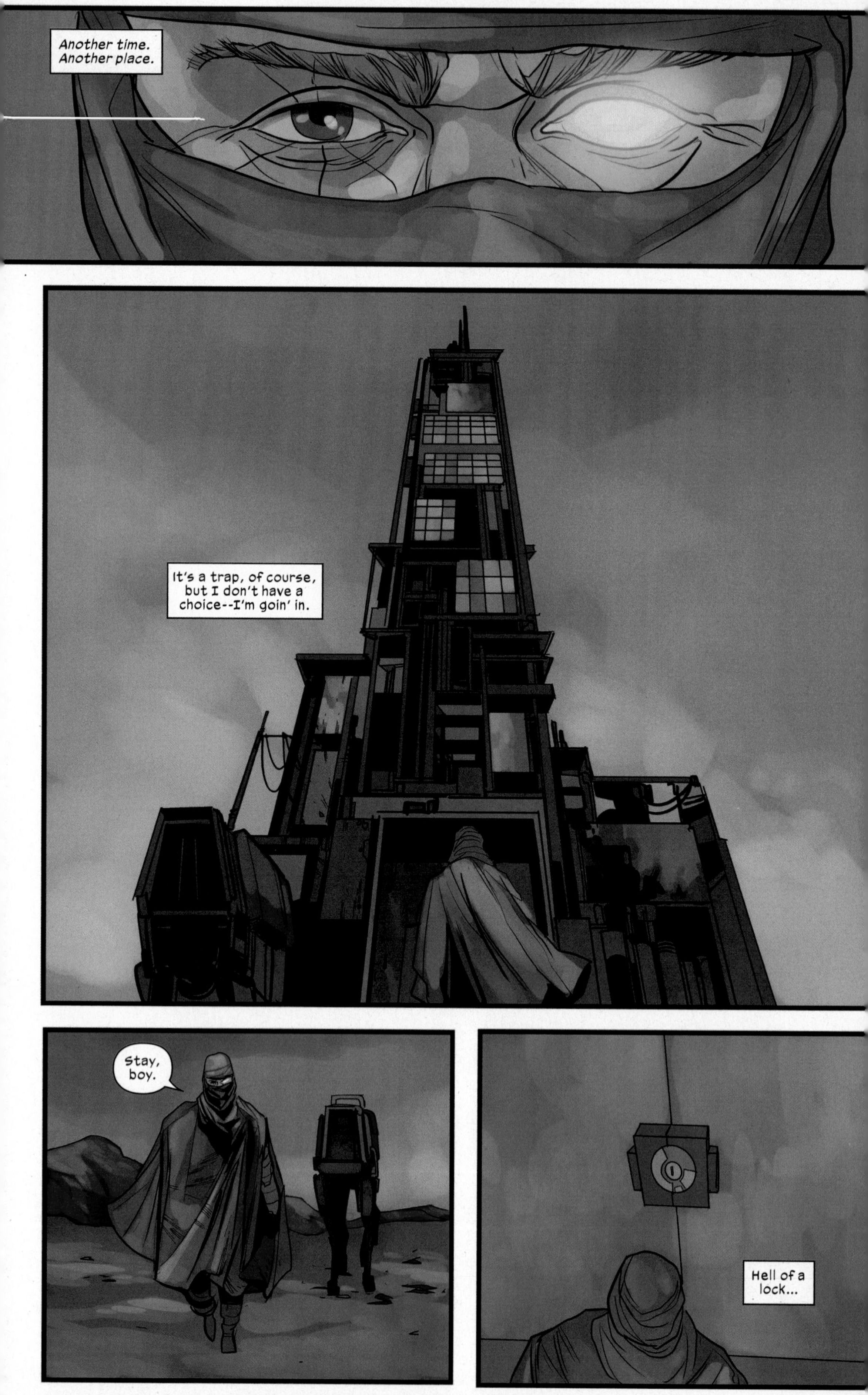

Another time.
Another place.
It's a trap, of course, but I don't have a choice--I'm goin' in.
Stay, boy.
Hell of a lock...

...I can do it the loud way or the quiet way.

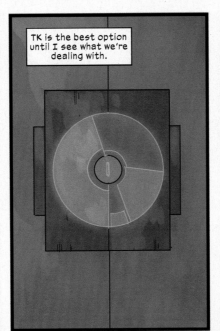

TK is the best option until I see what we're dealing with.

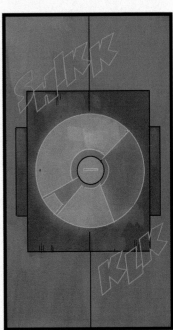

SHIKK

KLK

KLAK

No alarms. Stale air. Bad air. Decomp. I'd better not be too late.

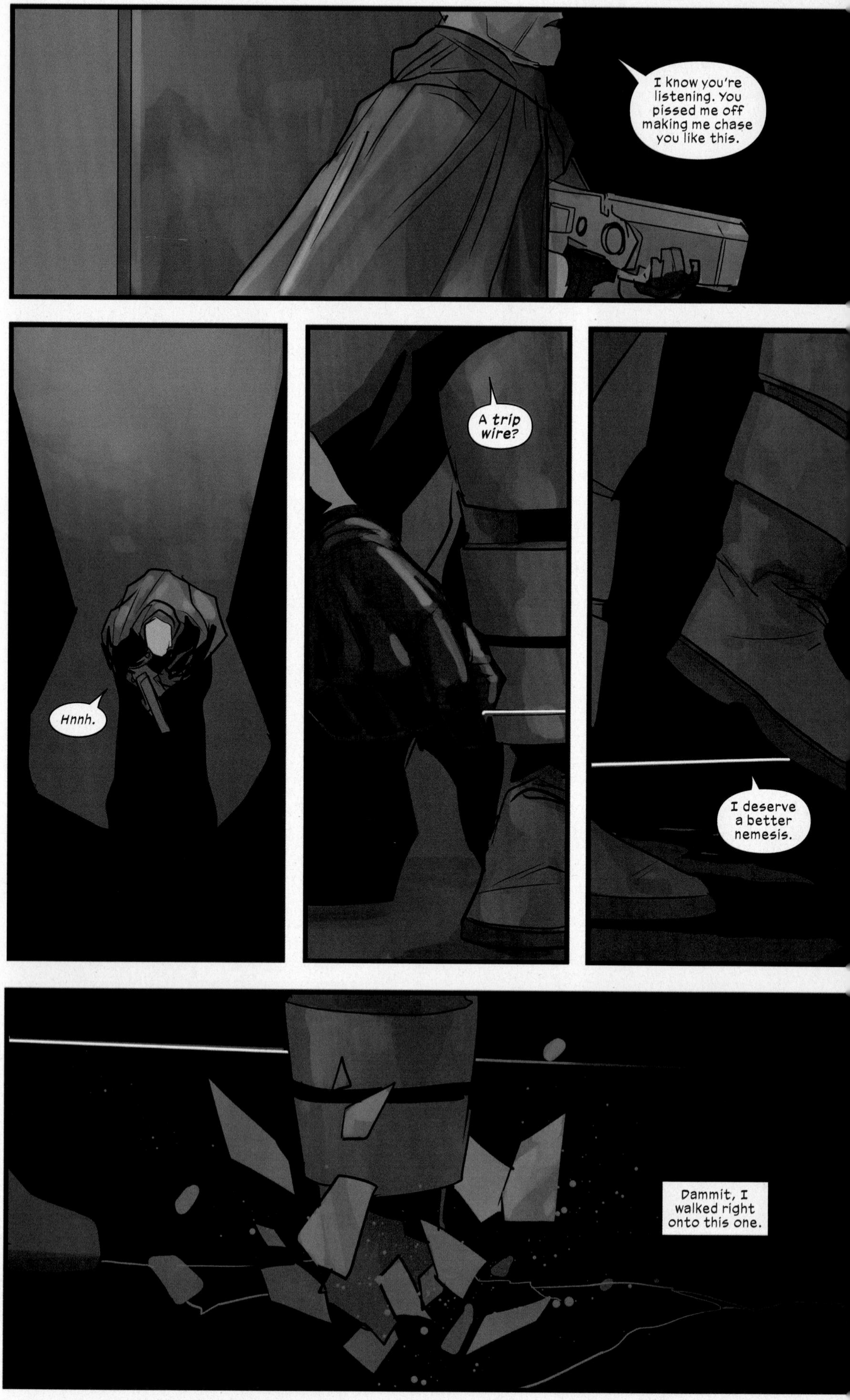
I know you're listening. You pissed me off making me chase you like this.
Hnnh.
A trip wire?
I deserve a better nemesis.
Dammit, I walked right onto this one.

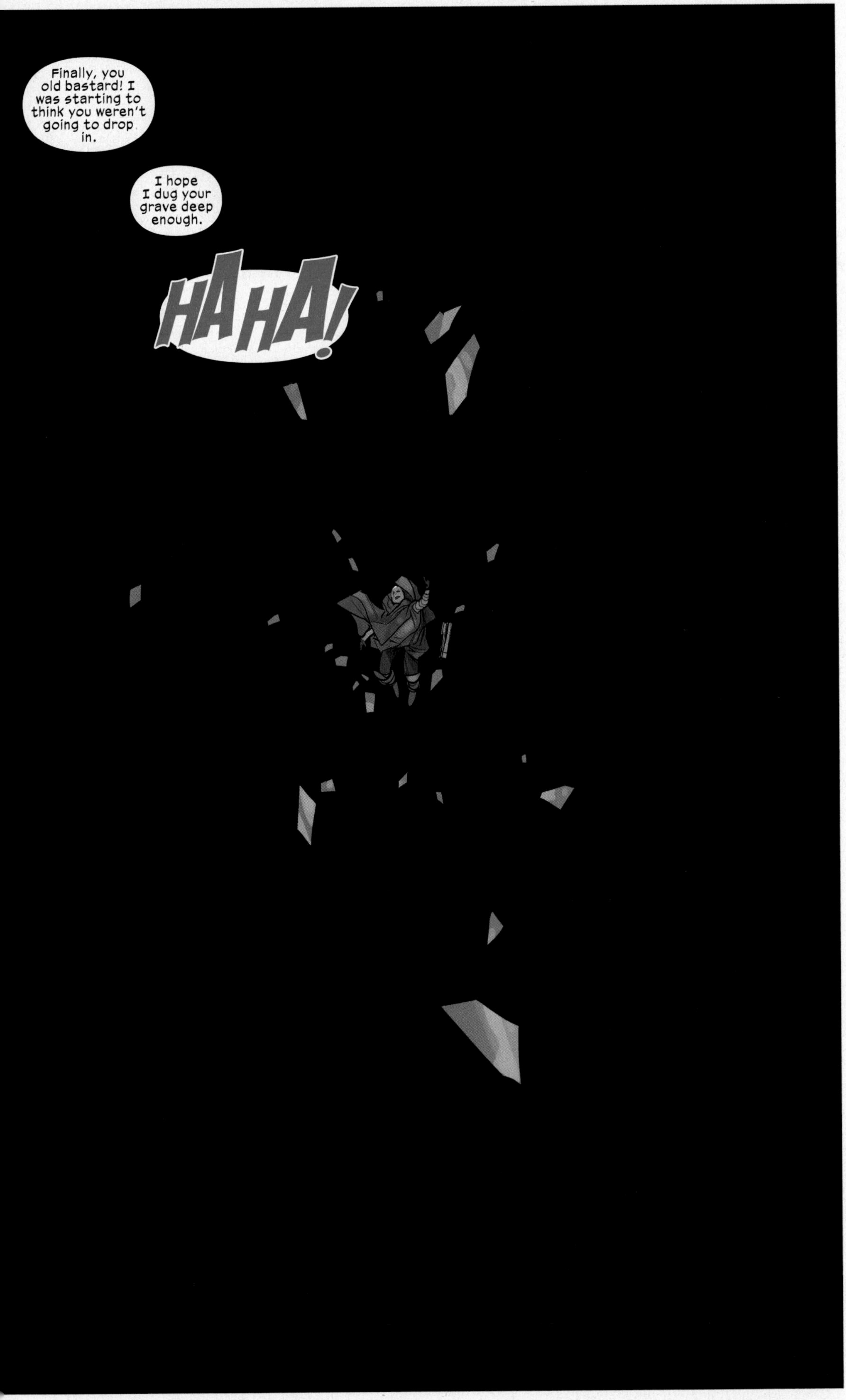
Finally, you old bastard! I was starting to think you weren't going to drop in.
I hope I dug your grave deep enough.
HAHA!

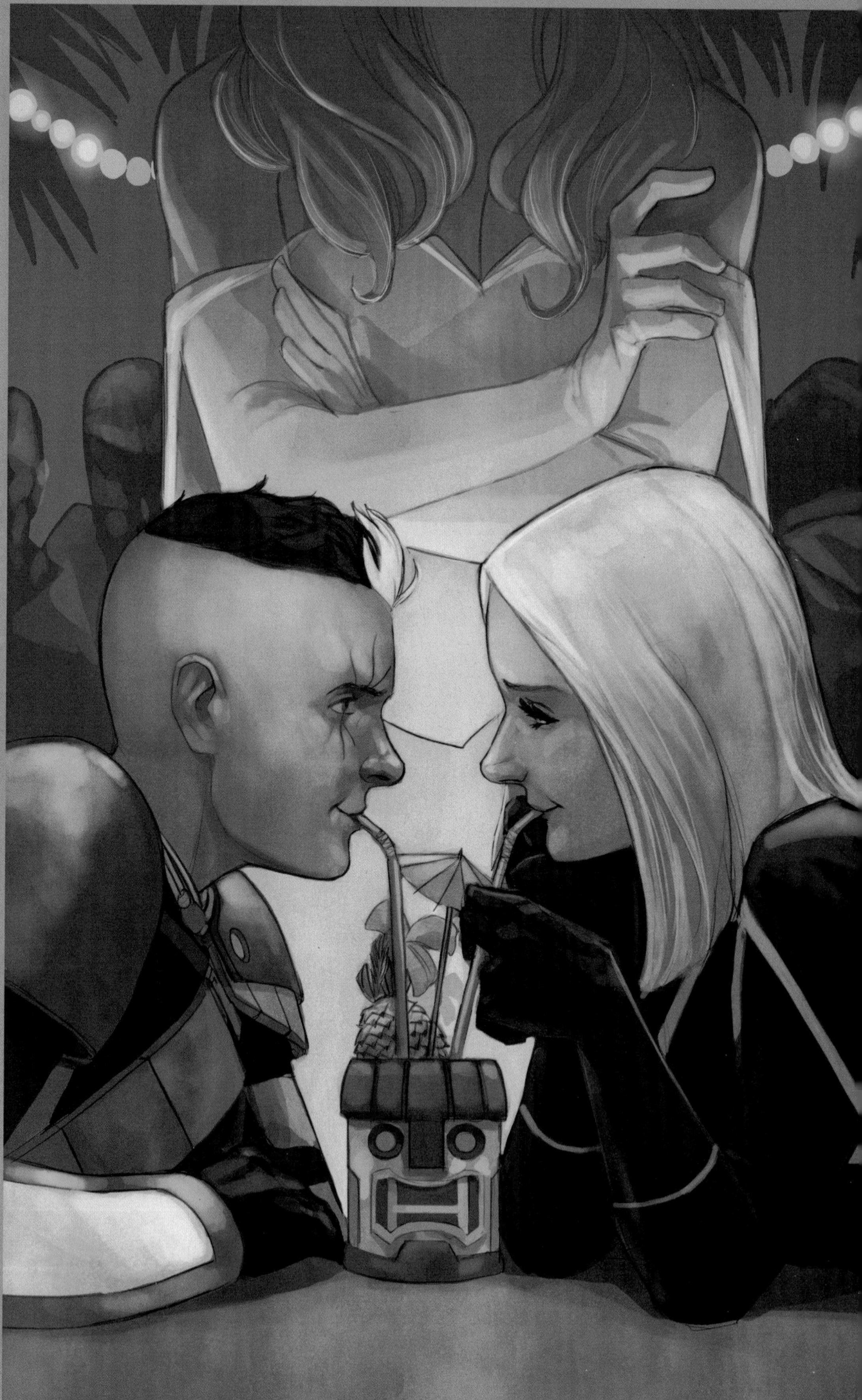

Bargaining

[ca__[0.9]
[ble_[0.9]

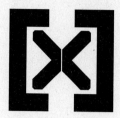

Cable? Everybody was scared of the old man...nobody is scared of the kid.

-- ANONYMOUS PATRON AT THE GREEN LAGOON

[ca__[0.X]
[ble_[0.X]

[ca__[0.9].....]
[ble_[0.9].....]

[Cable_alpha.]

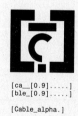

We detected her off the coast of Krakoa 25 minutes ago.

Telepaths like Emma and Esme could hear the thoughts of the beekeepers from the water off the island.

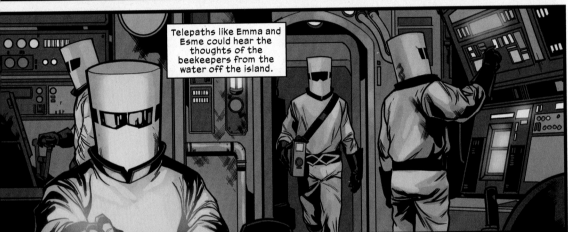

REACTOR ROOM

Usually we just ignore them, but today they came within 100 meters, so we decided to have some *fun.*

Hey! That's a no-go zone.

You're a no-go zone.

Don't worry-- our reactor inspection went great!

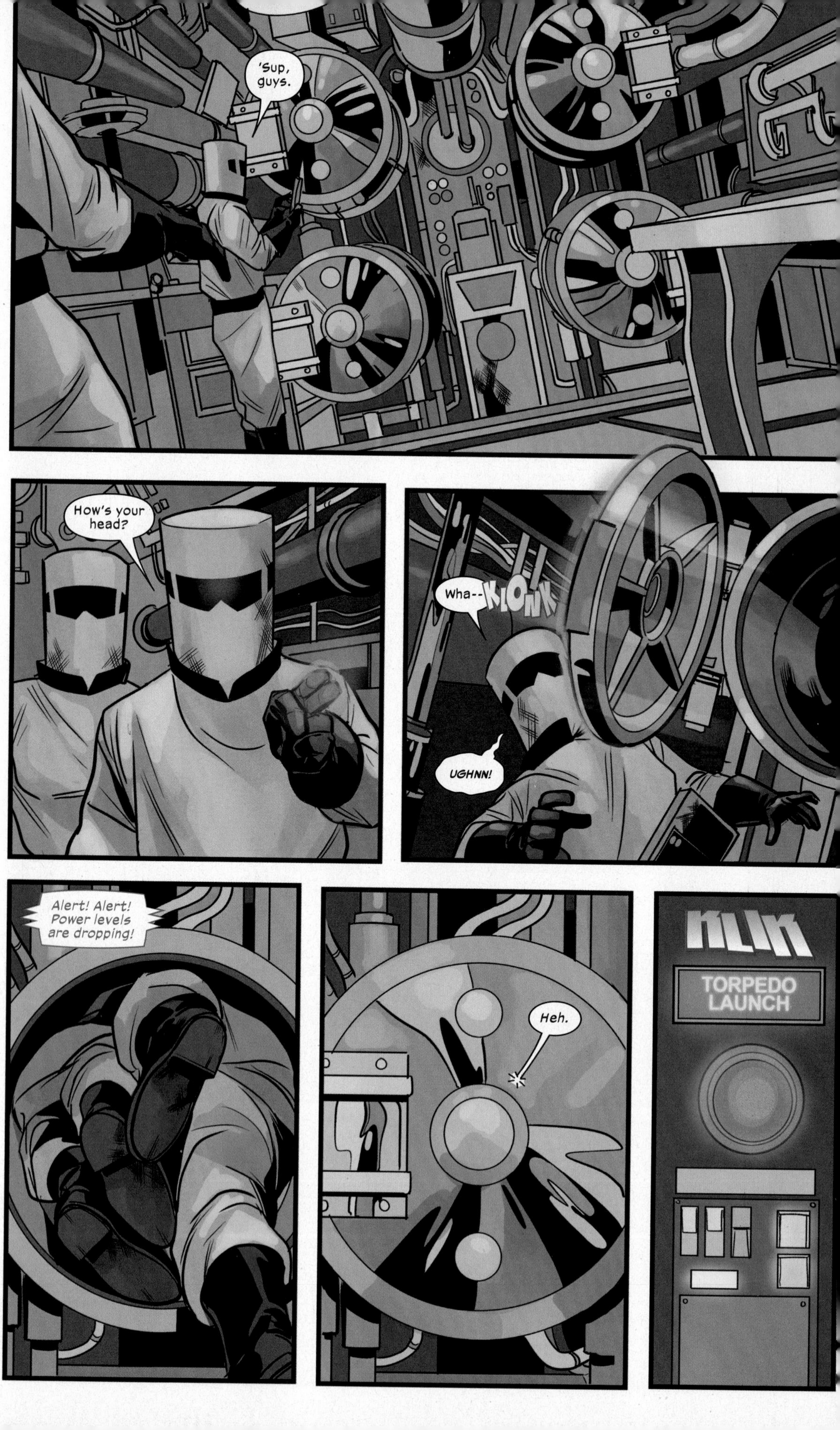
'Sup, guys.
How's your head?
Wha--
KLONK
UGHNN!
Alert! Alert! Power levels are dropping!
Heh.
KLIK
TORPEDO LAUNCH

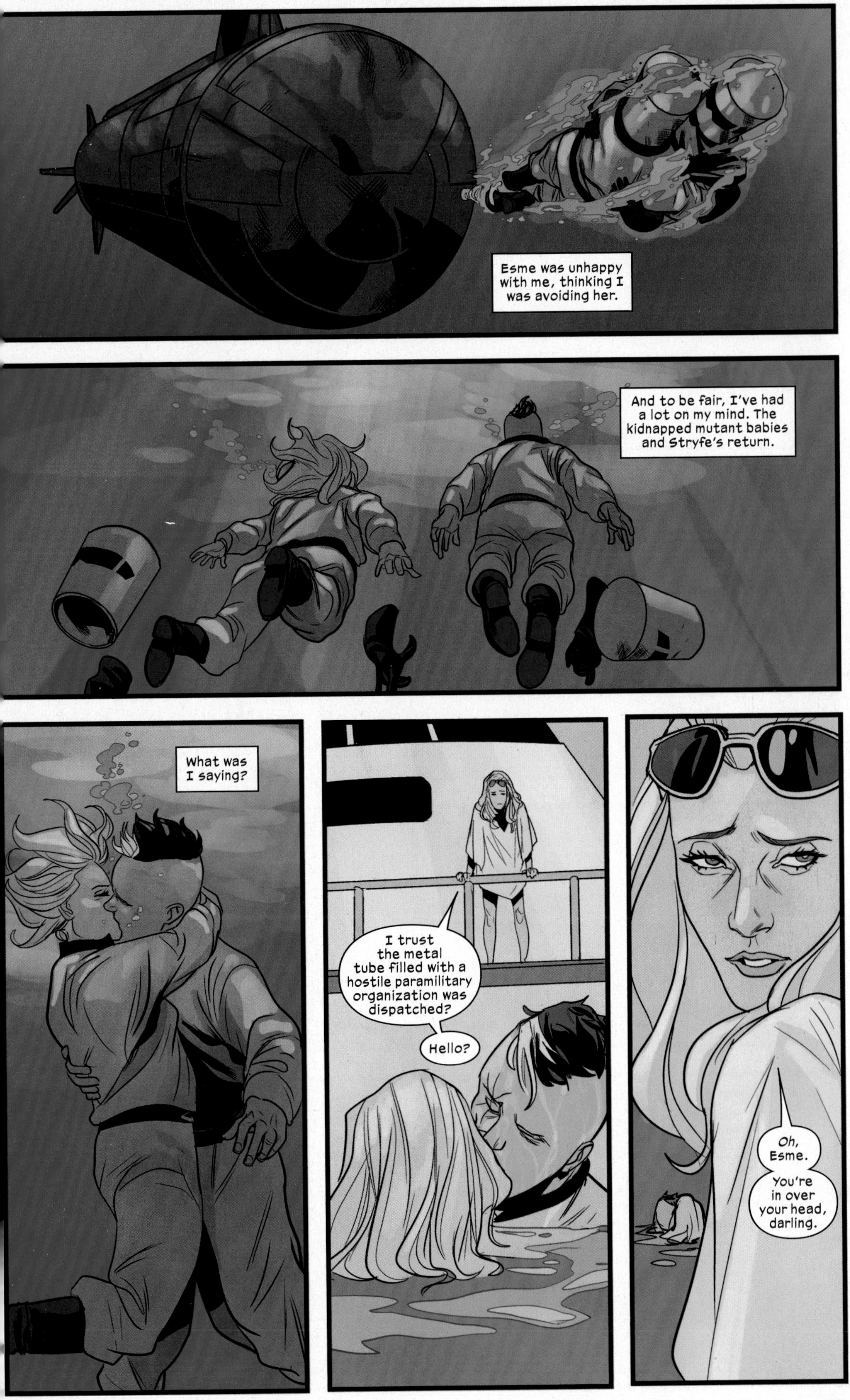
Esme was unhappy with me, thinking I was avoiding her.
And to be fair, I've had a lot on my mind. The kidnapped mutant babies and Stryfe's return.
What was I saying?
I trust the metal tube filled with a hostile paramilitary organization was dispatched?
Hello?
Oh, Esme.
You're in over your head, darling.

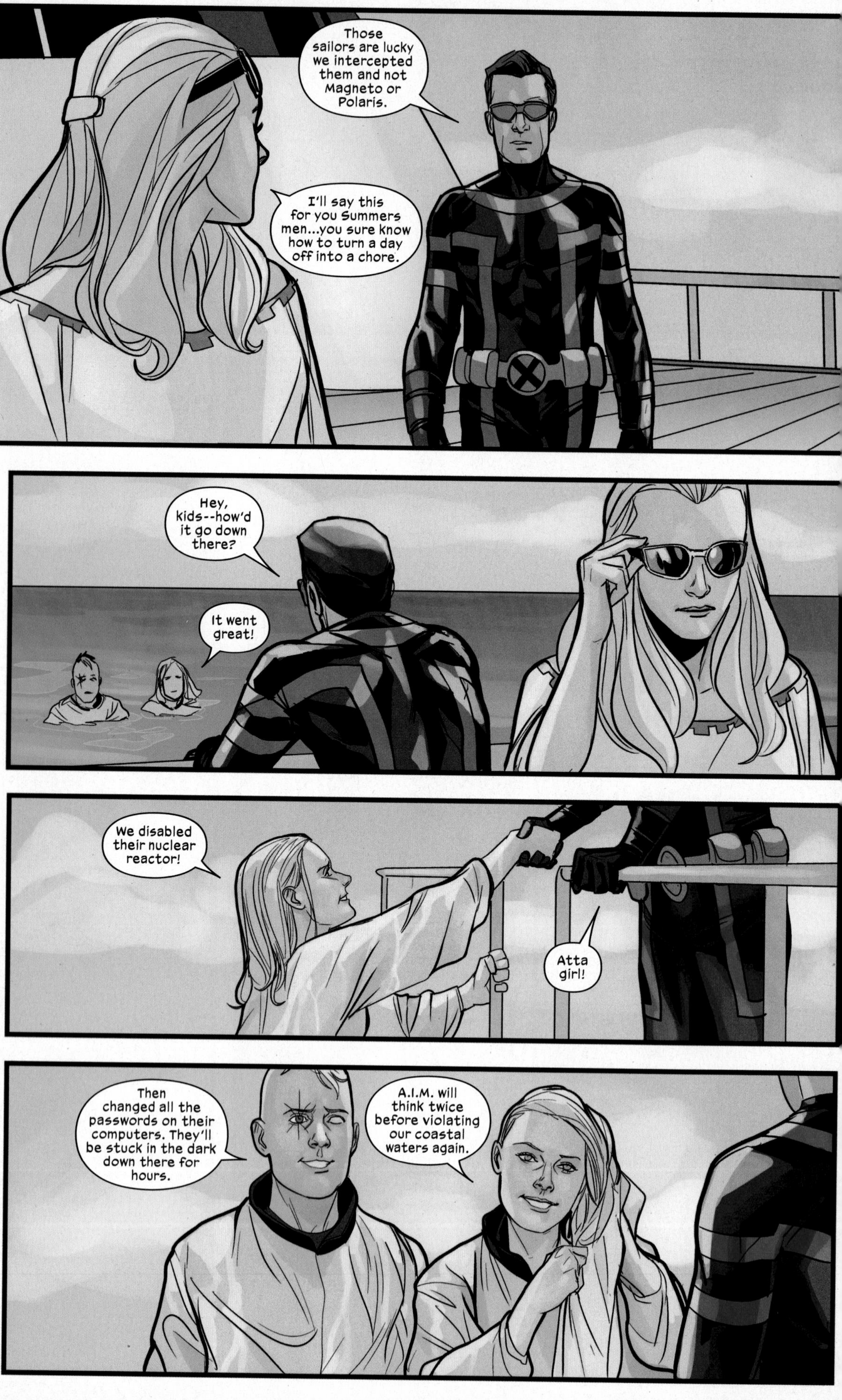
Those sailors are lucky we intercepted them and not Magneto or Polaris.
I'll say this for you Summers men...you sure know how to turn a day off into a chore.
Hey, kids--how'd it go down there?
It went great!
We disabled their nuclear reactor!
Atta girl!
Then changed all the passwords on their computers. They'll be stuck in the dark down there for hours.
A.I.M. will think twice before violating our coastal waters again.

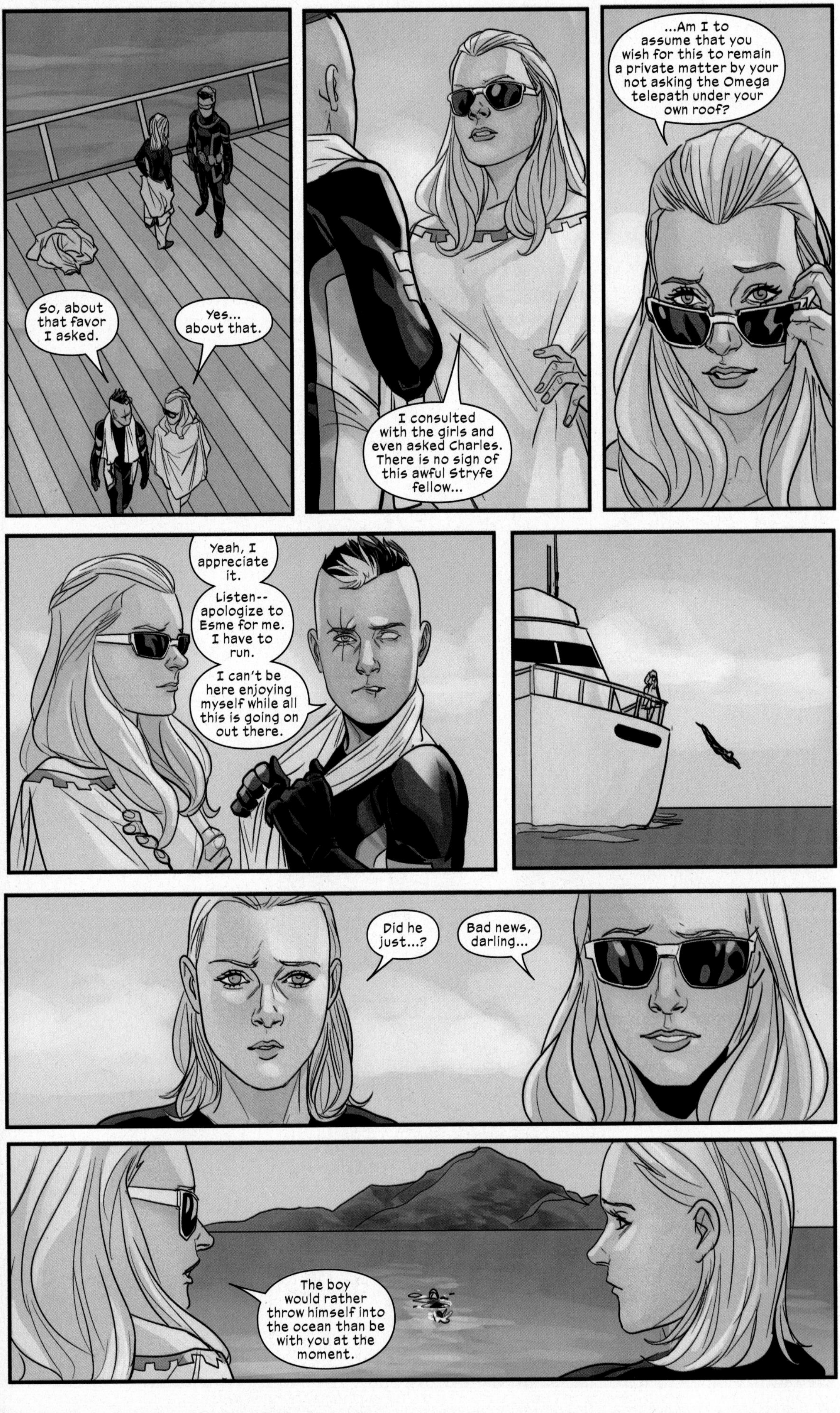
So, about that favor I asked.
Yes... about that.
I consulted with the girls and even asked Charles. There is no sign of this awful Stryfe fellow...
...Am I to assume that you wish for this to remain a private matter by your not asking the Omega telepath under your own roof?
Yeah, I appreciate it.
Listen-- apologize to Esme for me. I have to run.
I can't be here enjoying myself while all this is going on out there.
Did he just...?
Bad news, darling...
The boy would rather throw himself into the ocean than be with you at the moment.

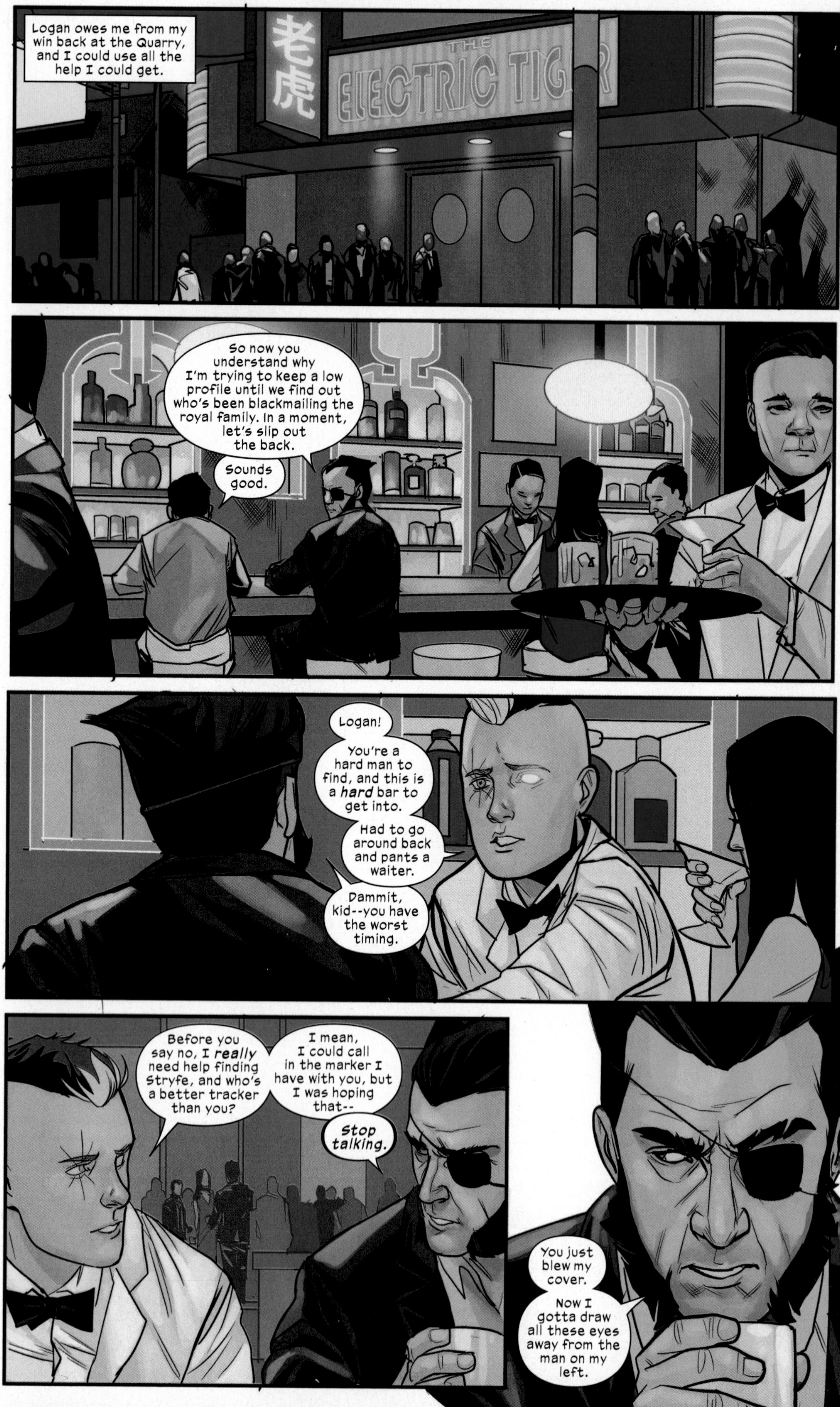

Logan owes me from my win back at the Quarry, and I could use all the help I could get.
老虎
THE ELECTRIC TIGER
So now you understand why I'm trying to keep a low profile until we find out who's been blackmailing the royal family. In a moment, let's slip out the back.
Sounds good.
Logan!
You're a hard man to find, and this is a *hard* bar to get into.
Had to go around back and pants a waiter.
Dammit, kid--you have the worst timing.
Before you say no, I *really* need help finding Stryfe, and who's a better tracker than you?
I mean, I could call in the marker I have with you, but I was hoping that--
Stop talking.
You just blew my cover.
Now I gotta draw all these eyes away from the man on my left.

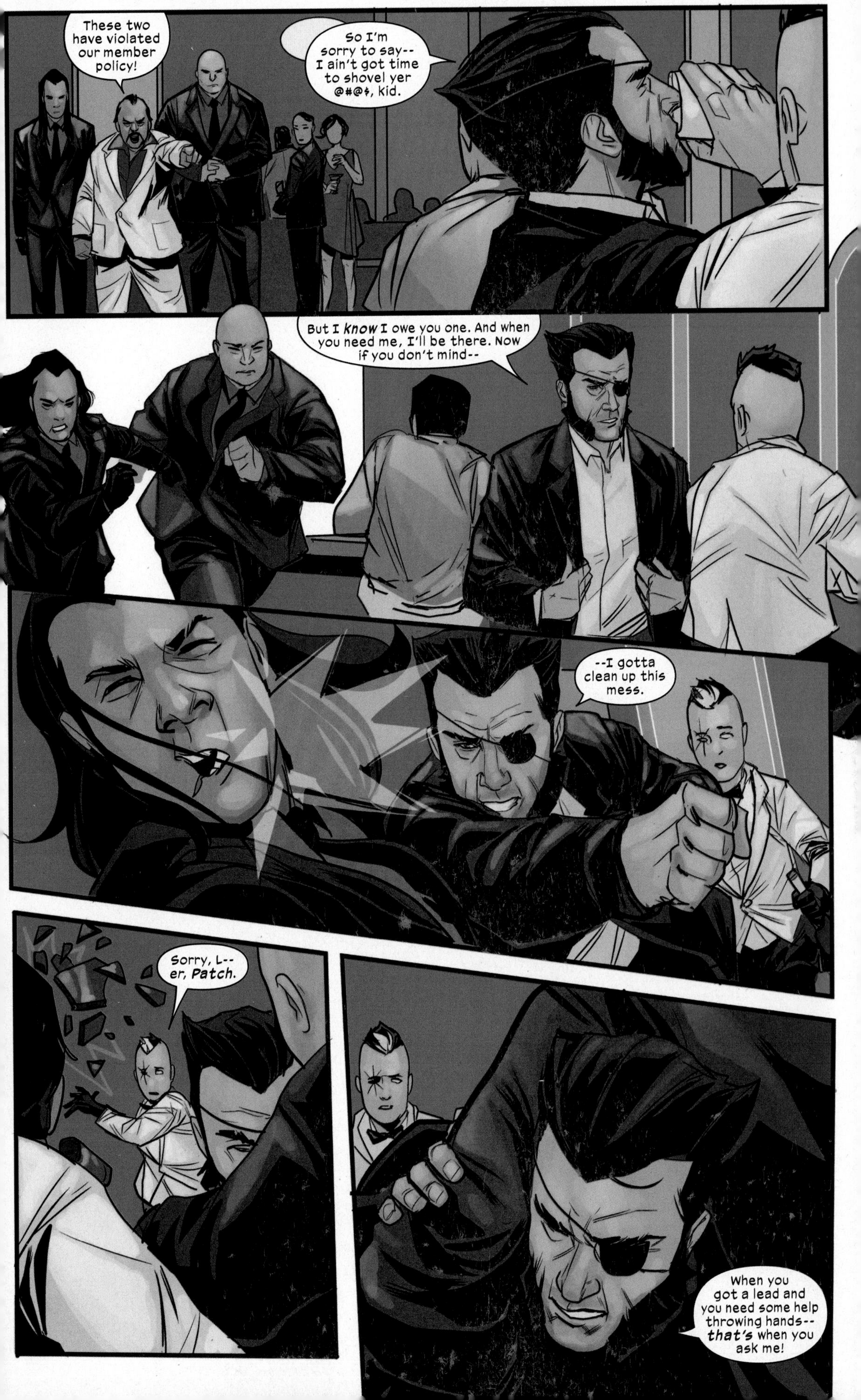
These two have violated our member policy!
So I'm sorry to say-- I ain't got time to shovel yer @#@$, kid.
But I *know* I owe you one. And when you need me, I'll be there. Now if you don't mind--
--I gotta clean up this mess.
Sorry, L-- er, *Patch.*
When you got a lead and you need some help throwing hands-- *that's* when you ask me!

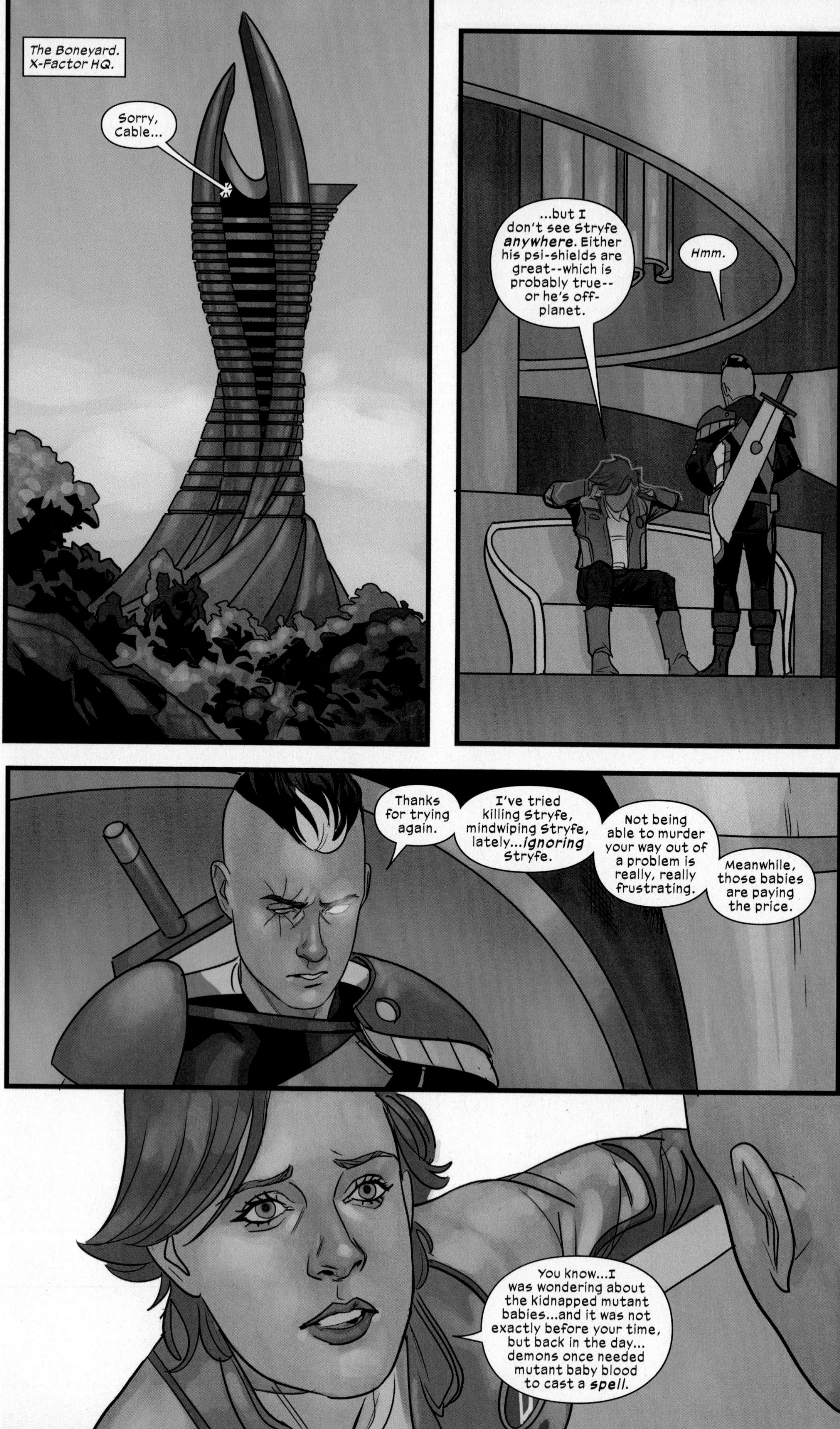
The Boneyard. X-Factor HQ.
Sorry, Cable...
...but I don't see Stryfe *anywhere*. Either his psi-shields are great--which is probably true--or he's off-planet.
Hmm.
Thanks for trying again.
I've tried killing Stryfe, mindwiping Stryfe, lately...*ignoring* Stryfe.
Not being able to murder your way out of a problem is really, really frustrating.
Meanwhile, those babies are paying the price.
You know...I was wondering about the kidnapped mutant babies...and it was not exactly before your time, but back in the day... demons once needed mutant baby blood to cast a *spell*.

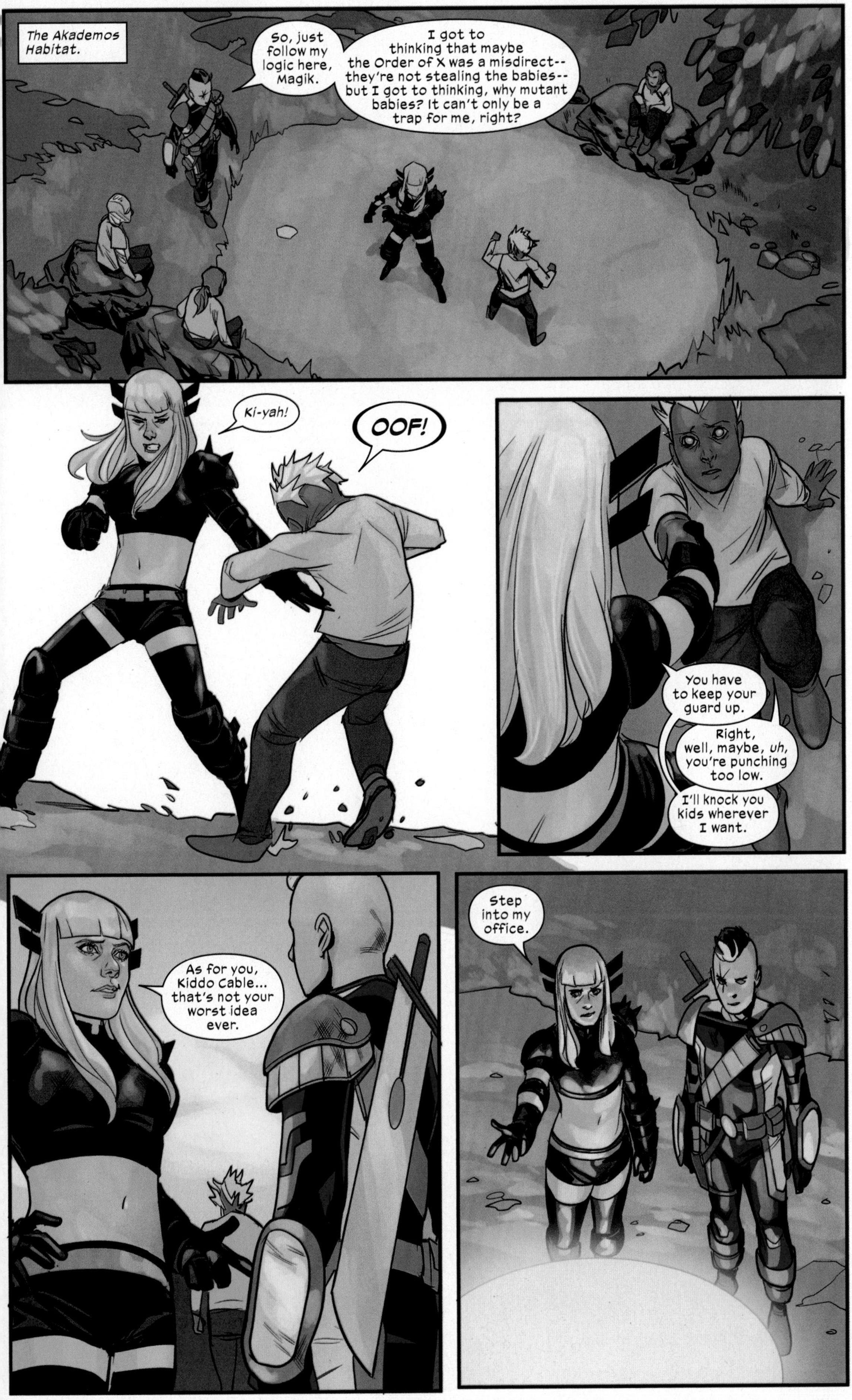
The Akademos Habitat.
So, just follow my logic here, Magik.
I got to thinking that maybe the Order of X was a misdirect--they're not stealing the babies--but I got to thinking, why mutant babies? It can't only be a trap for me, right?
Ki-yah!
OOF!
You have to keep your guard up.
Right, well, maybe, uh, you're punching too low.
I'll knock you kids wherever I want.
As for you, Kiddo Cable... that's not your worst idea ever.
Step into my office.

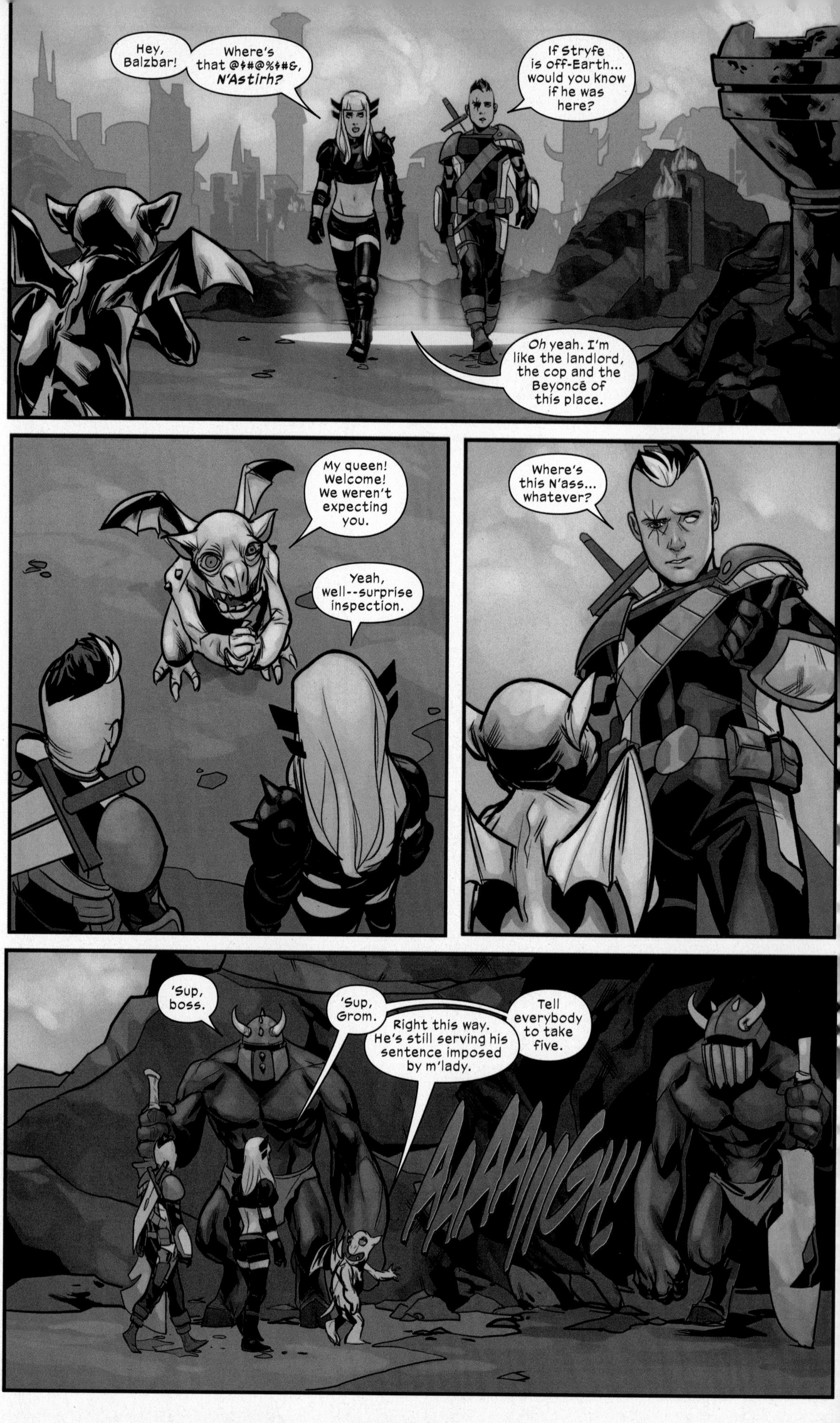
Hey, Balzbar!
Where's that @$#@%$#&, N'Astirh?
If Stryfe is off-Earth... would you know if he was here?
Oh yeah. I'm like the landlord, the cop and the Beyoncé of this place.
My queen! Welcome! We weren't expecting you.
Yeah, well--surprise inspection.
Where's this N'ass... whatever?
'Sup, boss.
'Sup, Grom.
Right this way. He's still serving his sentence imposed by m'lady.
Tell everybody to take five.
AAAAUGH!

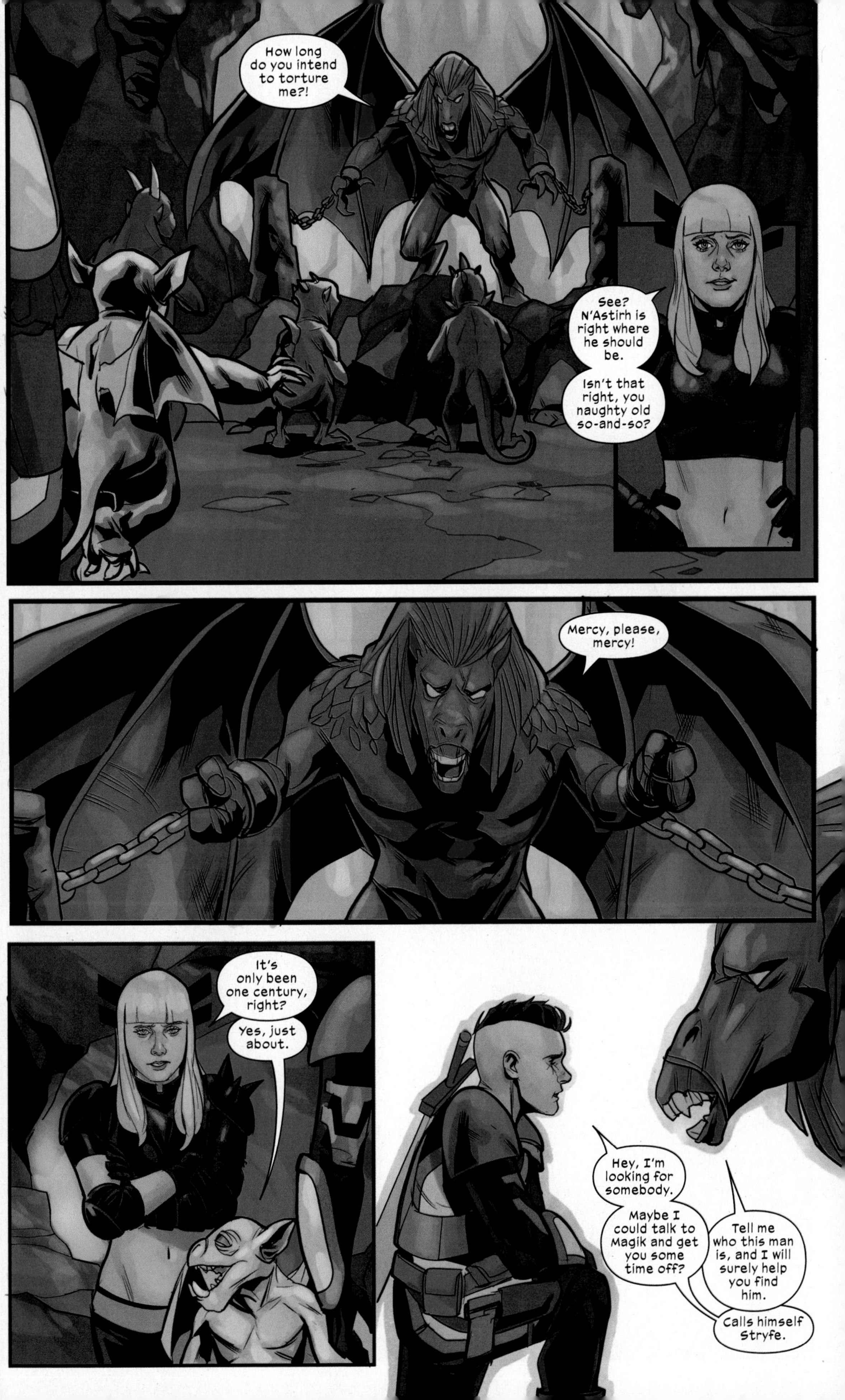
How long do you intend to torture me?!
See? N'Astirh is right where he should be.
Isn't that right, you naughty old so-and-so?
Mercy, please, mercy!
It's only been one century, right?
Yes, just about.
Hey, I'm looking for somebody.
Maybe I could talk to Magik and get you some time off?
Tell me who this man is, and I will surely help you find him.
Calls himself Stryfe.

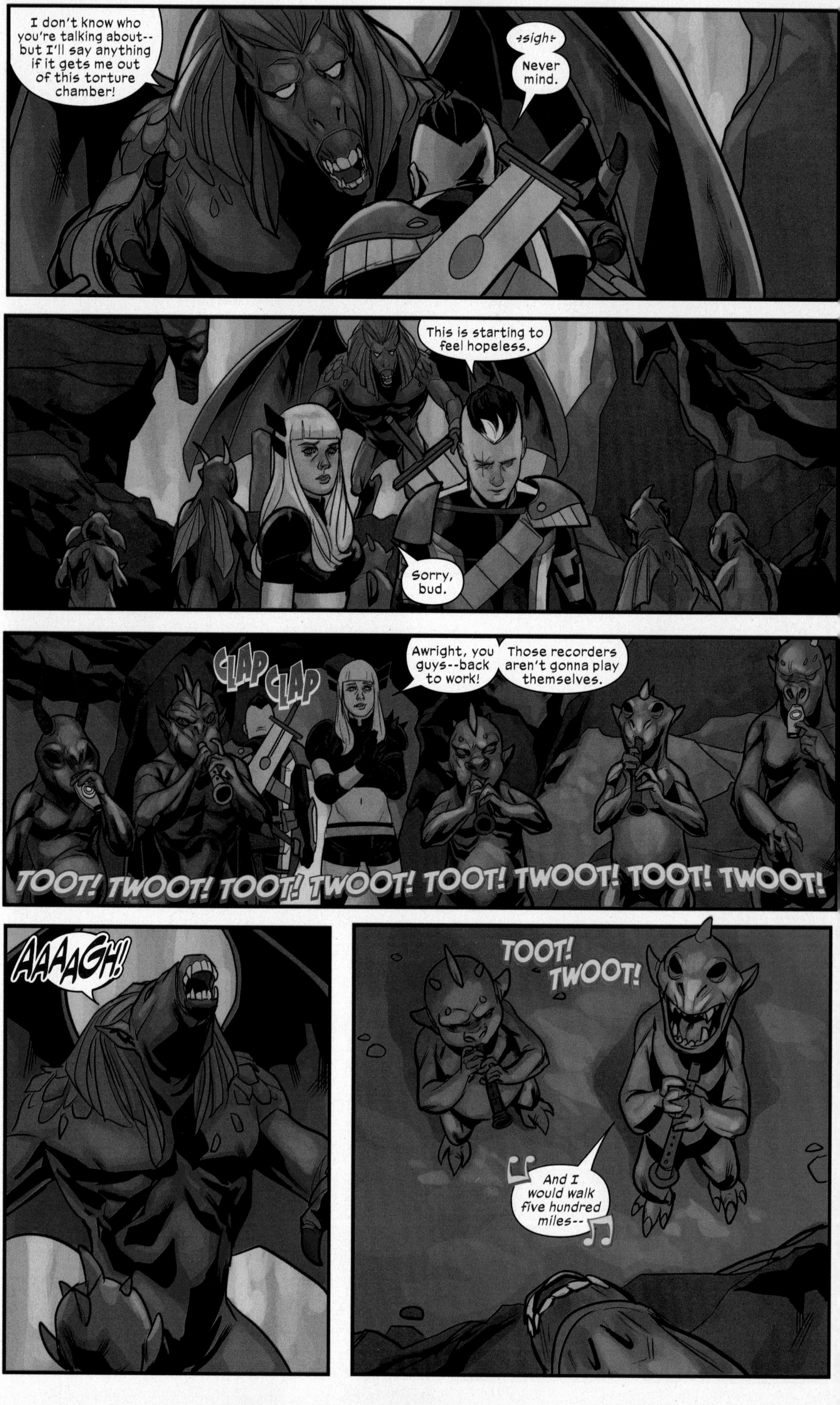

I don't know who you're talking about--but I'll say anything if it gets me out of this torture chamber!
-sigh-
Never mind.
This is starting to feel hopeless.
Sorry, bud.
CLAP CLAP
Awright, you guys--back to work!
Those recorders aren't gonna play themselves.
TOOT! TWOOT! TOOT! TWOOT! TOOT! TWOOT! TOOT! TWOOT!
AAAAGH!
TOOT! TWOOT!
And I would walk five hundred miles--

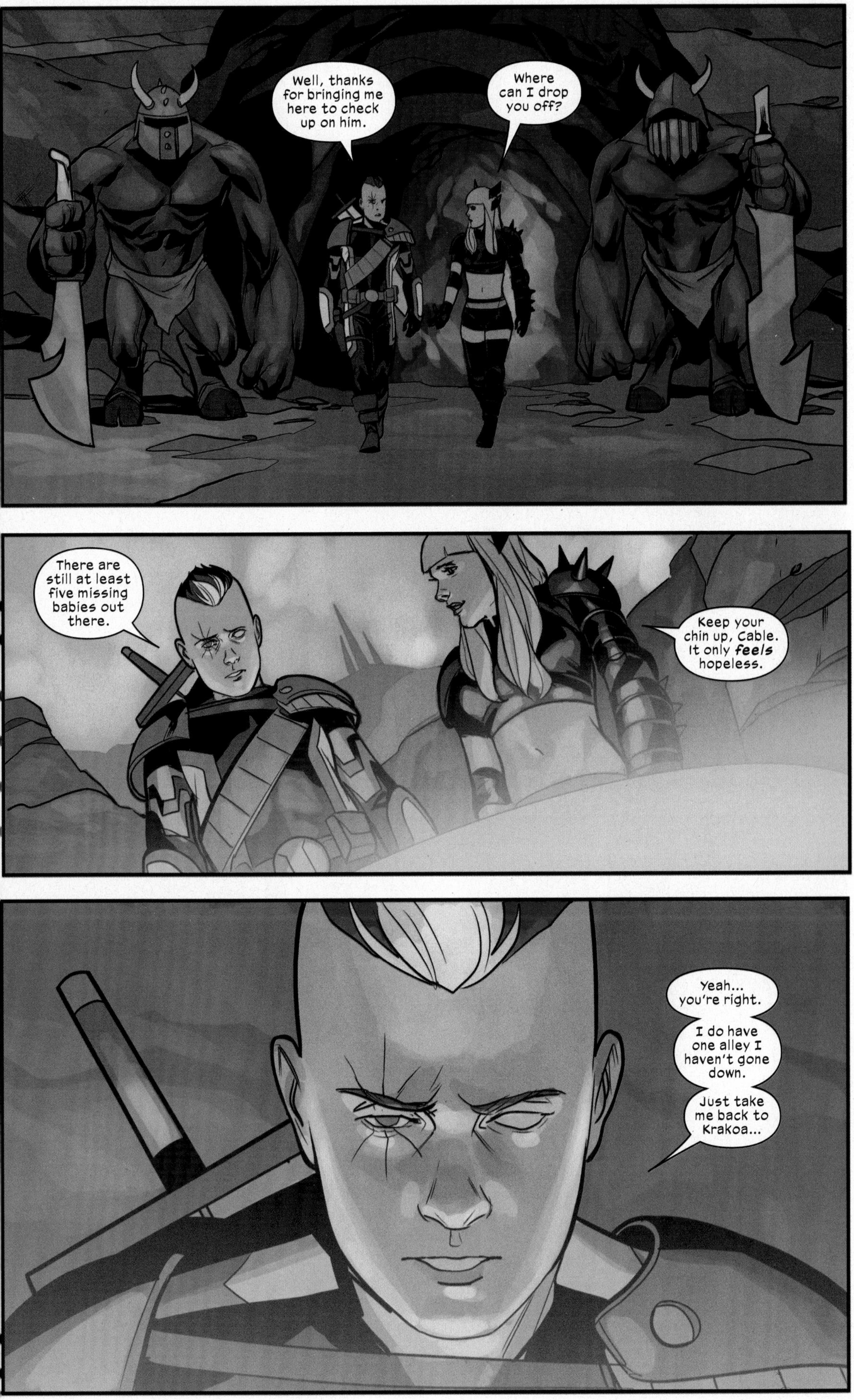
Well, thanks for bringing me here to check up on him.
Where can I drop you off?
There are still at least five missing babies out there.
Keep your chin up, Cable. It only *feels* hopeless.
Yeah... you're right.
I do have one alley I haven't gone down.
Just take me back to Krakoa...

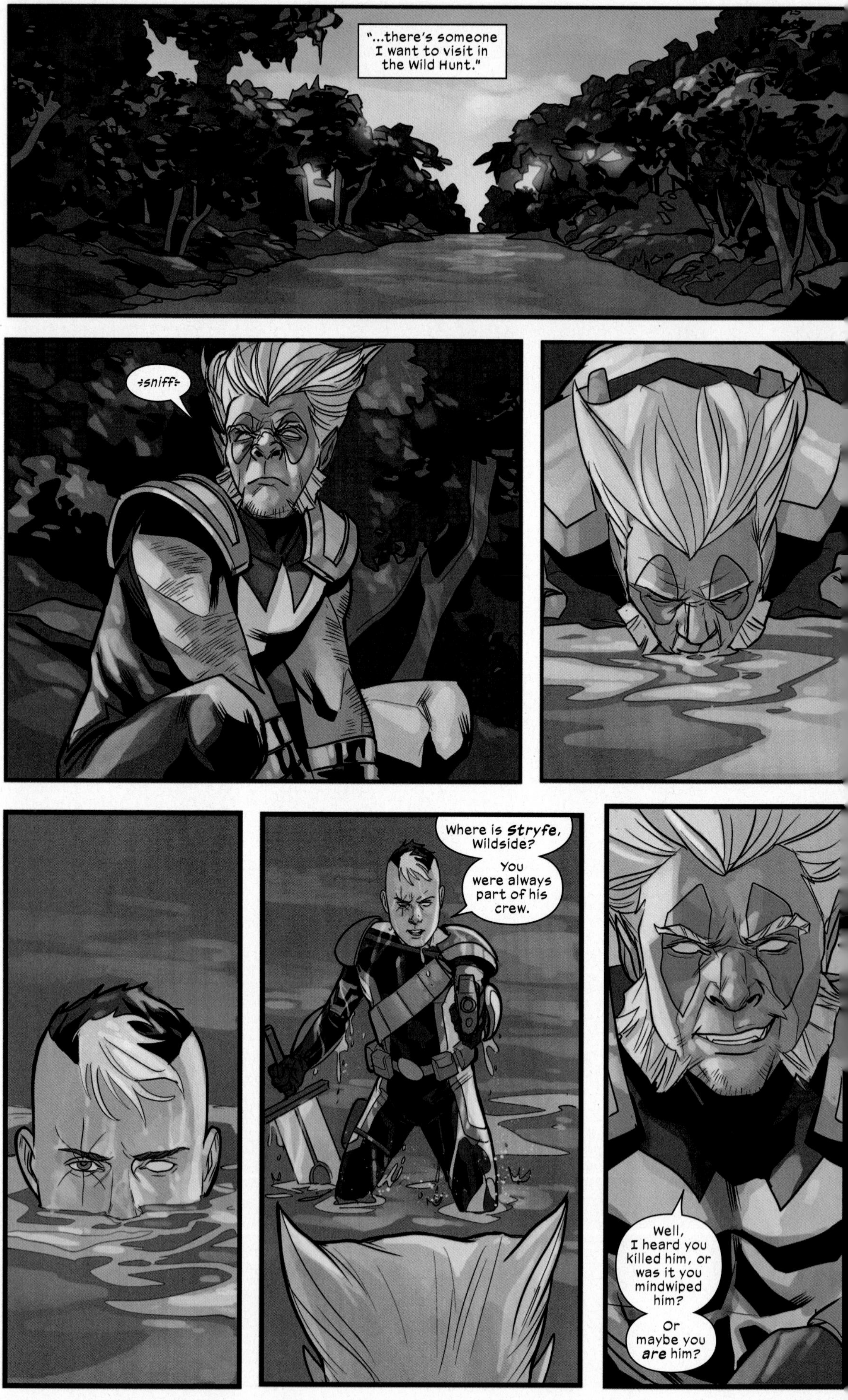
"...there's someone I want to visit in the Wild Hunt."
sniff
Where is Stryfe, Wildside?
You were always part of his crew.
Well, I heard you killed him, or was it you mindwiped him?
Or maybe you are him?

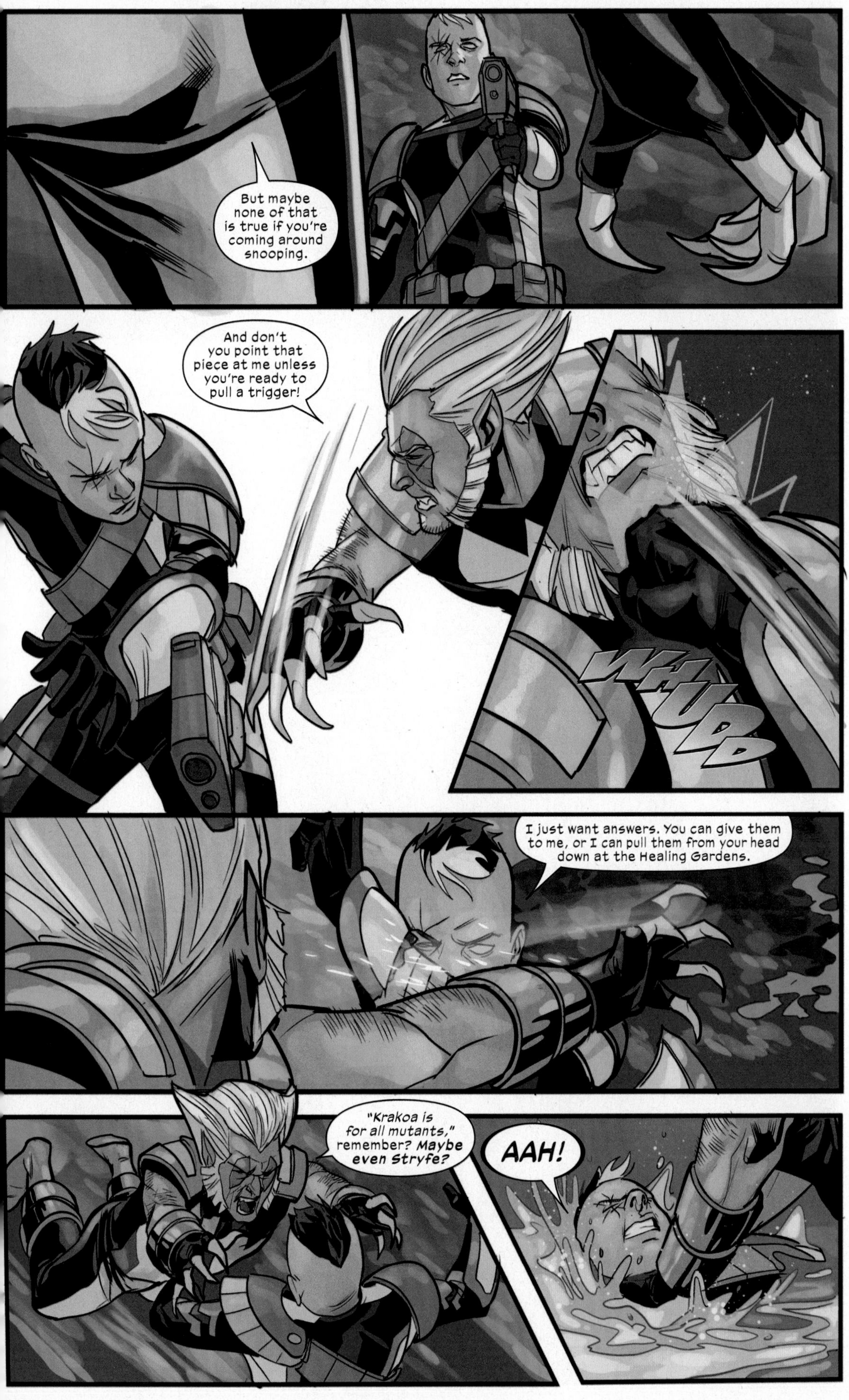
But maybe none of that is true if you're coming around snooping.
And don't you point that piece at me unless you're ready to pull a trigger!
WHUDD
I just want answers. You can give them to me, or I can pull them from your head down at the Healing Gardens.
"Krakoa is for all mutants," remember? Maybe even Stryfe?
AAH!

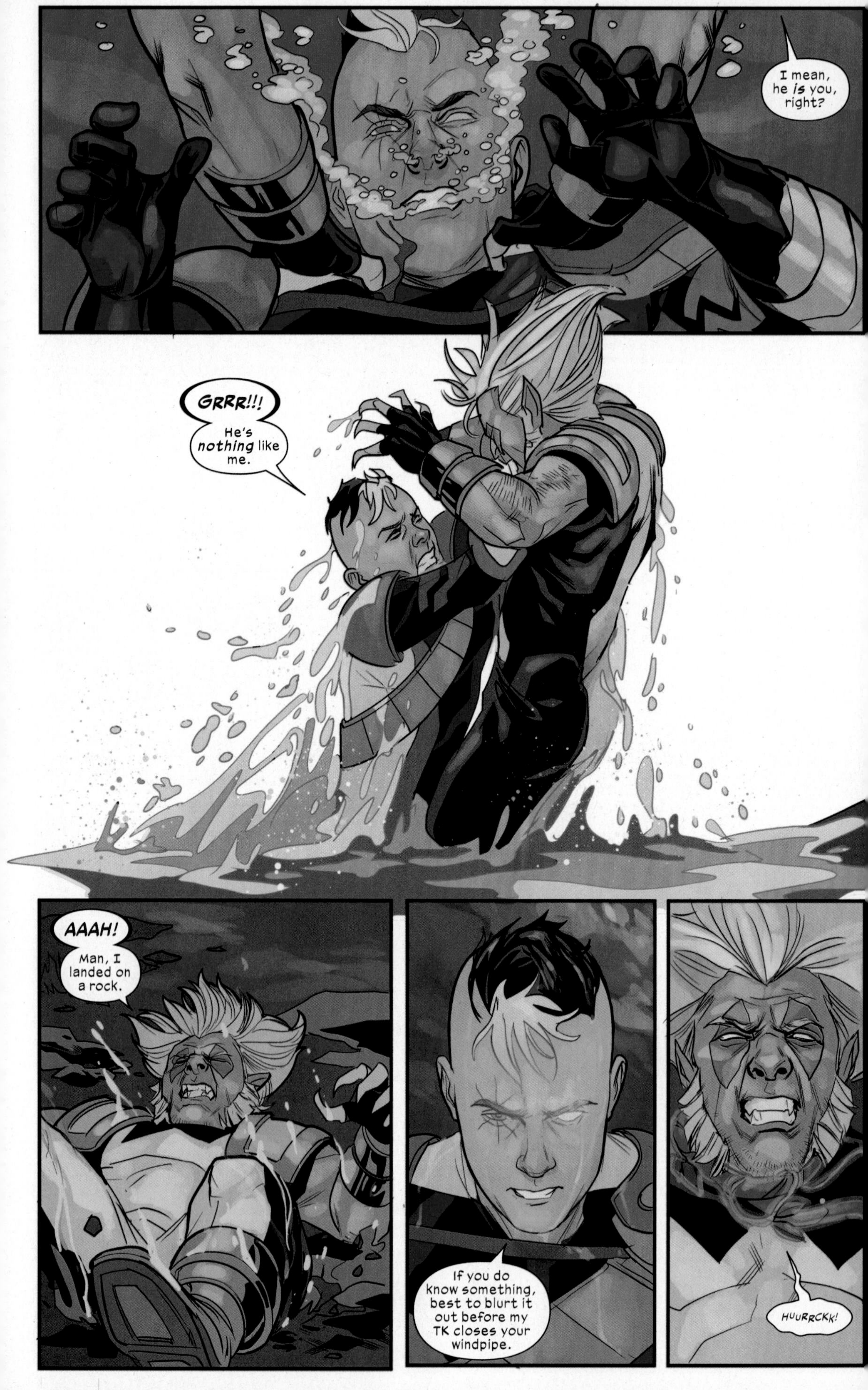
I mean, he *is* you, right?
GRRR!!!
He's *nothing* like me.
AAAH!
Man, I landed on a rock.
If you do know something, best to blurt it out before my TK closes your windpipe.
HUURRCKK!

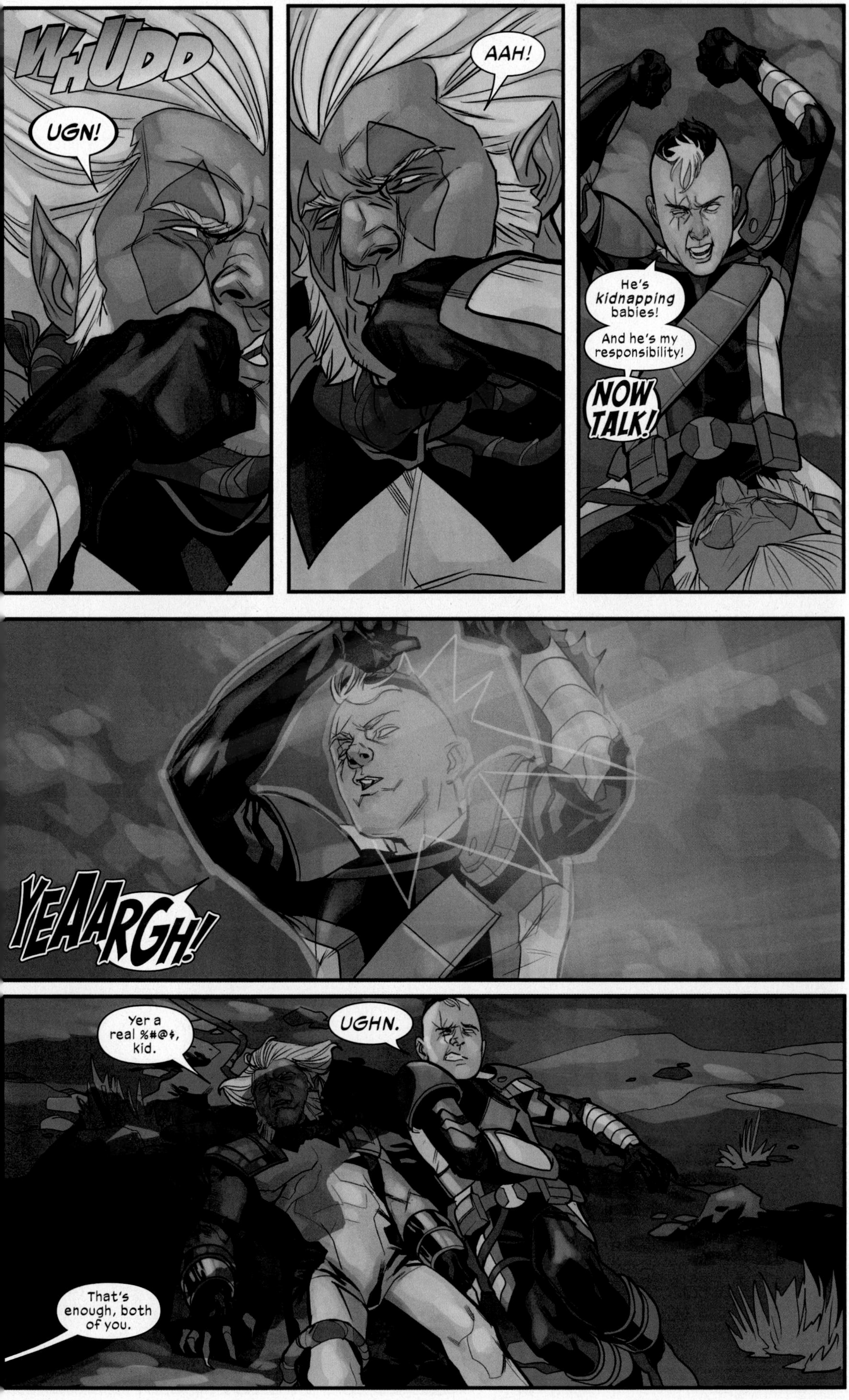
WHUDD
UGN!
AAH!
He's *kidnapping* babies!
And he's my responsibility!
NOW TALK!
YEAARGH!
Yer a real %#@$, kid.
UGHN.
That's enough, both of you.

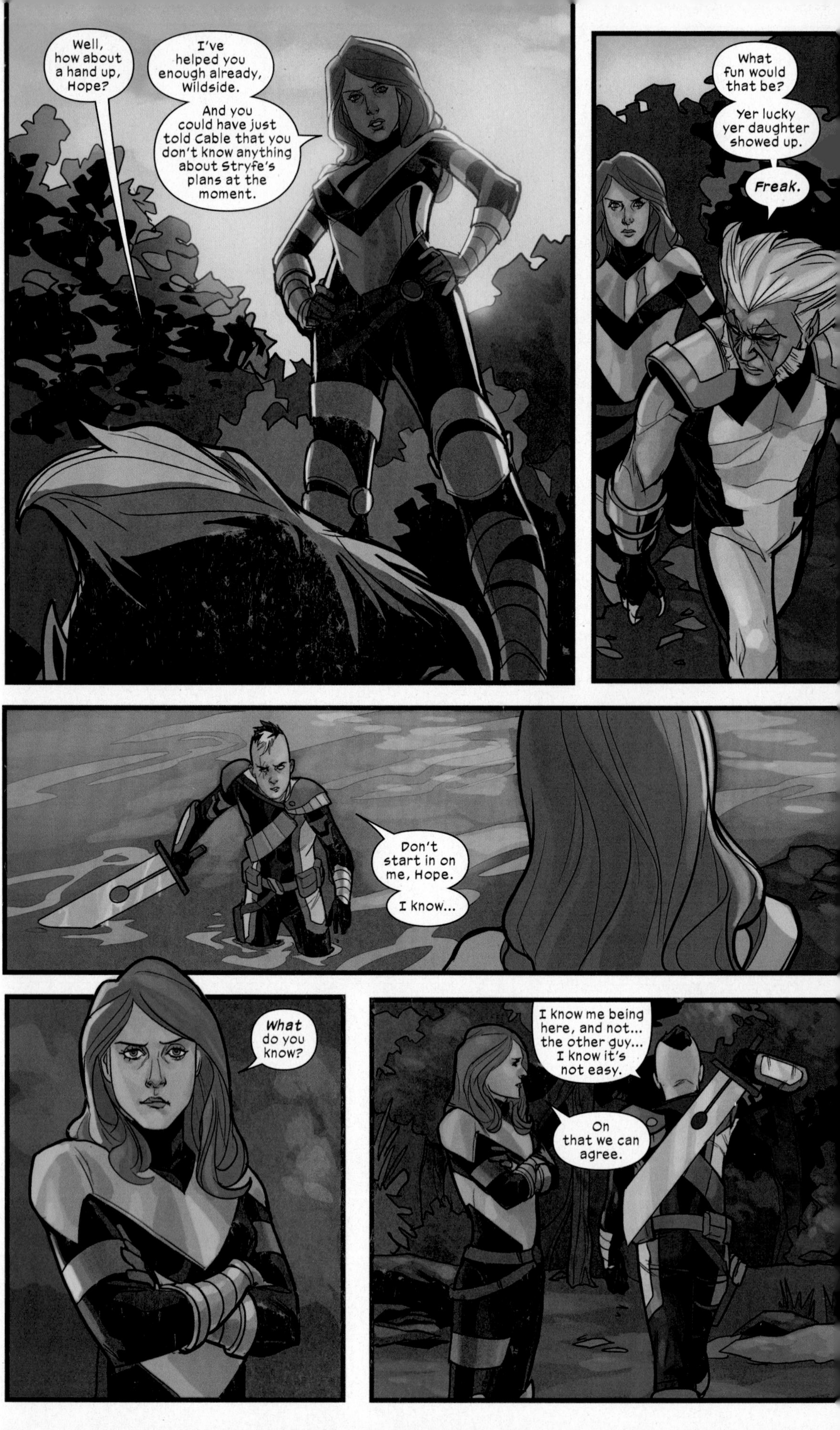
Well, how about a hand up, Hope?
I've helped you enough already, Wildside.
And you could have just told Cable that you don't know anything about Stryfe's plans at the moment.
What fun would that be?
Yer lucky yer daughter showed up.
Freak.
Don't start in on me, Hope.
I know...
What do you know?
I know me being here, and not... the other guy... I know it's not easy.
On that we can agree.

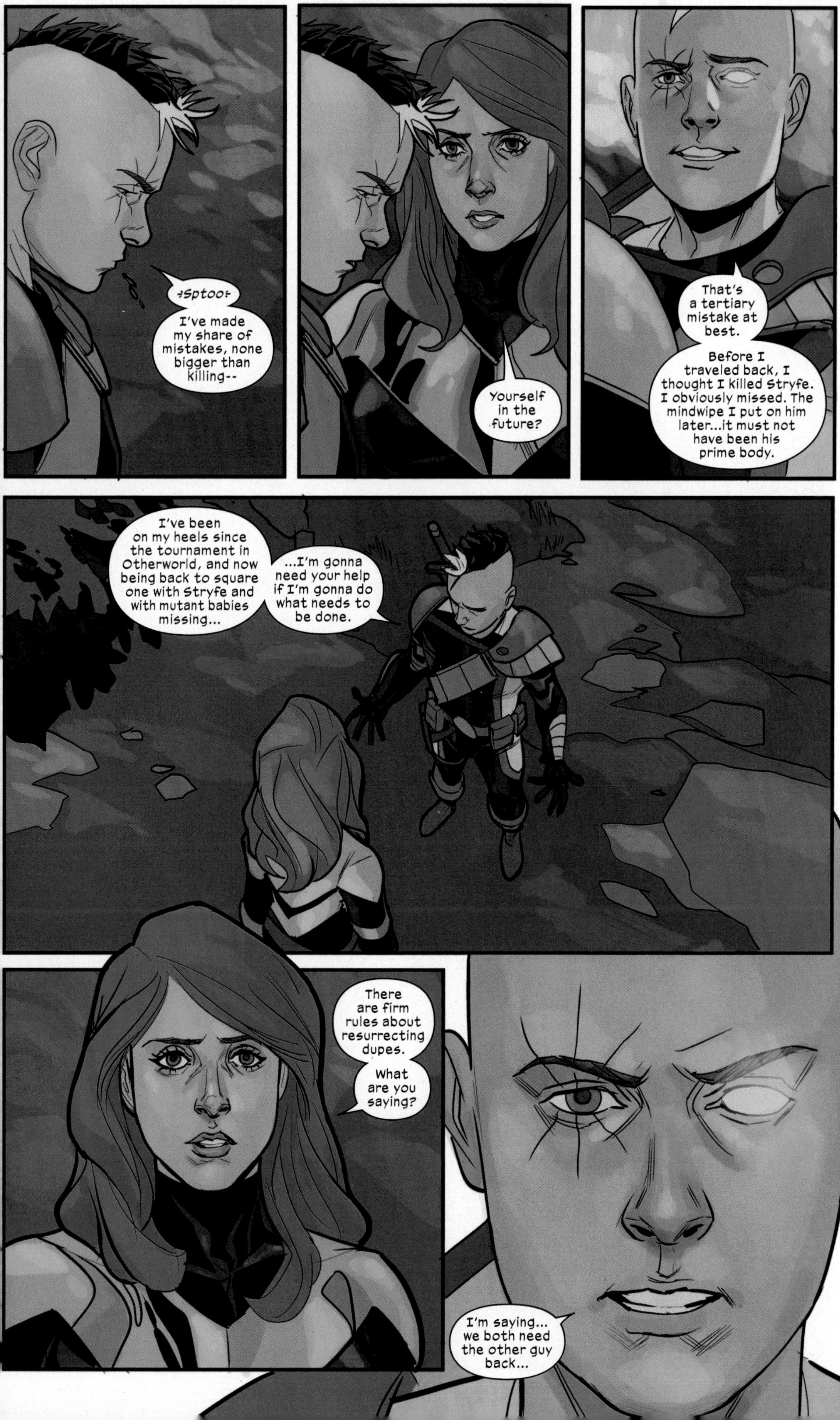

-Sptoo-
I've made my share of mistakes, none bigger than killing--
Yourself in the future?
That's a tertiary mistake at best.
Before I traveled back, I thought I killed Stryfe. I obviously missed. The mindwipe I put on him later...it must not have been his prime body.
I've been on my heels since the tournament in Otherworld, and now being back to square one with Stryfe and with mutant babies missing...
...I'm gonna need your help if I'm gonna do what needs to be done.
There are firm rules about resurrecting dupes.
What are you saying?
I'm saying... we both need the other guy back...

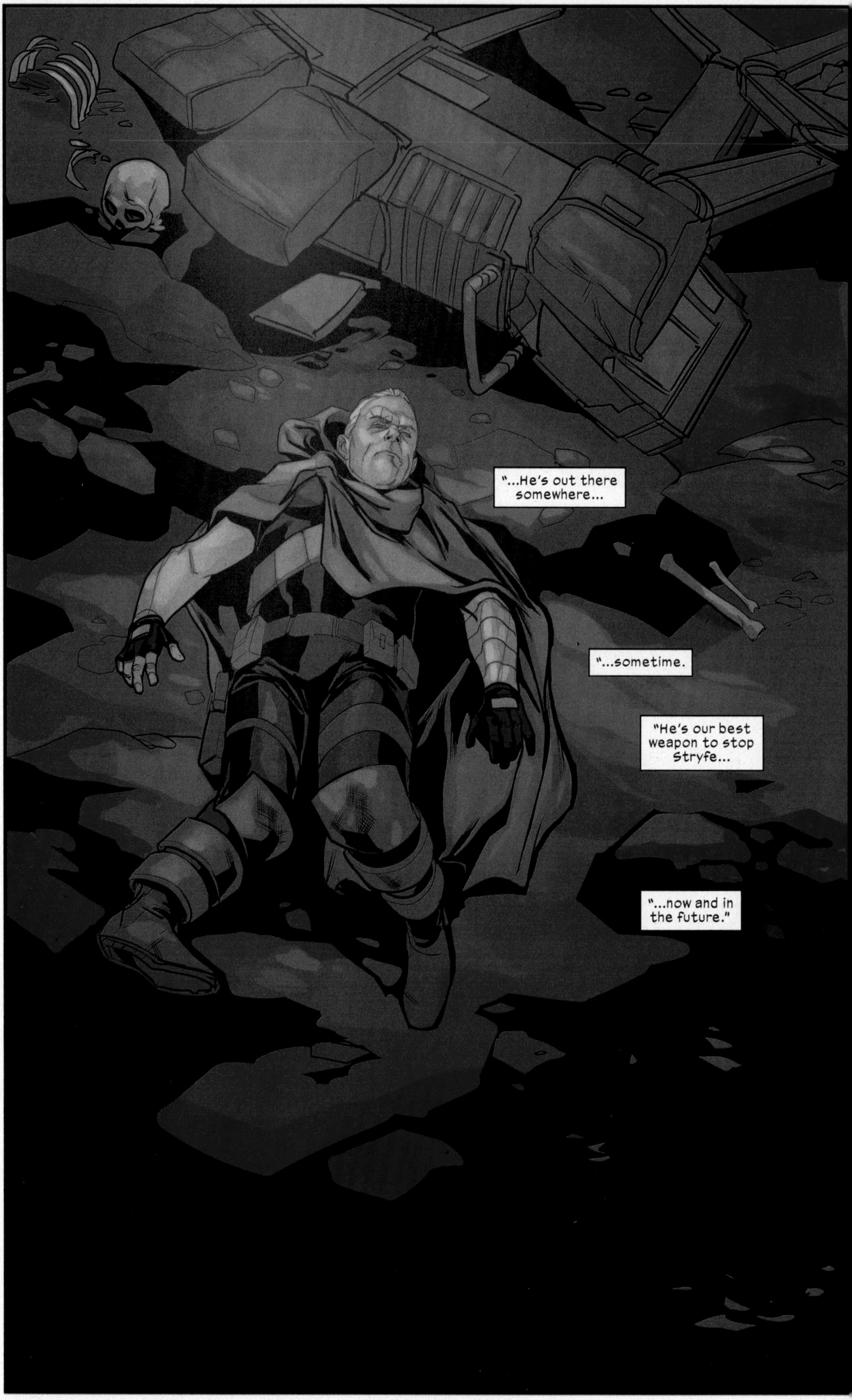
"...He's out there somewhere...
"...sometime.
"He's our best weapon to stop Stryfe...
"...now and in the future."

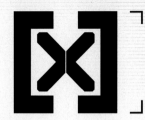

Re: Duplicates

When the resurrection process was solidified one of the first questions that came up was that of duplicates. It was decided that it would undermine the validity of the protocols if multiple versions of the same person were to be produced. This decision was then extended out to the concept of duplicates in general, that other forms -- clones, versions from alternate dimensions, or time-travelling doubles -- would also not be eligible for resurrection. Or perhaps, to put a finer point on it, only one of the duplicates would be eligible.

(Exceptions were made in cases where "duplication" is an extension of mutant gifts -- e.g. the Stepford Cuckoos being able to be resurrected back to their five selves or Madrox Prime being able to be resurrected even if one or more of his dupes have survived.)

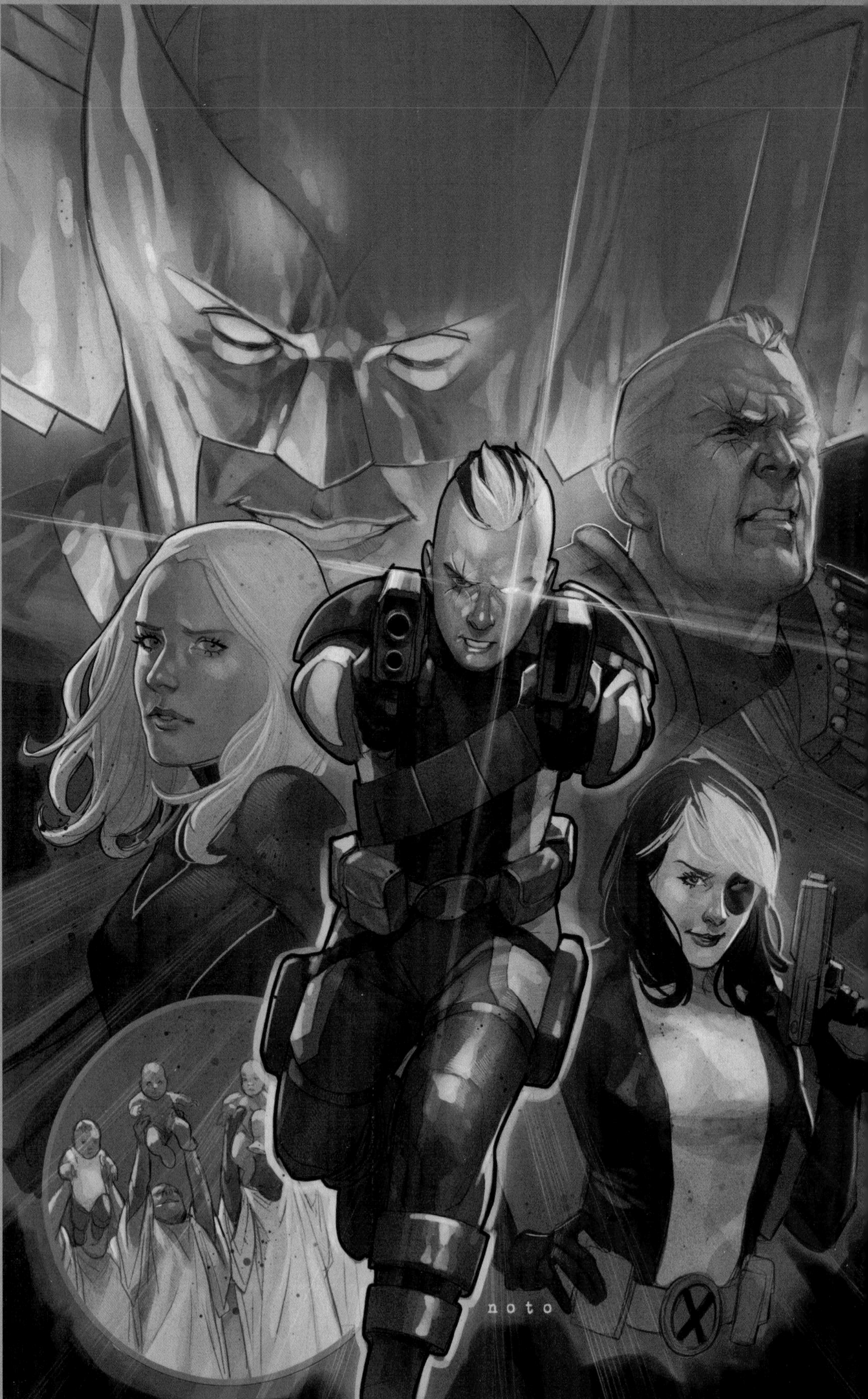
noto

Depression

[ca__[0.10]
[ble_[0.10]

More important than how you kill Cable is *when* you kill Cable.

-- ANCIENT STRYFE PROVERB FROM THE FUTURE

[ca__[0.XX]
[ble_[0.XX]

[ca__[0.10].....]
[ble_[0.10].....]

[Cable_alpha.]

I have to be war ready.

And I know now that means being ready to fight...

...and to make the hard decisions.

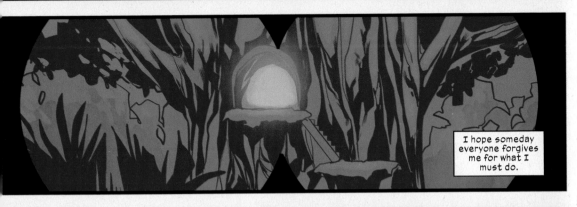

I hope someday everyone forgives me for what I must do.

Tsk.

Nathan, there are less painful paths to exile...

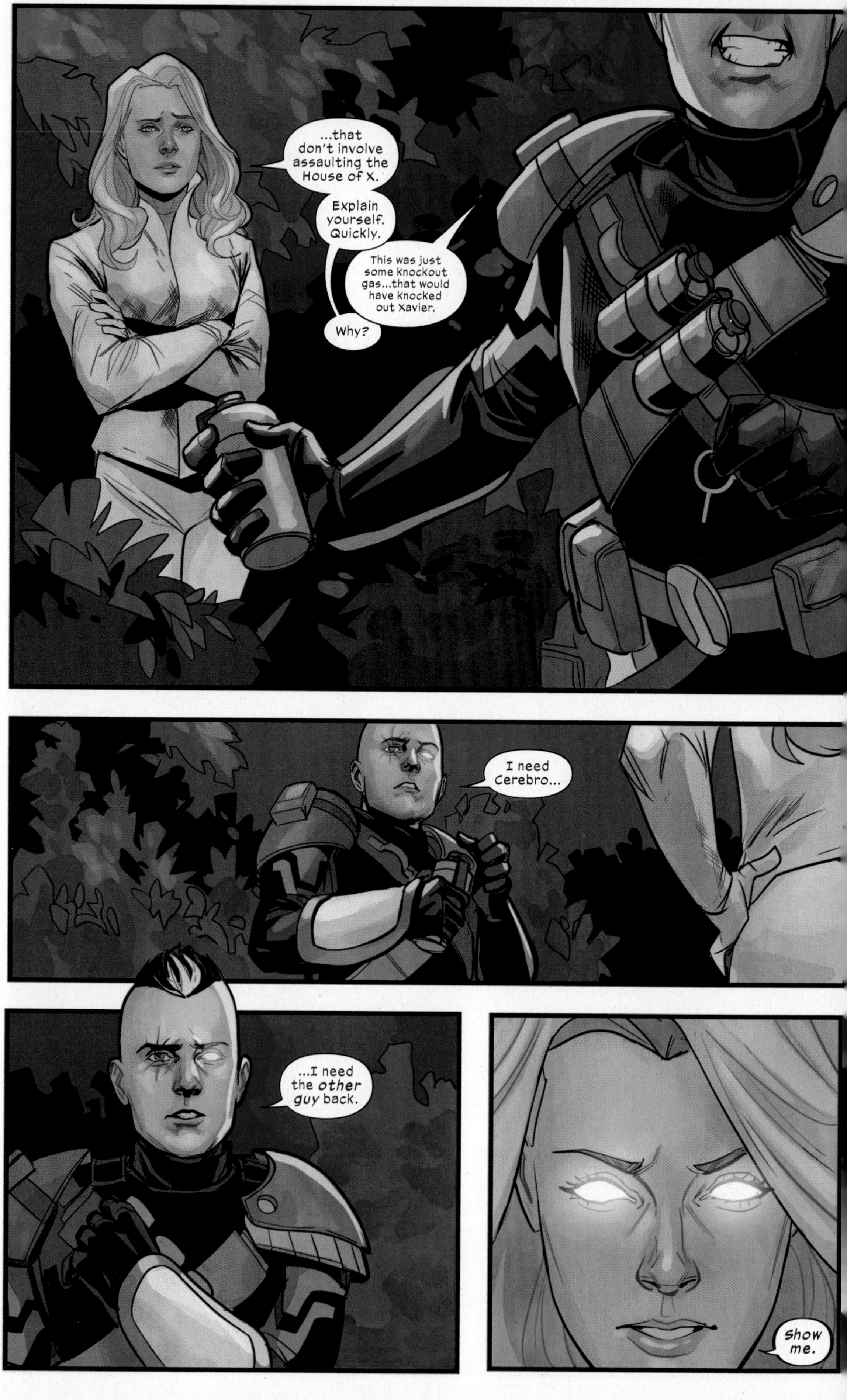
...that don't involve assaulting the House of X.
Explain yourself. Quickly.
This was just some knockout gas...that would have knocked out Xavier.
Why?
I need Cerebro...
...I need the *other guy* back.
Show me.

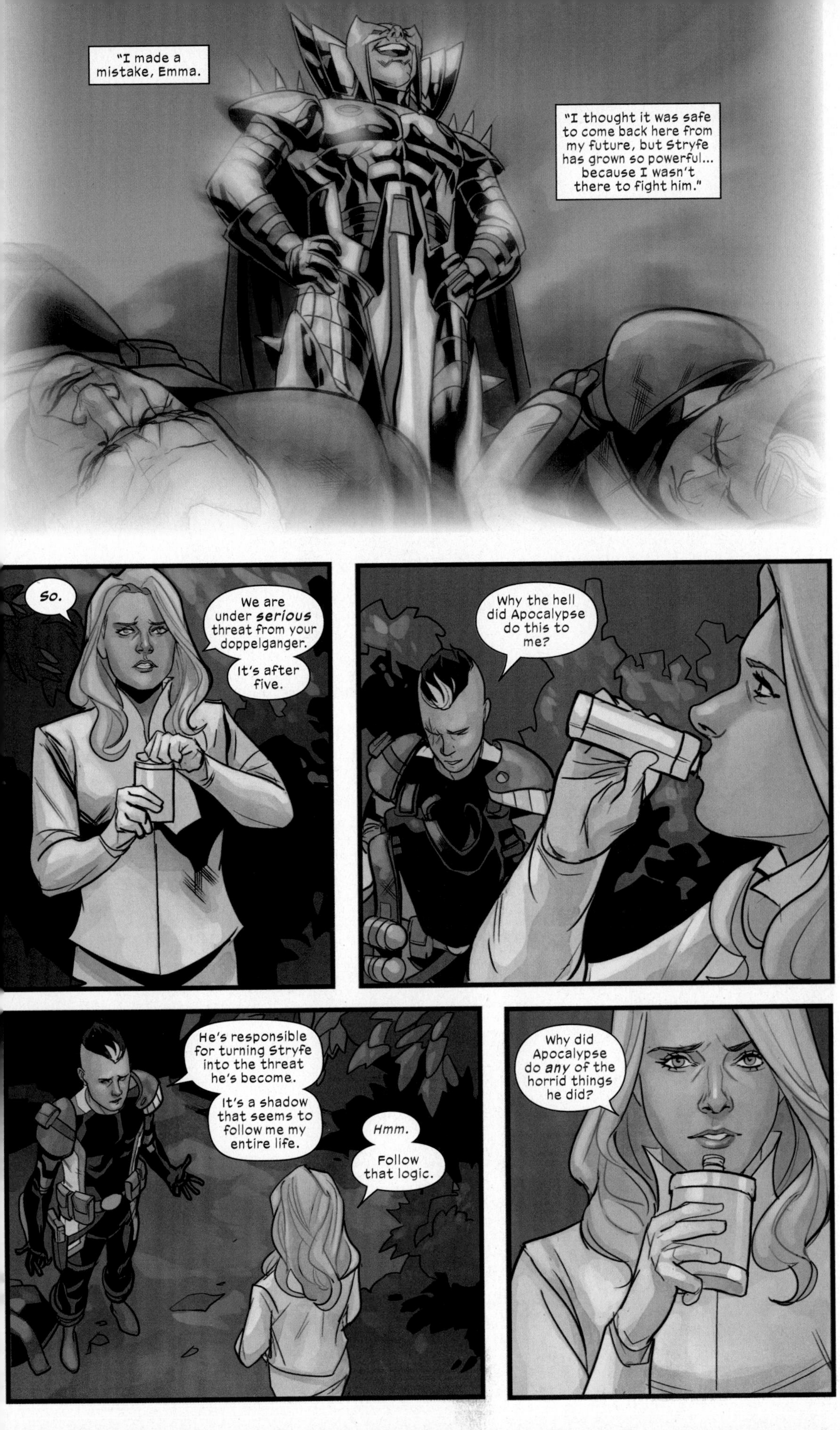
"I made a mistake, Emma.
"I thought it was safe to come back here from my future, but Stryfe has grown so powerful... because I wasn't there to fight him."
So.
We are under *serious* threat from your doppelganger.
It's after five.
Why the hell did Apocalypse do this to me?
He's responsible for turning Stryfe into the threat he's become.
It's a shadow that seems to follow me my entire life.
Hmm.
Follow that logic.
Why did Apocalypse do *any* of the horrid things he did?

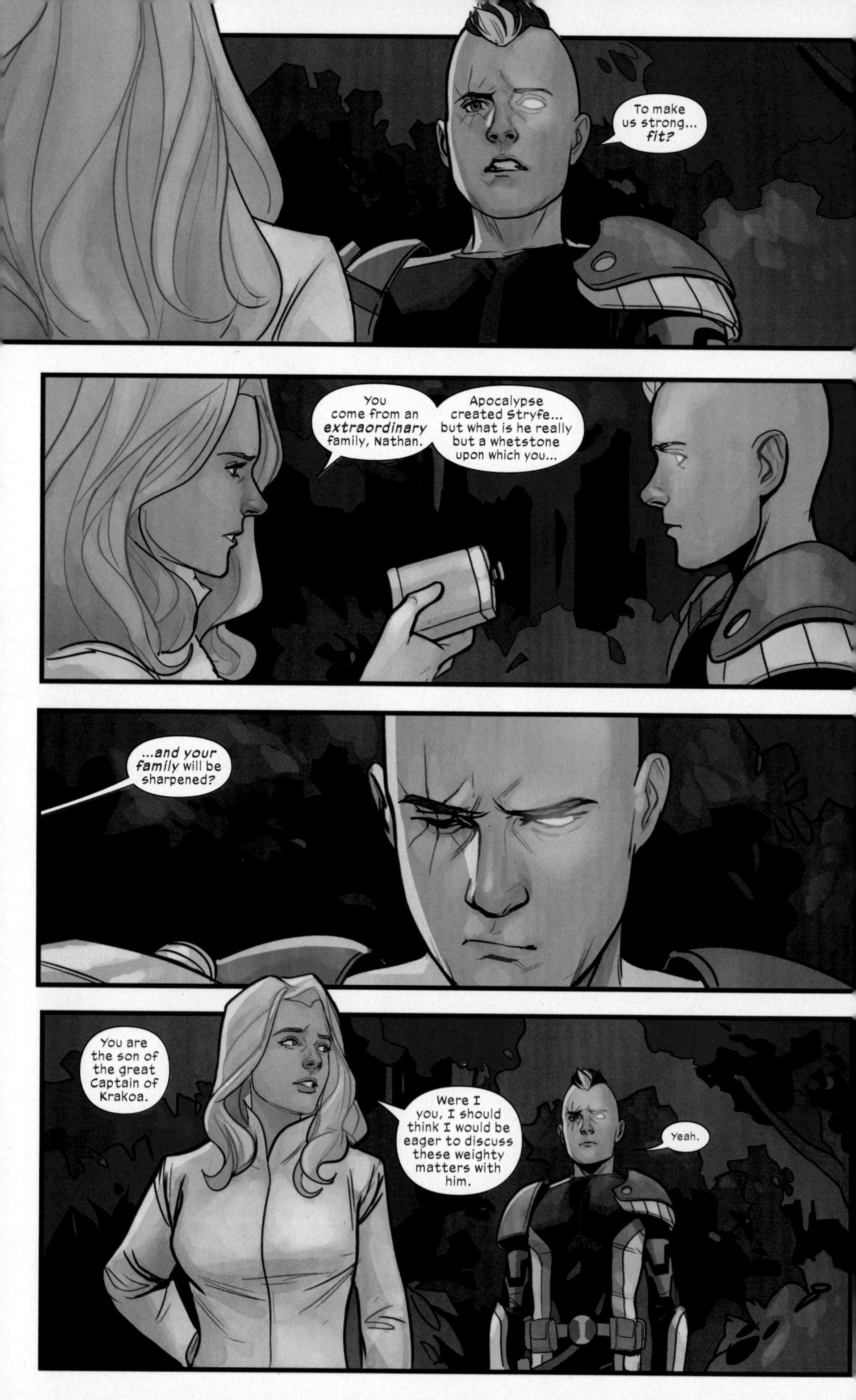
To make us strong... fit?
You come from an extraordinary family, Nathan.
Apocalypse created Stryfe... but what is he really but a whetstone upon which you...
...and your family will be sharpened?
You are the son of the great Captain of Krakoa.
Were I you, I should think I would be eager to discuss these weighty matters with him.
Yeah.

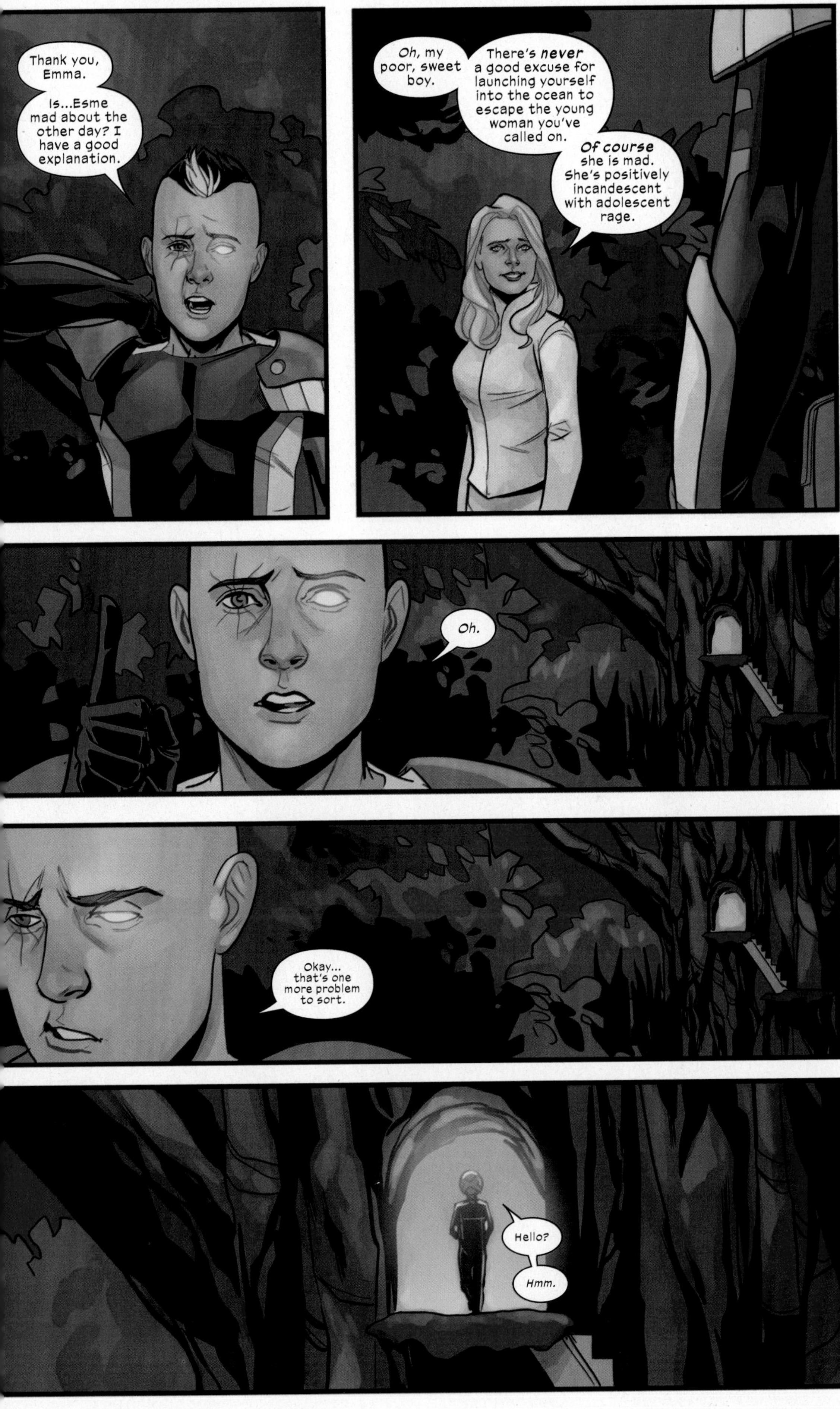

Thank you, Emma.
Is...Esme mad about the other day? I have a good explanation.
Oh, my poor, sweet boy.
There's *never* a good excuse for launching yourself into the ocean to escape the young woman you've called on.
Of course she is mad. She's positively incandescent with adolescent rage.
Oh.
Okay... that's one more problem to sort.
Hello?
Hmm.

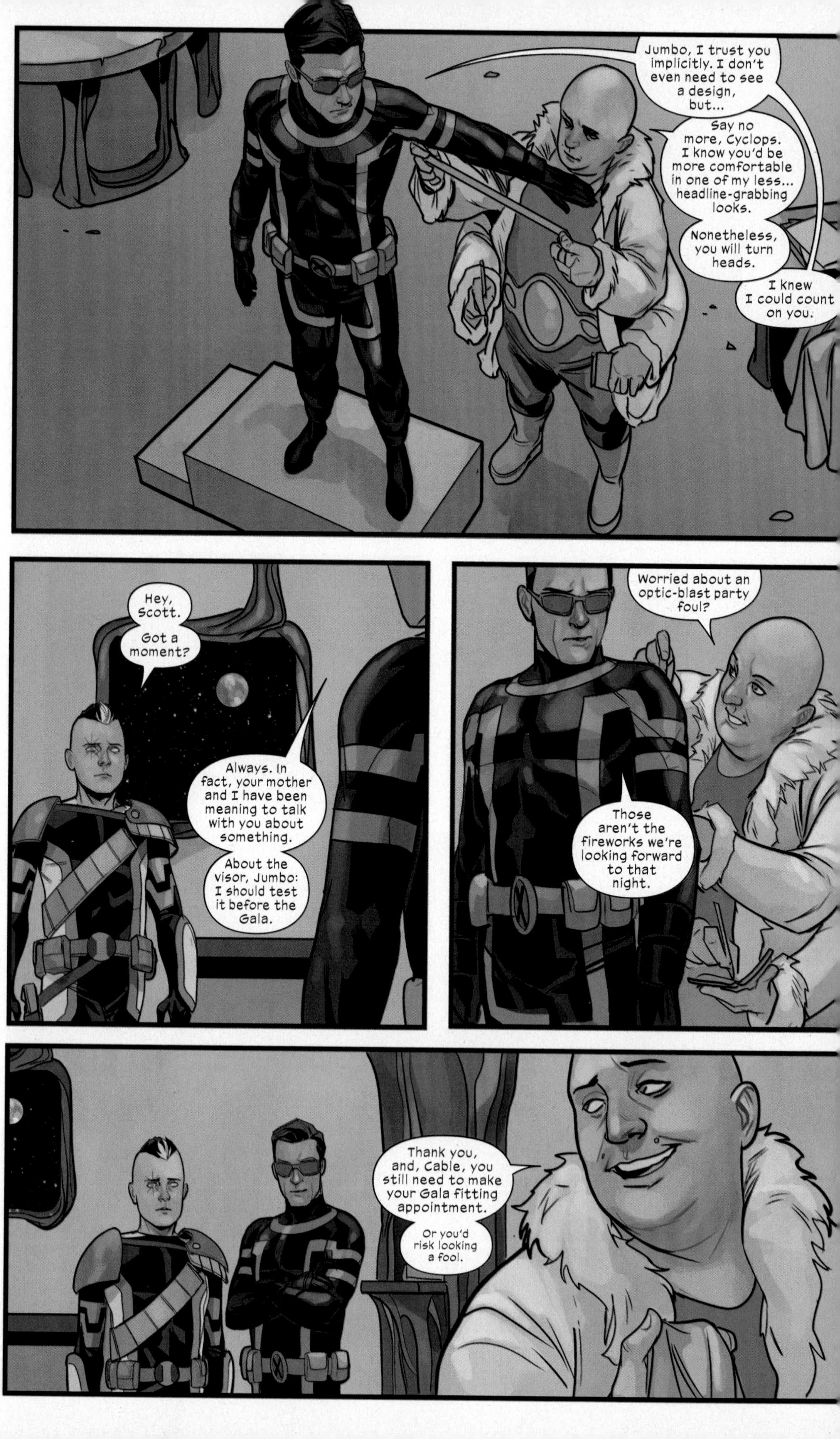
Jumbo, I trust you implicitly. I don't even need to see a design, but...
Say no more, Cyclops. I know you'd be more comfortable in one of my less... headline-grabbing looks.
Nonetheless, you will turn heads.
I knew I could count on you.
Hey, Scott.
Got a moment?
Always. In fact, your mother and I have been meaning to talk with you about something.
About the visor, Jumbo: I should test it before the Gala.
Worried about an optic-blast party foul?
Those aren't the fireworks we're looking forward to that night.
Thank you, and, Cable, you still need to make your Gala fitting appointment.
Or you'd risk looking a fool.

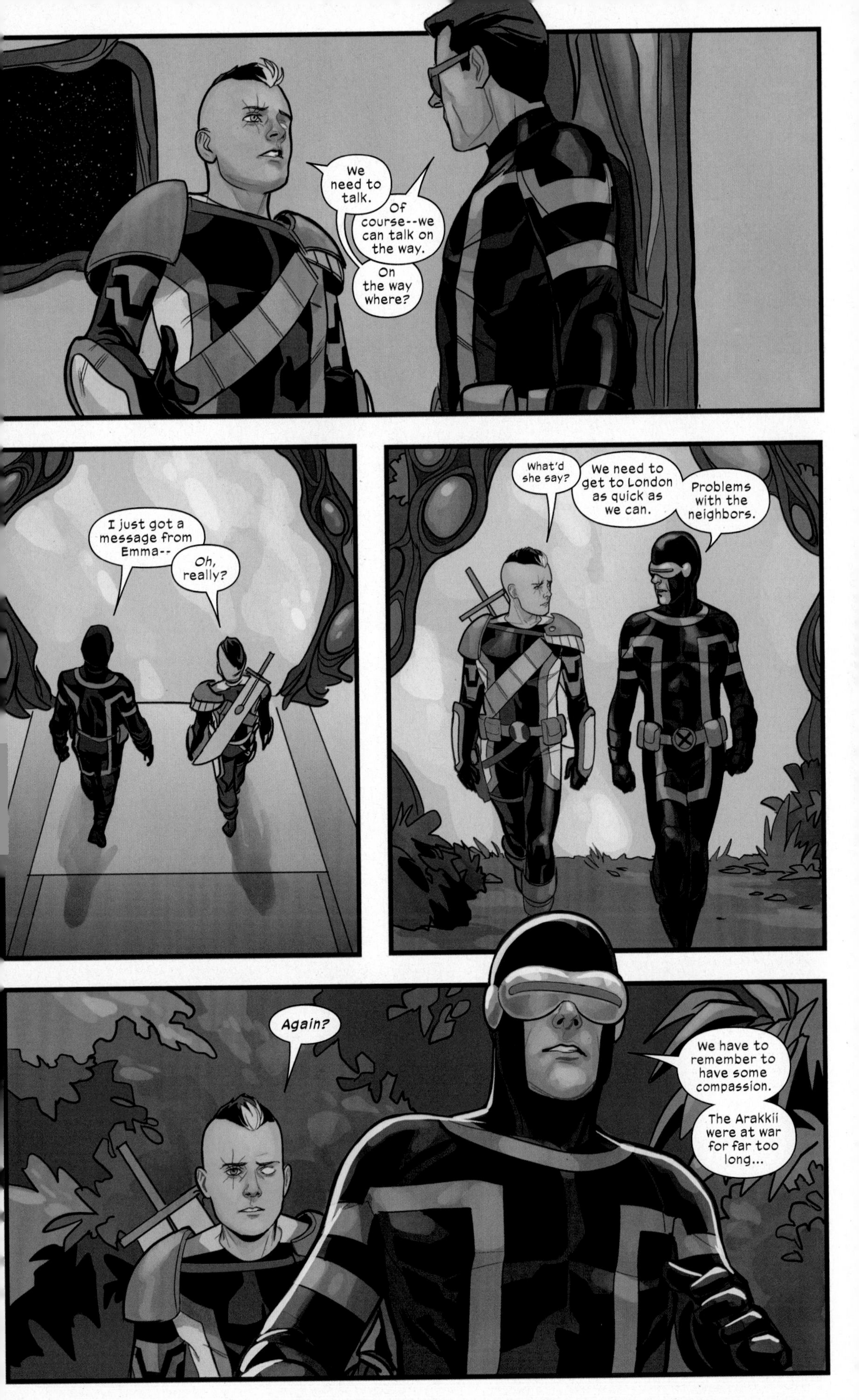
We need to talk.
Of course--we can talk on the way.
On the way where?
I just got a message from Emma--
Oh, really?
What'd she say?
We need to get to London as quick as we can.
Problems with the neighbors.
Again?
We have to remember to have some compassion.
The Arakkii were at war for far too long...

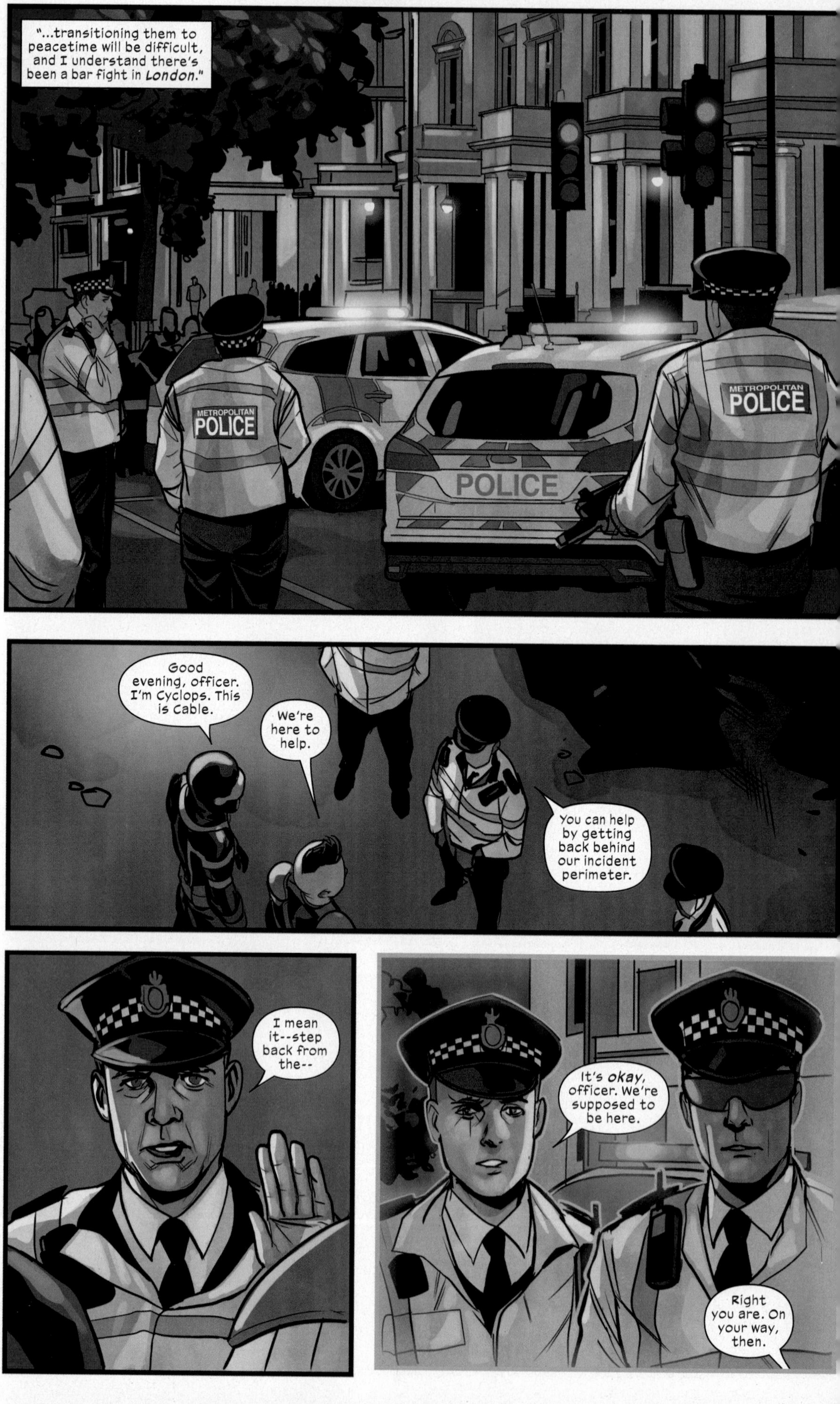
"...transitioning them to peacetime will be difficult, and I understand there's been a bar fight in *London*."
METROPOLITAN POLICE
POLICE
METROPOLITAN POLICE
Good evening, officer. I'm Cyclops. This is Cable.
We're here to help.
You can help by getting back behind our incident perimeter.
I mean it--step back from the--
It's *okay*, officer. We're supposed to be here.
Right you are. On your way, then.

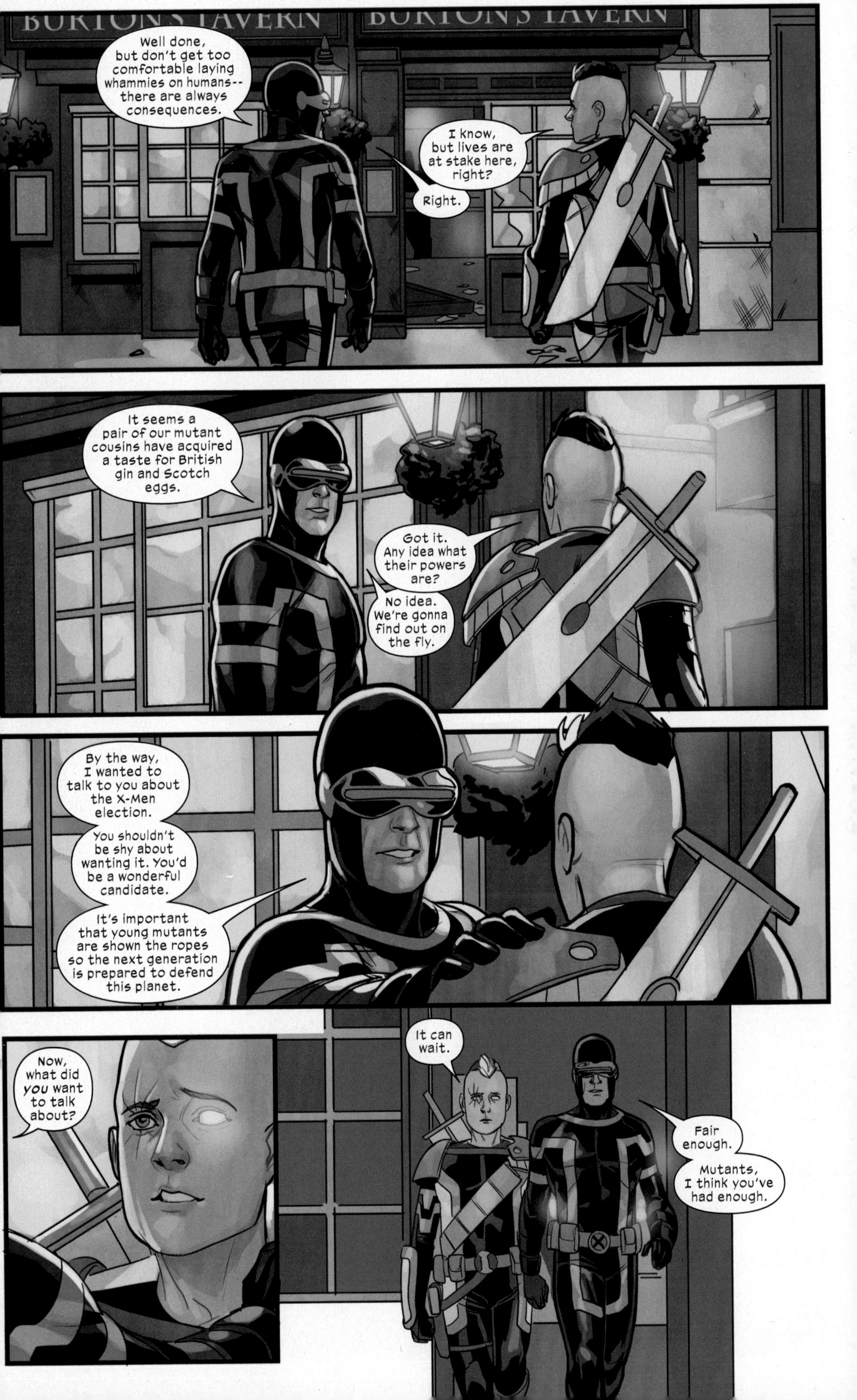
BURTON'S TAVERN
BURTON'S TAVERN
Well done, but don't get too comfortable laying whammies on humans--there are always consequences.
I know, but lives are at stake here, right?
Right.
It seems a pair of our mutant cousins have acquired a taste for British gin and Scotch eggs.
Got it. Any idea what their powers are?
No idea. We're gonna find out on the fly.
By the way, I wanted to talk to you about the X-Men election.
You shouldn't be shy about wanting it. You'd be a wonderful candidate.
It's important that young mutants are shown the ropes so the next generation is prepared to defend this planet.
Now, what did *you* want to talk about?
It can wait.
Fair enough.
Mutants, I think you've had enough.

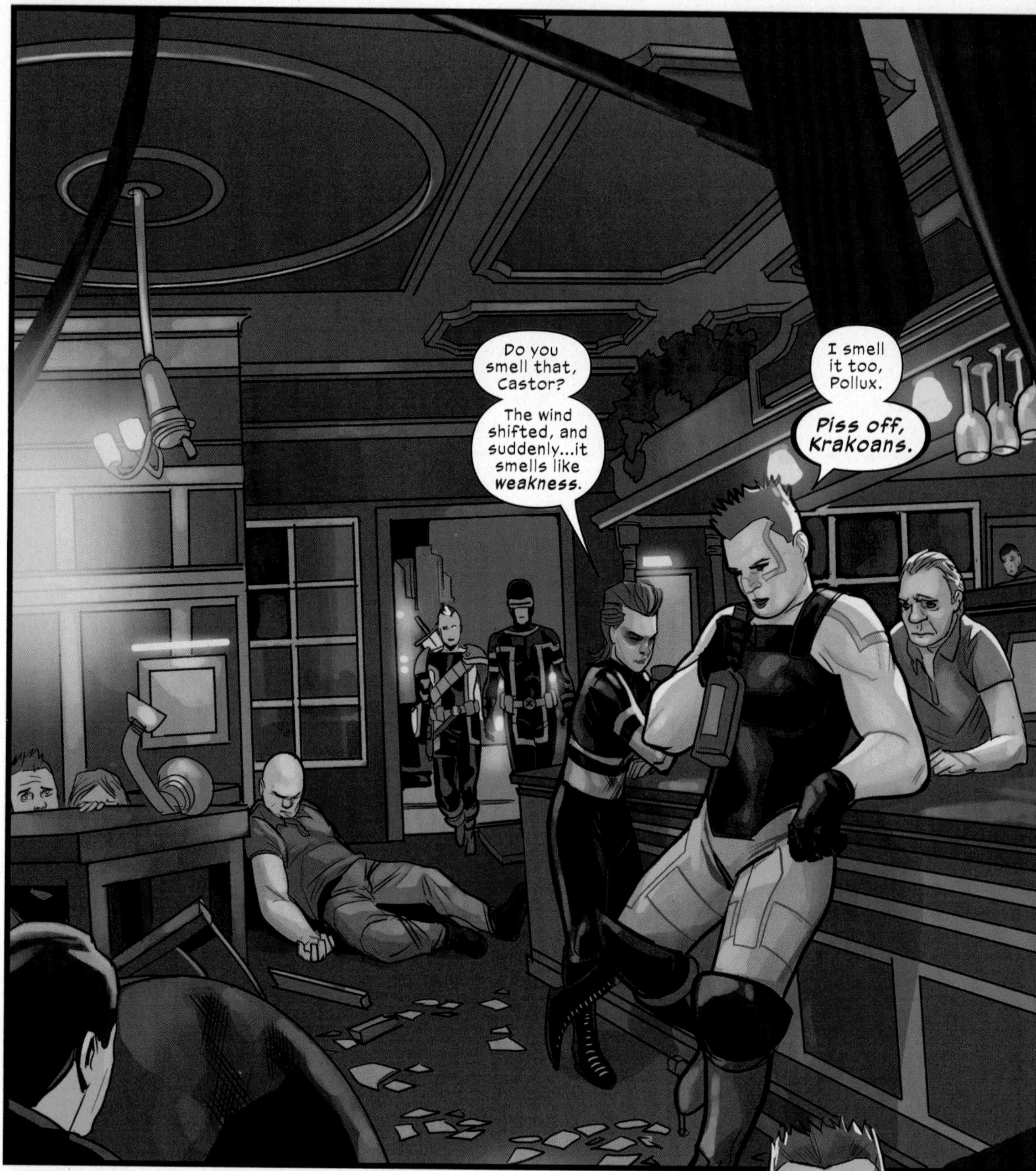
Do you smell that, Castor?
The wind shifted, and suddenly...it smells like *weakness*.
I smell it too, Pollux.
Piss off, Krakoans.

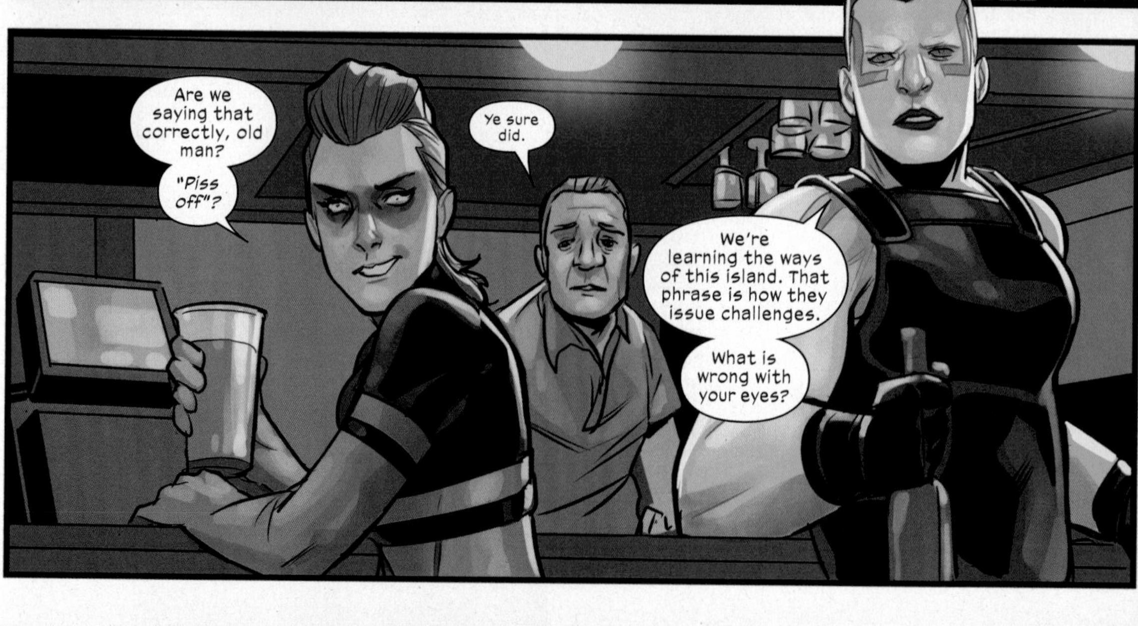
Are we saying that correctly, old man?
"Piss off"?
Ye sure did.
We're learning the ways of this island. That phrase is how they issue challenges.
What is wrong with your eyes?

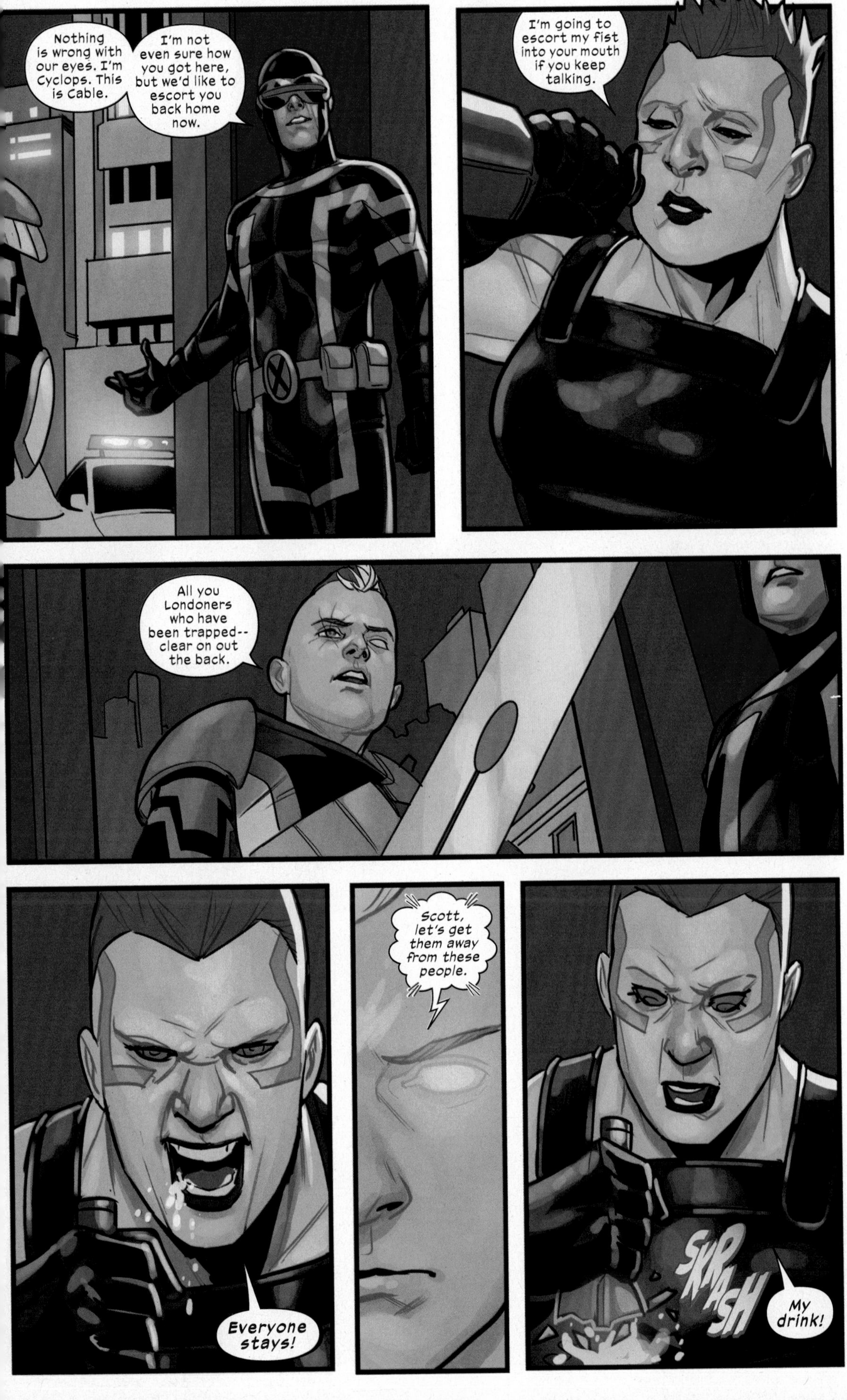
Nothing is wrong with our eyes. I'm Cyclops. This is Cable.
I'm not even sure how you got here, but we'd like to escort you back home now.
I'm going to escort my fist into your mouth if you keep talking.
All you Londoners who have been trapped--clear on out the back.
Everyone stays!
Scott, let's get them away from these people.
SKRASH
My drink!

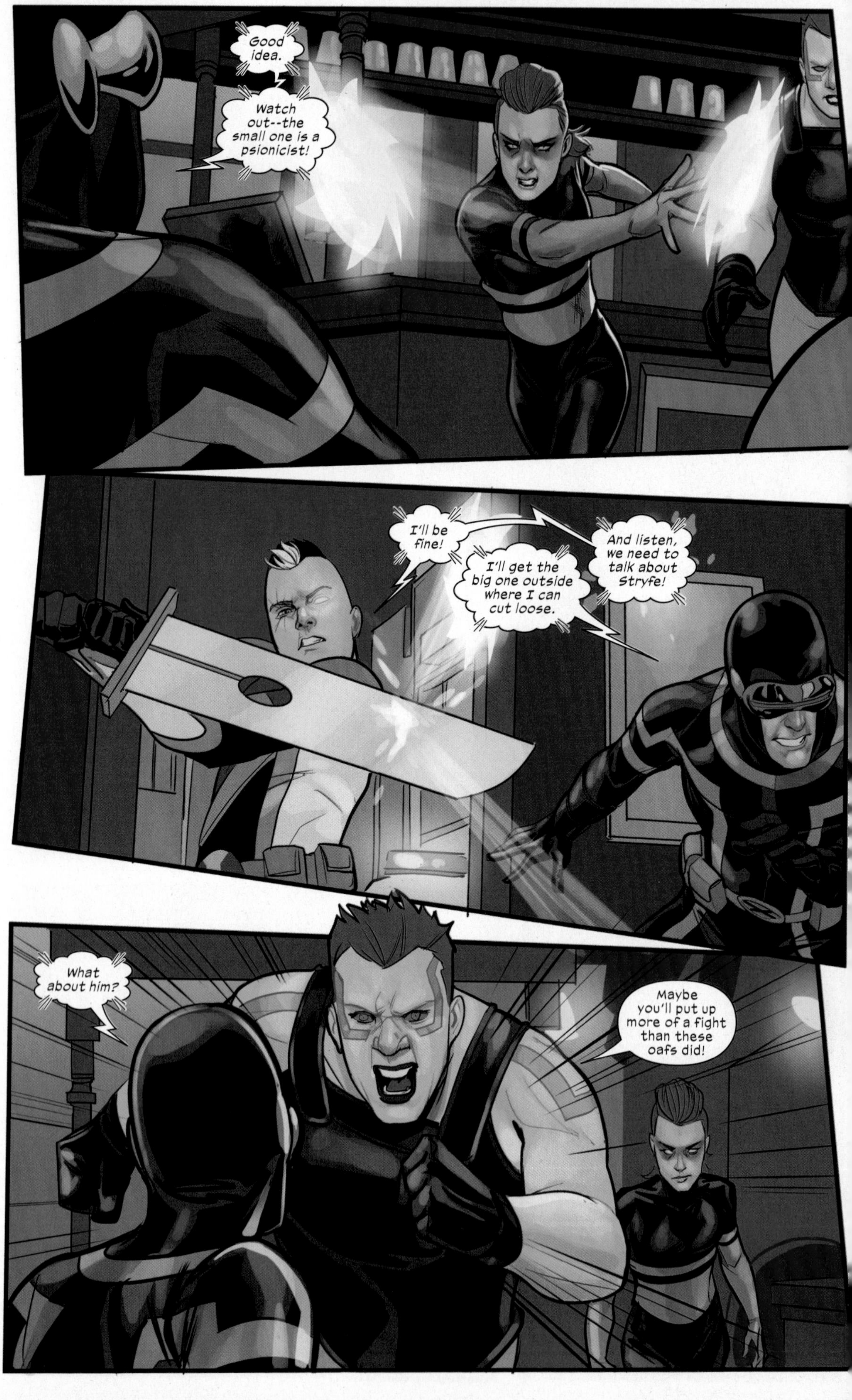
Good idea.
Watch out--the small one is a psionicist!
I'll be fine!
I'll get the big one outside where I can cut loose.
And listen, we need to talk about Stryfe!
What about him?
Maybe you'll put up more of a fight than these oafs did!

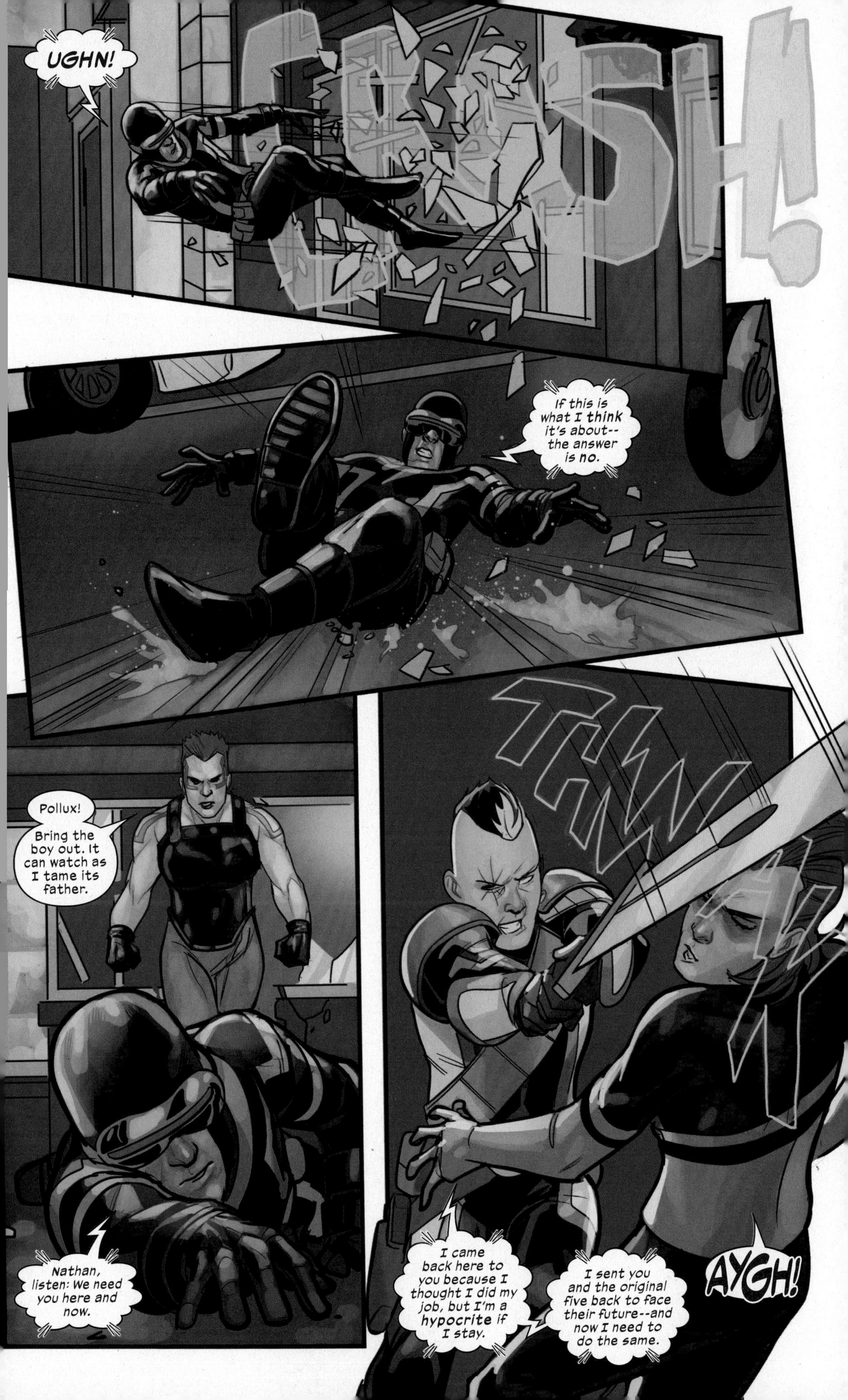
UGHN!
CRASH!
If this is what I think it's about--the answer is no.
Pollux!
Bring the boy out. It can watch as I tame its father.
Nathan, listen: We need you here and now.
THWAK
I came back here to you because I thought I did my job, but I'm a hypocrite if I stay.
I sent you and the original five back to face their future--and now I need to do the same.
AYGH!

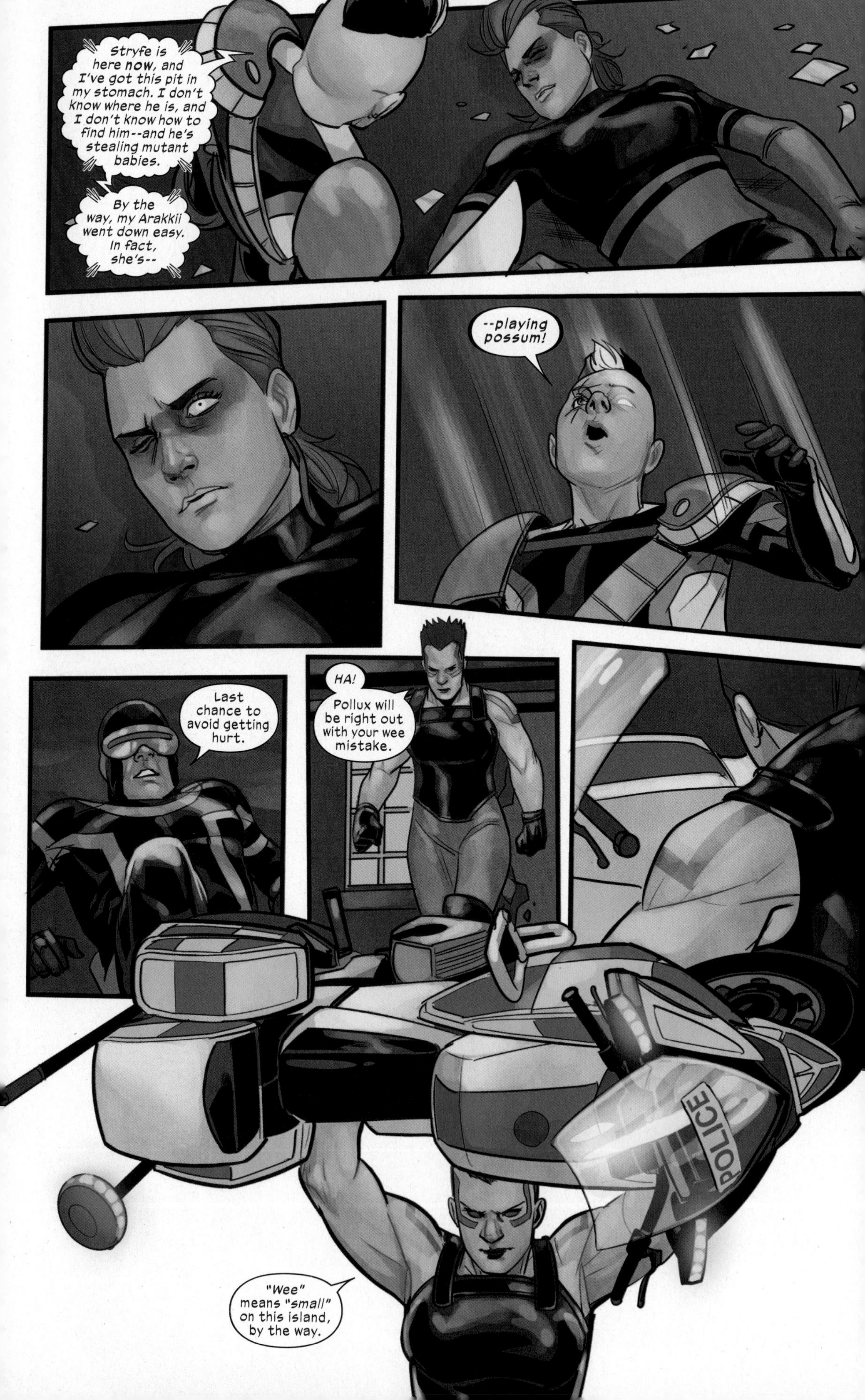
Stryfe is here now, and I've got this pit in my stomach. I don't know where he is, and I don't know how to find him--and he's stealing mutant babies.
By the way, my Arakkii went down easy. In fact, she's--
--playing possum!
Last chance to avoid getting hurt.
HA!
Pollux will be right out with your wee mistake.
POLICE
"Wee" means "small" on this island, by the way.

Yes, I know. Sleep well.

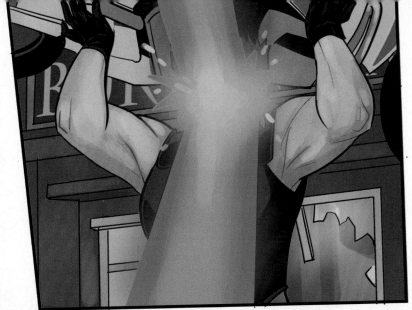

BURTON'S TAVERN

CLAP CLAP CLAP

Well served.

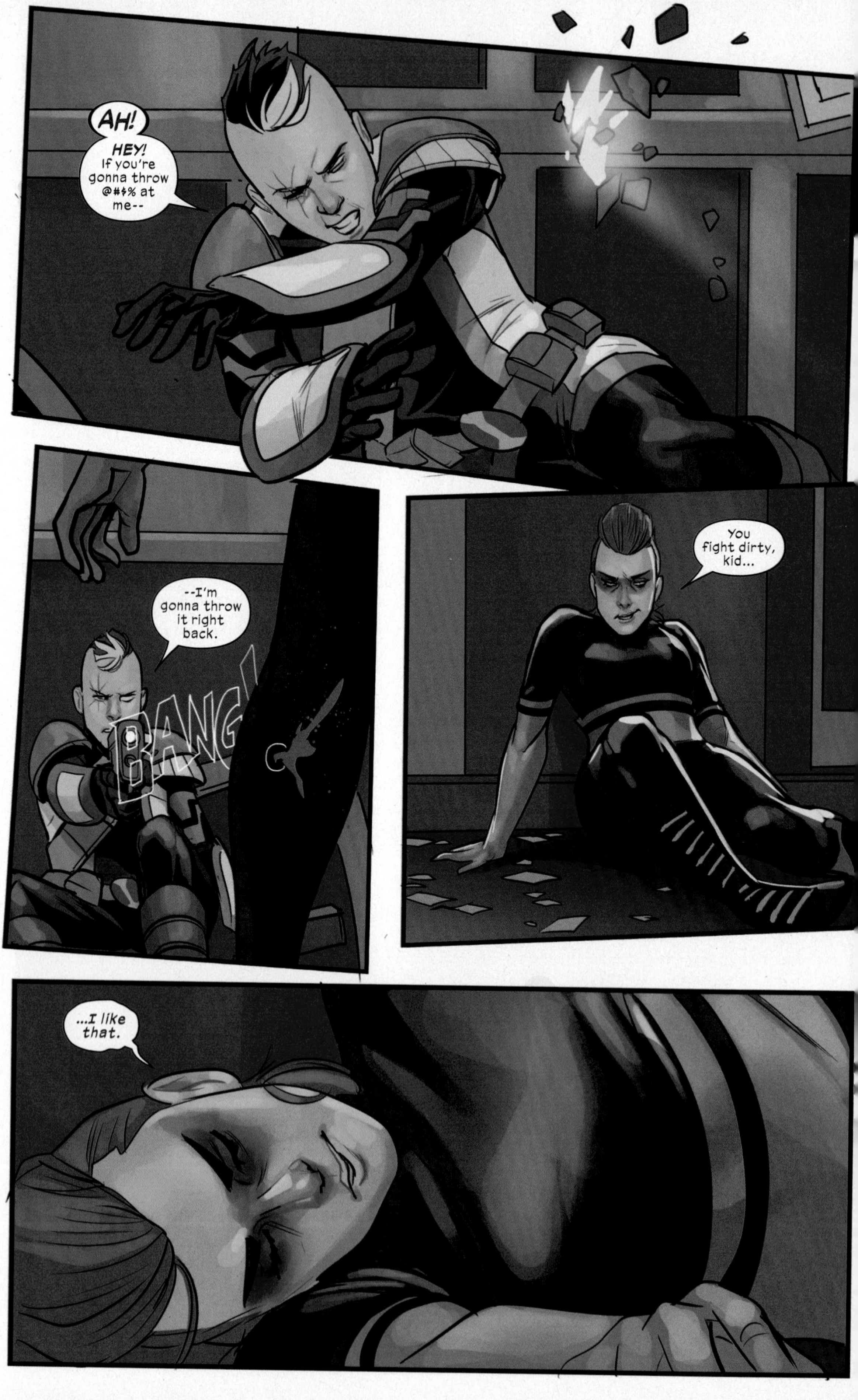
AH!
HEY! If you're gonna throw @#$% at me--
--I'm gonna throw it right back.
BANG!
You fight dirty, kid...
...I like that.

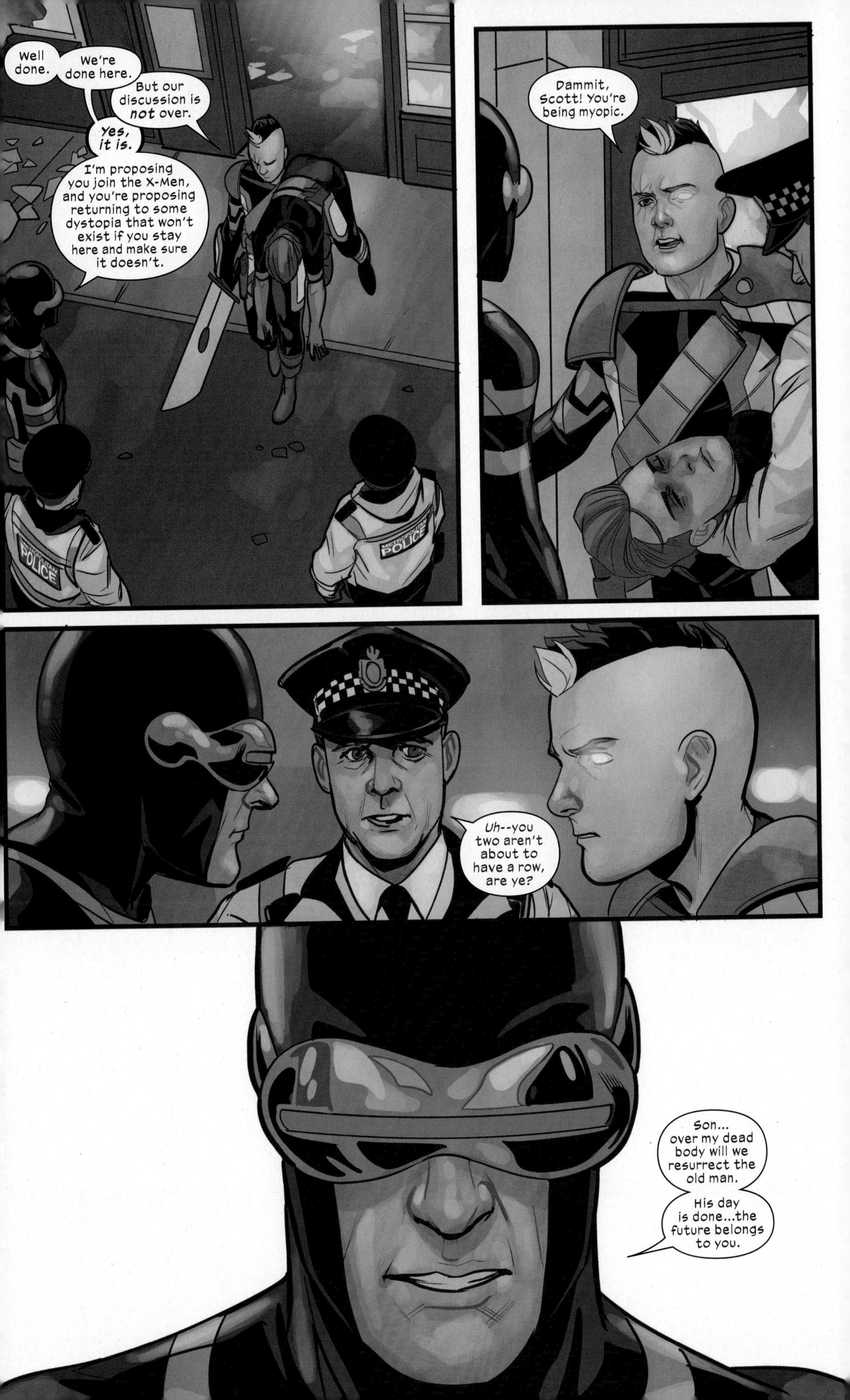
Well done.
We're done here.
But our discussion is *not* over.
Yes, it is.
I'm proposing you join the X-Men, and you're proposing returning to some dystopia that won't exist if you stay here and make sure it doesn't.
METROPOLITAN POLICE
METROPOLITAN POLICE
Dammit, Scott! You're being myopic.
Uh--you two aren't about to have a row, are ye?
Son... over my dead body will we resurrect the old man.
His day is done...the future belongs to you.

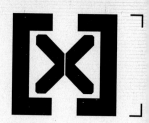

When Cable was slain by his younger self just before the Dawn of Krakoa, it initiated the old man's Casket Protocols.

The most immediate concern Cable had over his eventual death was to secure his remains. This was accomplished on his behalf by Deadpool.

This action was accompanied by a change in defensive posture. Cable's safe houses shredded data and removed safeties from all traps.

Cable's Graymalkin Station remained cloaked in high Earth orbit. The station had been reconstituted in secrecy from the spoils of technology seized during the second Great Armor Wars of the 3030s.

It was highly likely that Stryfe had compromised Cable's first artificial intelligence, the Professor, at some point, and Cable never fully trusted it again. He turned to his home-brewed A.I. Belle to run point on the sleeping station. Belle's initial determination that Stryfe was responsible for killing Cable in the department store was revealed to be false after seeing the exploits of "Kid Cable" A.K. (AFTER KRAKOA) in the media.

Belle gained additional situational knowledge of the mutant baby kidnappings after Cable and Esme Cuckoo inserted themselves into the Philadelphia police department investigation. Belle skimmed info from the servers and concluded before Cable did that an attack was underway by Stryfe.

The assumption that Stryfe was attacking backward through time and seeking to replace Kid Cable with a clone of himself was proven true when Cable and Domino found and destroyed the clone pods hidden in Tokyo, Japan.

The middle-aged Stryfe clones inserted into the pro-mutant human cult "the Order of X" and the one safeguarding the Tokyo clone pod were killed by Cable. It's unknown if any sleeper Stryfe clones are still embedded in human society.

Five mutant babies remain missing, and it's not clear if there is a larger plan for them or if they were simply bait for Cable.

The first Hellfire Gala of the Krakoan Age is days away, and Cable has not discovered any of his safe houses or Graymalkin Station.

Belle watches, waits, observes and remains on guard.

Another time.
Another place.

Wake up, old man.
The boss wants a chat.

Oh, I've been awake the whole time.

I'm guessing you filth don't have any possums in this @#@$&%#$...

...If you did, you might have done a better job of pacifying me-- and searching my robot hound...

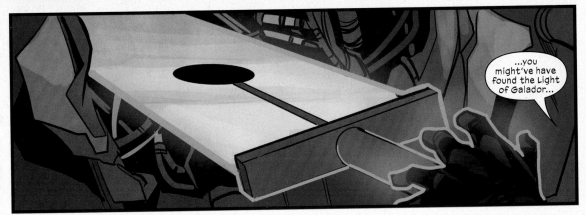

...you might've have found the Light of Galador...

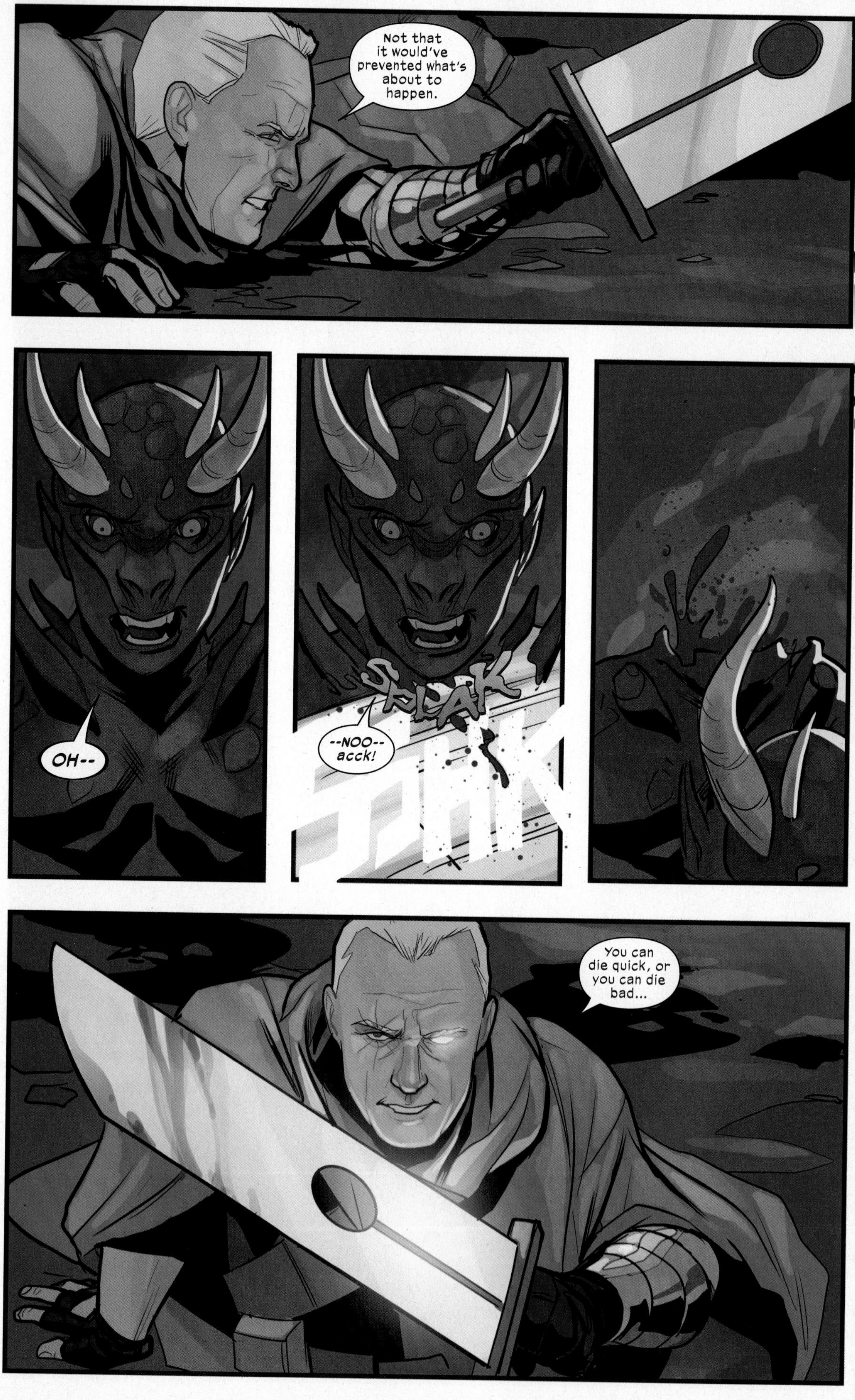
Not that it would've prevented what's about to happen.
OH--
SPLAK
--NOO-- acck!
You can die quick, or you can die bad...

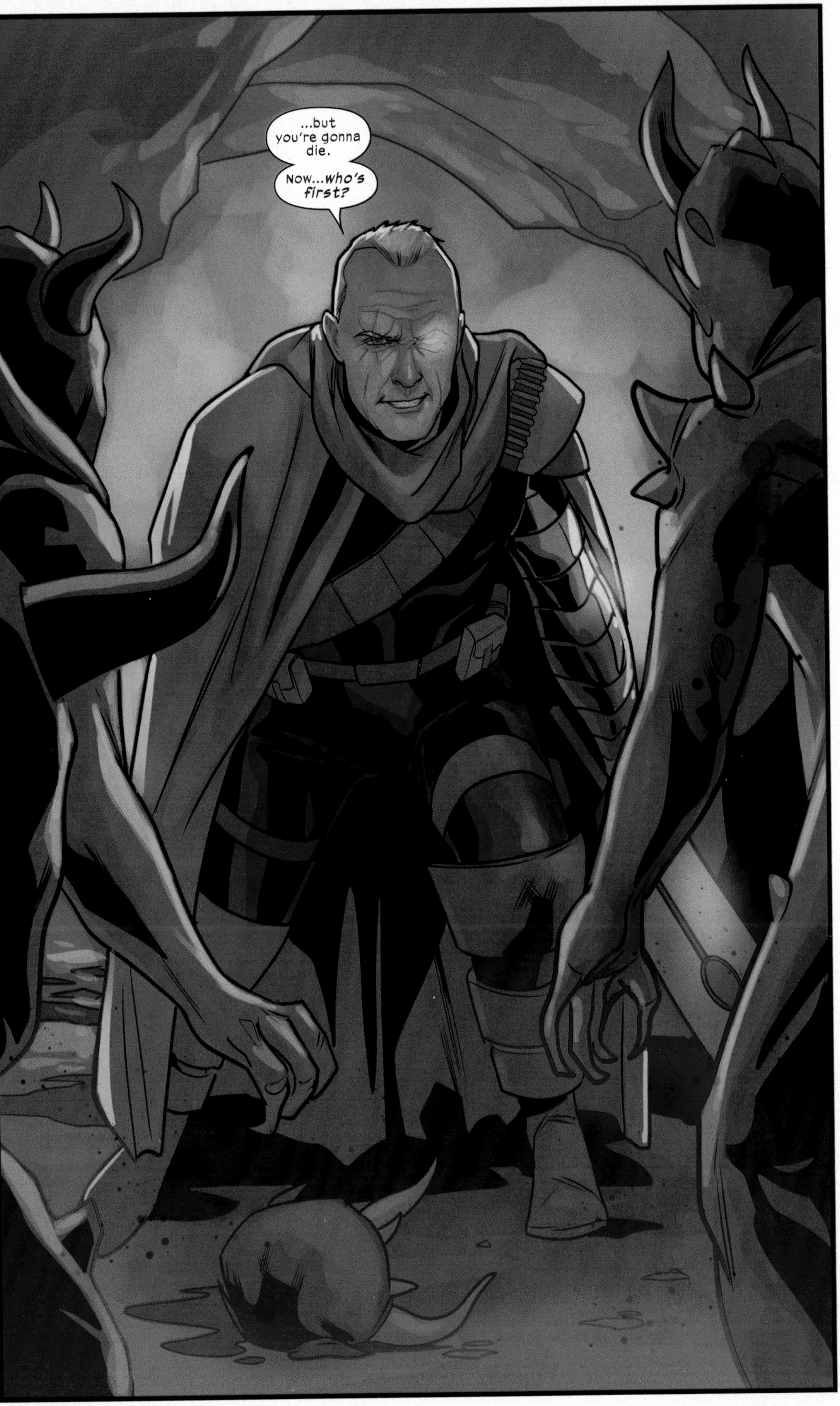
...but you're gonna die.
Now...who's first?

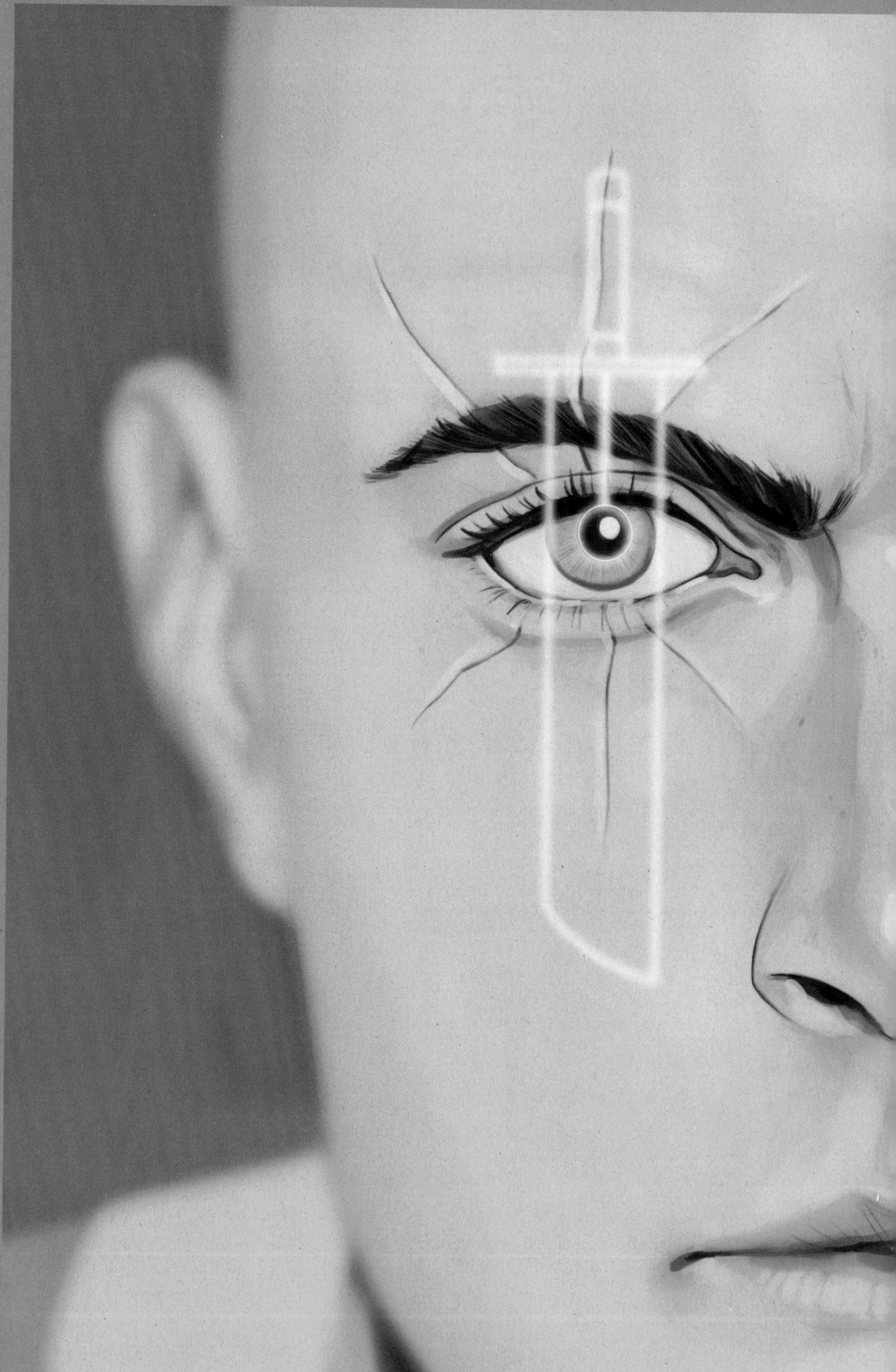
noto

Acceptance

11

[ca__[0.11]
[ble_[0.11]

You know what's about to happen, right?

-- CYCLOPS

[ca__[0.XX]
[ble_[0.XX]

[ca__[0.11]....]
[ble_[0.11]....]

[Cable_alpha.]

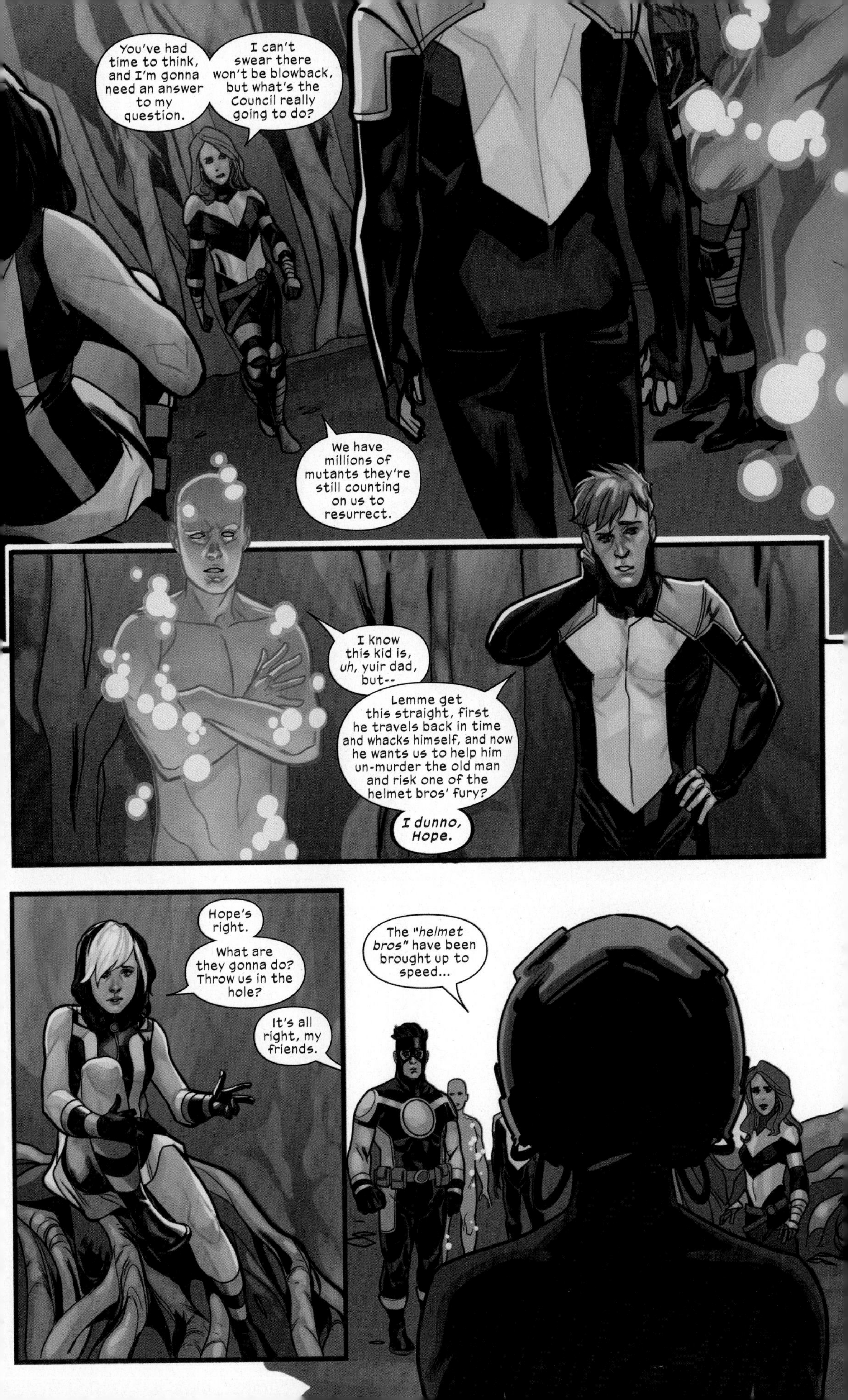

You've had time to think, and I'm gonna need an answer to my question.
I can't swear there won't be blowback, but what's the Council really going to do?
We have millions of mutants they're still counting on us to resurrect.
I know this kid is, *uh,* yuir dad, but--
Lemme get this straight, first he travels back in time and whacks himself, and now he wants us to help him un-murder the old man and risk one of the helmet bros' fury?
I dunno, Hope.
Hope's right.
What are they gonna do? Throw us in the hole?
It's all right, my friends.
The "*helmet bros*" have been brought up to speed...

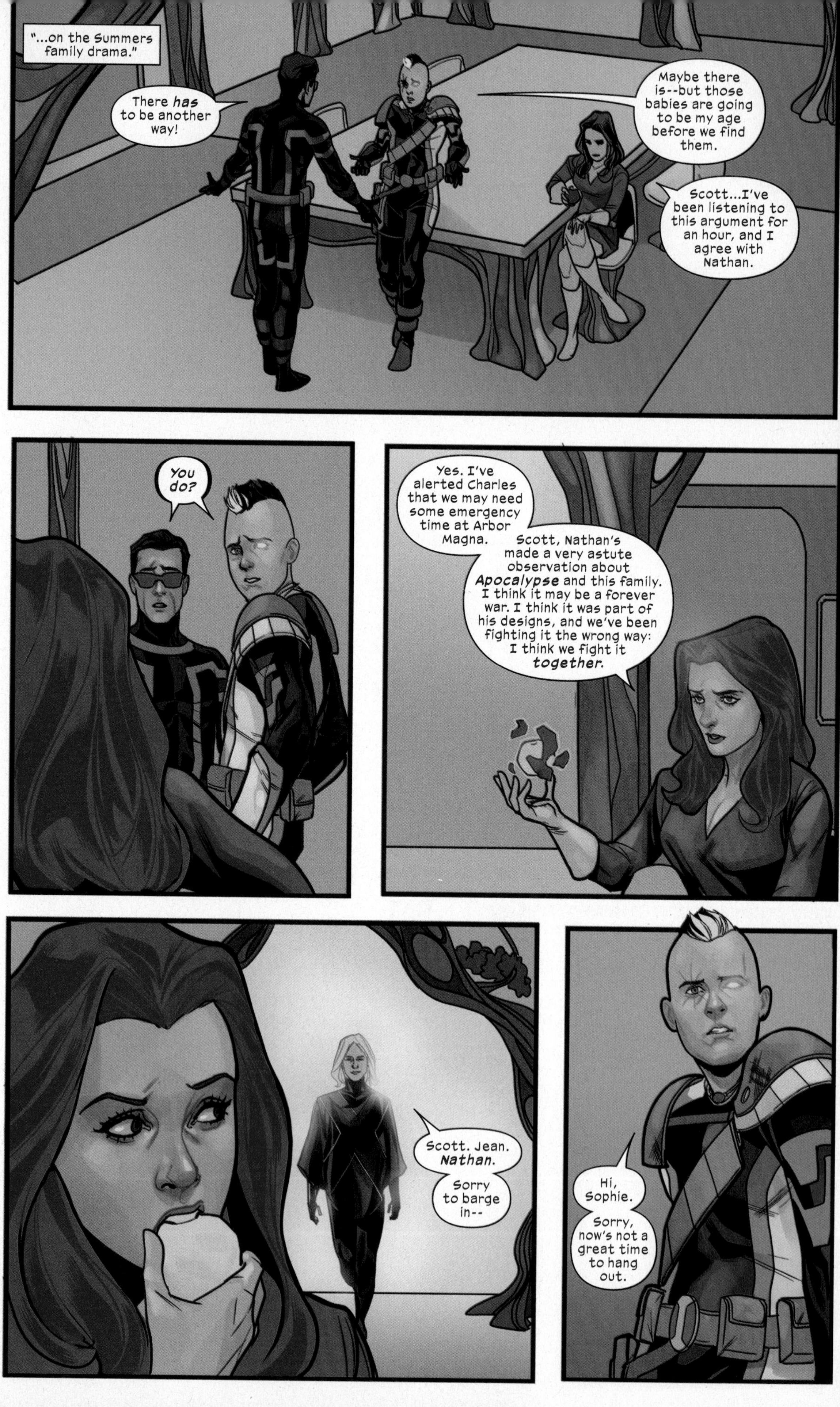
"...on the Summers family drama."
There *has* to be another way!
Maybe there is--but those babies are going to be my age before we find them.
Scott...I've been listening to this argument for an hour, and I agree with Nathan.
You do?
Yes. I've alerted Charles that we may need some emergency time at Arbor Magna.
Scott, Nathan's made a very astute observation about *Apocalypse* and this family. I think it may be a forever war. I think it was part of his designs, and we've been fighting it the wrong way: I think we fight it *together*.
Scott. Jean. *Nathan*.
Sorry to barge in--
Hi, Sophie.
Sorry, now's not a great time to hang out.

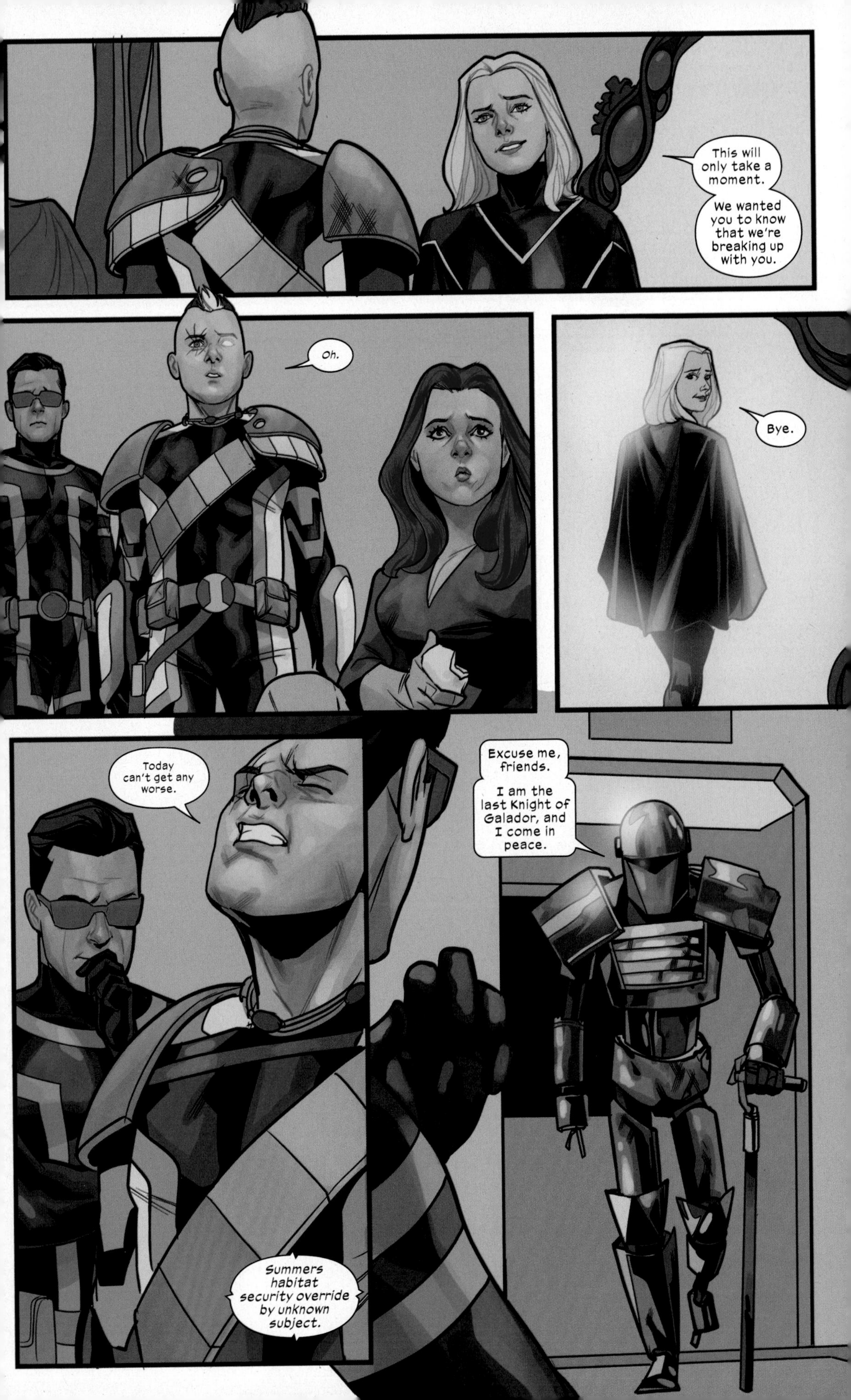
This will only take a moment.
We wanted you to know that we're breaking up with you.
Oh.
Bye.
Today can't get any worse.
Excuse me, friends.
I am the last Knight of Galador, and I come in peace.
Summers habitat security override by unknown subject.

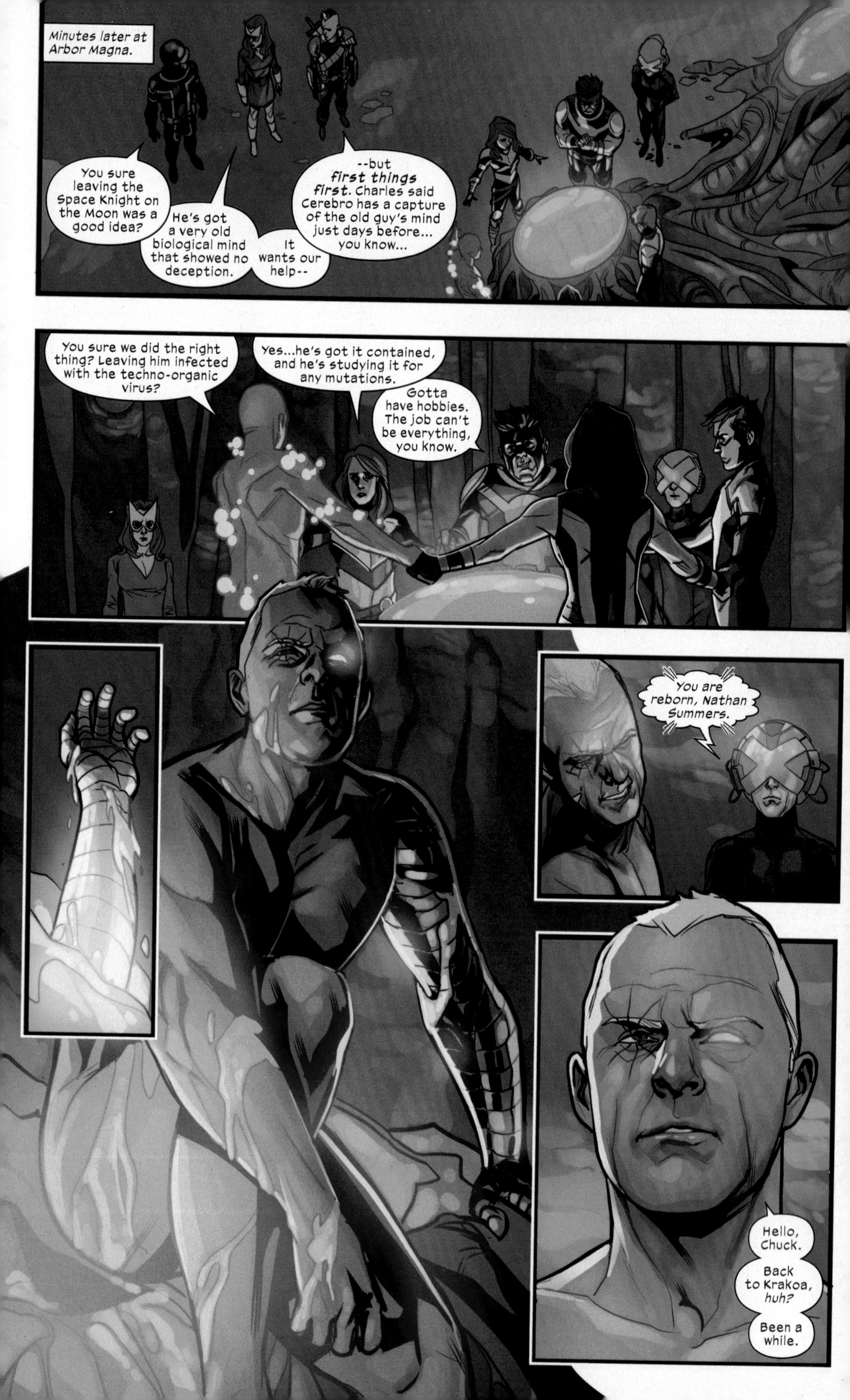
Minutes later at Arbor Magna.
You sure leaving the Space Knight on the Moon was a good idea?
He's got a very old biological mind that showed no deception.
It wants our help--
--but first things first. Charles said Cerebro has a capture of the old guy's mind just days before... you know...
You sure we did the right thing? Leaving him infected with the techno-organic virus?
Yes...he's got it contained, and he's studying it for any mutations.
Gotta have hobbies. The job can't be everything, you know.
You are reborn, Nathan Summers.
Hello, Chuck.
Back to Krakoa, huh?
Been a while.

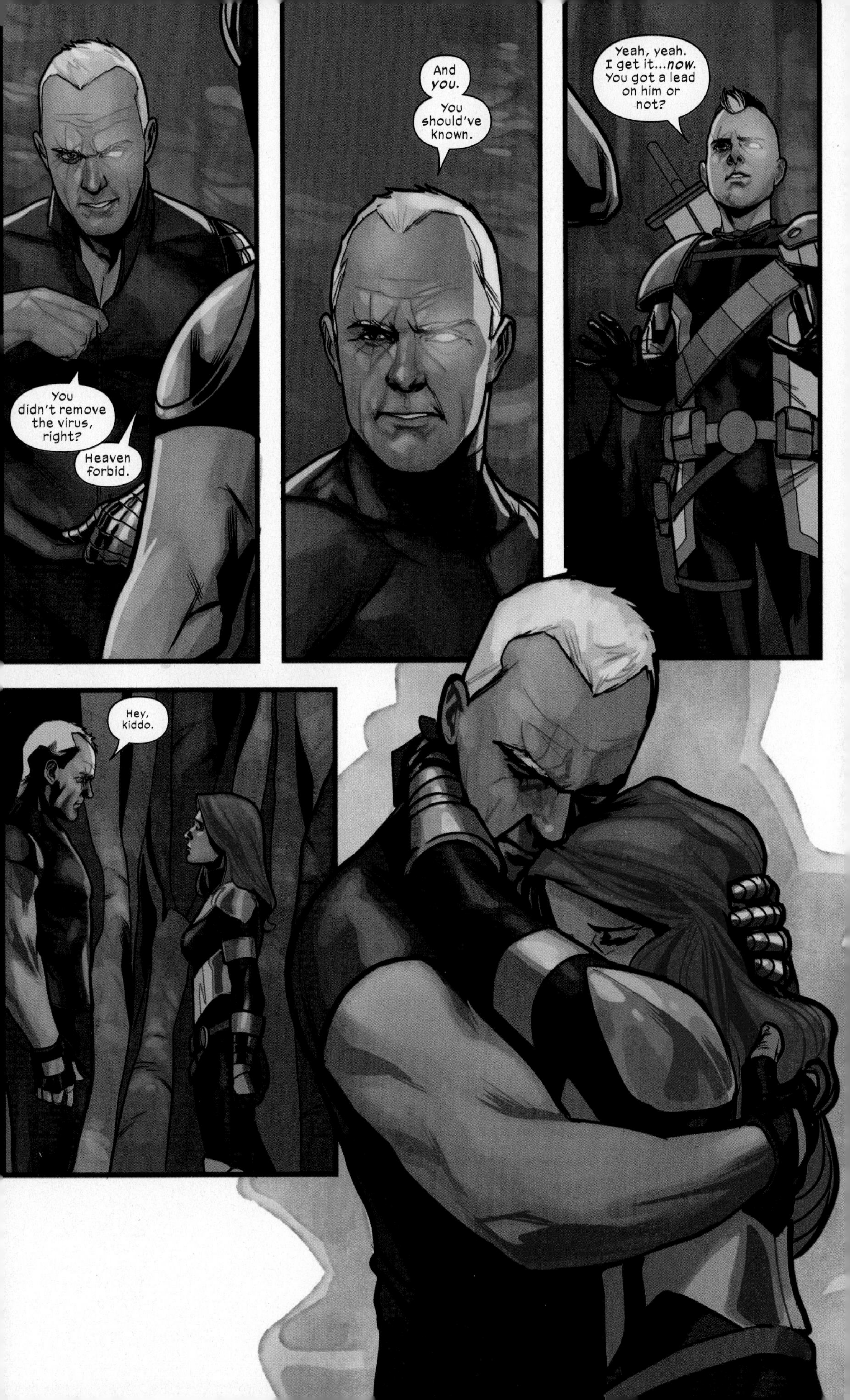
You didn't remove the virus, right?
Heaven forbid.
And *you*.
You should've known.
Yeah, yeah. I get it...*now*. You got a lead on him or not?
Hey, kiddo.

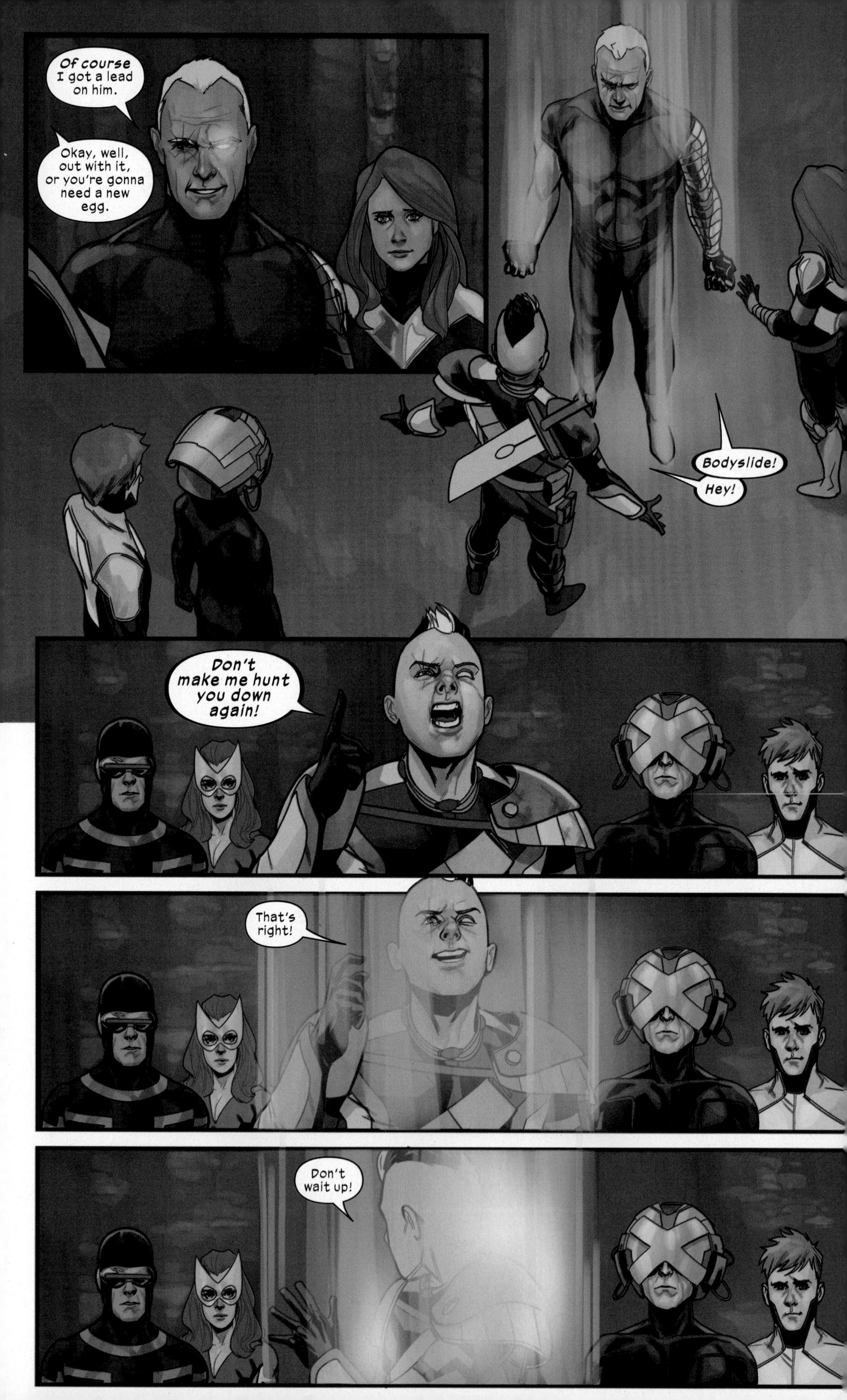
Of course I got a lead on him.
Okay, well, out with it, or you're gonna need a new egg.
Bodyslide!
Hey!
Don't make me hunt you down again!
That's right!
Don't wait up!

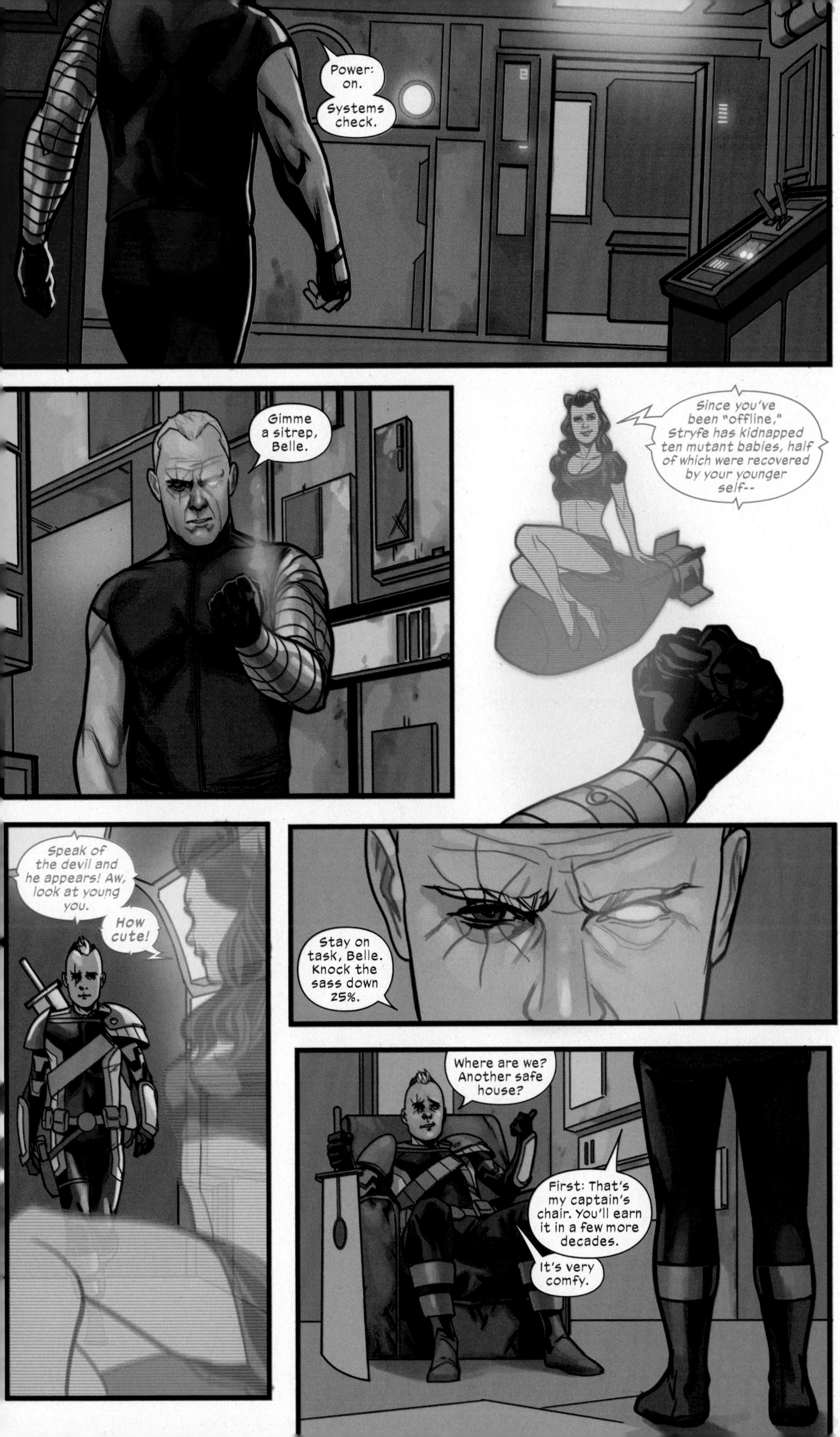
Power: on.
Systems check.
Gimme a sitrep, Belle.
Since you've been "offline," Stryfe has kidnapped ten mutant babies, half of which were recovered by your younger self--
Speak of the devil and he appears! Aw, look at young you.
How cute!
Stay on task, Belle. Knock the sass down 25%.
Where are we? Another safe house?
First: That's my captain's chair. You'll earn it in a few more decades.
It's very comfy.

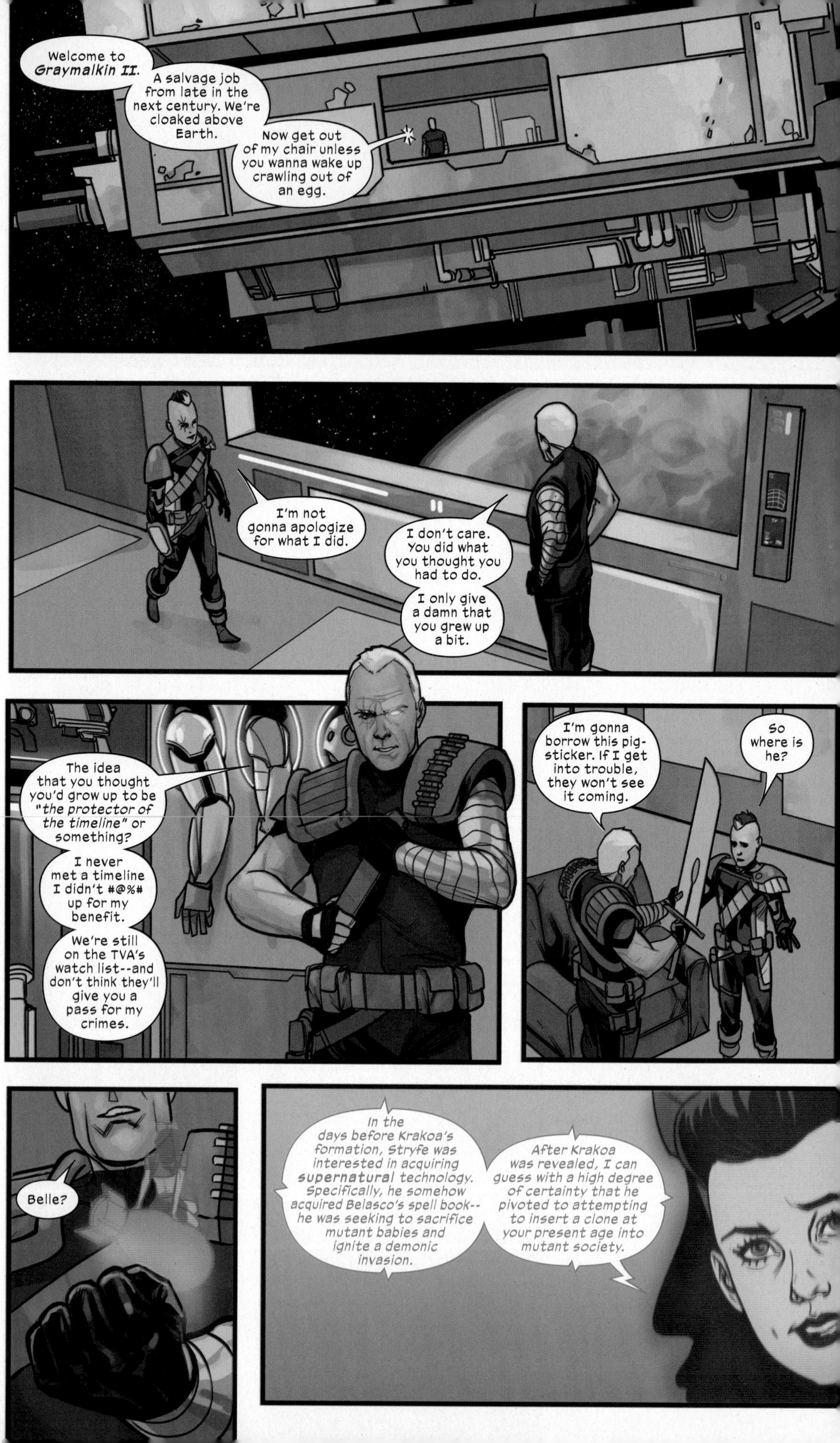
Welcome to Graymalkin II.
A salvage job from late in the next century. We're cloaked above Earth.
Now get out of my chair unless you wanna wake up crawling out of an egg.
I'm not gonna apologize for what I did.
I don't care. You did what you thought you had to do.
I only give a damn that you grew up a bit.
The idea that you thought you'd grow up to be "the protector of the timeline" or something?
I never met a timeline I didn't #@%# up for my benefit.
We're still on the TVA's watch list--and don't think they'll give you a pass for my crimes.
I'm gonna borrow this pig-sticker. If I get into trouble, they won't see it coming.
So where is he?
Belle?
In the days before Krakoa's formation, Stryfe was interested in acquiring supernatural technology. Specifically, he somehow acquired Belasco's spell book--he was seeking to sacrifice mutant babies and ignite a demonic invasion.
After Krakoa was revealed, I can guess with a high degree of certainty that he pivoted to attempting to insert a clone at your present age into mutant society.

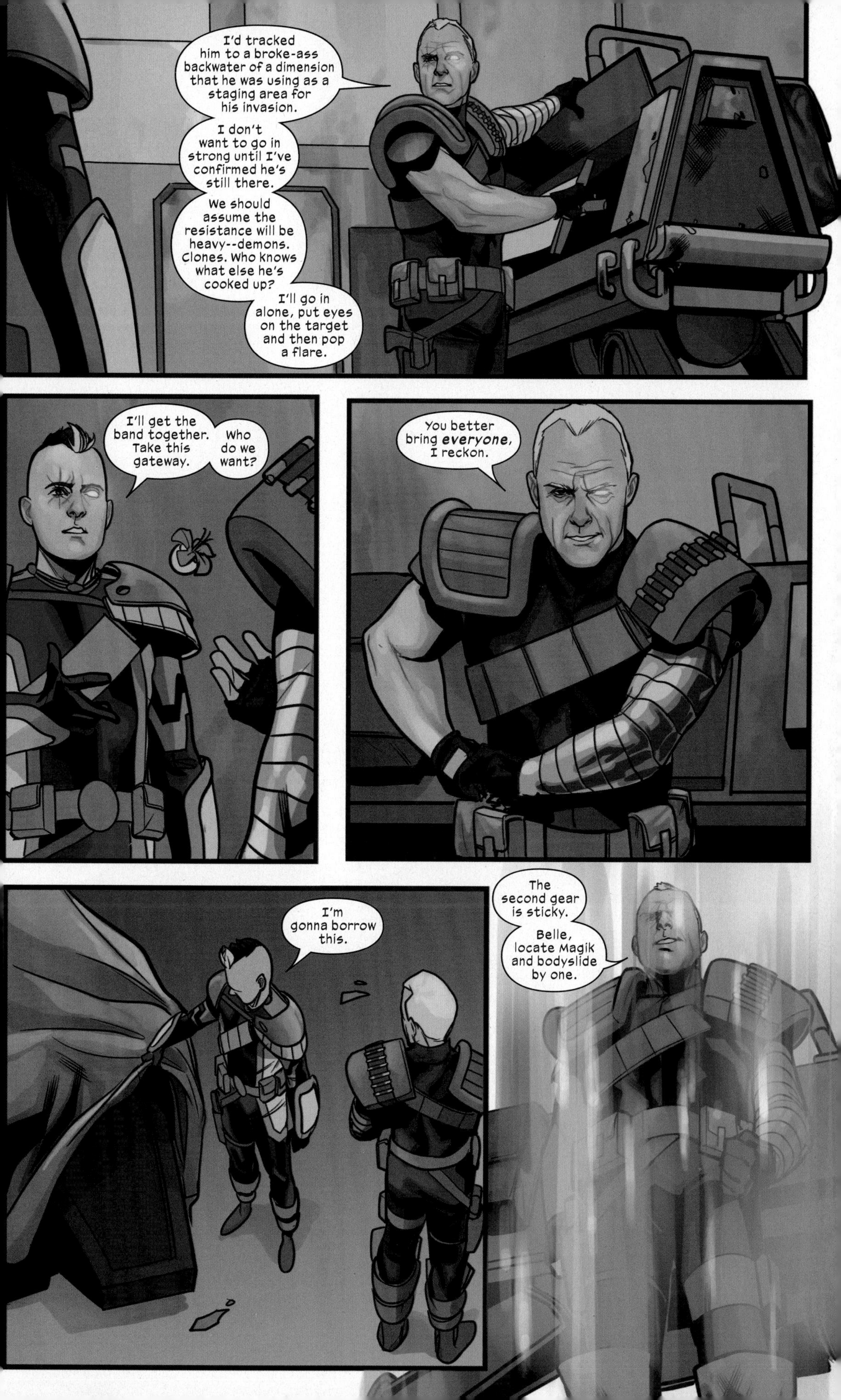
I'd tracked him to a broke-ass backwater of a dimension that he was using as a staging area for his invasion.
I don't want to go in strong until I've confirmed he's still there.
We should assume the resistance will be heavy--demons. Clones. Who knows what else he's cooked up?
I'll go in alone, put eyes on the target and then pop a flare.
I'll get the band together. Take this gateway.
Who do we want?
You better bring *everyone*, I reckon.
I'm gonna borrow this.
The second gear is sticky.
Belle, locate Magik and bodyslide by one.

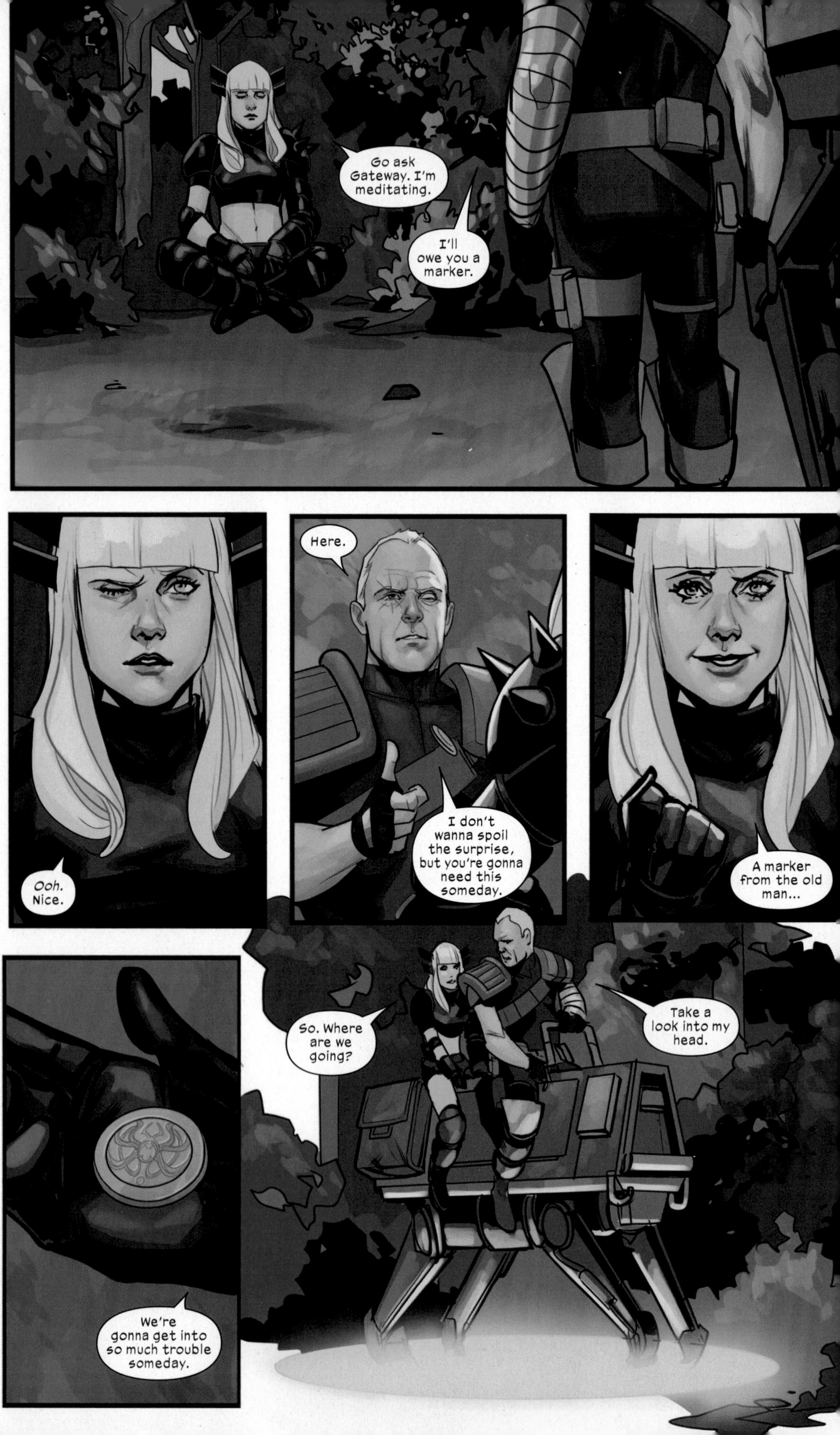
Go ask Gateway. I'm meditating.
I'll owe you a marker.
Ooh. Nice.
Here.
I don't wanna spoil the surprise, but you're gonna need this someday.
A marker from the old man...
We're gonna get into so much trouble someday.
So. Where are we going?
Take a look into my head.

[Cable....[LOG]_00]
[Wagon....[WAR]_11]

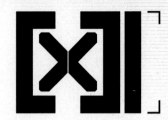

CABLE'S WAR WAGON DEPLOYMENT LOG

1992: The War Wagon was constructed.

2021: "The Summers War" in the demon lands against Stryfe.

2023: [redacted]

1918: Tunguska racing catastrophe.

2901: Impounded during the attack on a corrupt Time Variance Authority.

1978: NYC blackout caused by assault on Stryfe in the Bronx.

2099: War Wagon II debuts, with a new AI selected from a contest in the Mojoverse.

2015: Secret War Wagons. Admittedly, this was more of a Deadpool story.

All events are untold tales in chronological order. All of this has happened already, you just don't know it yet.

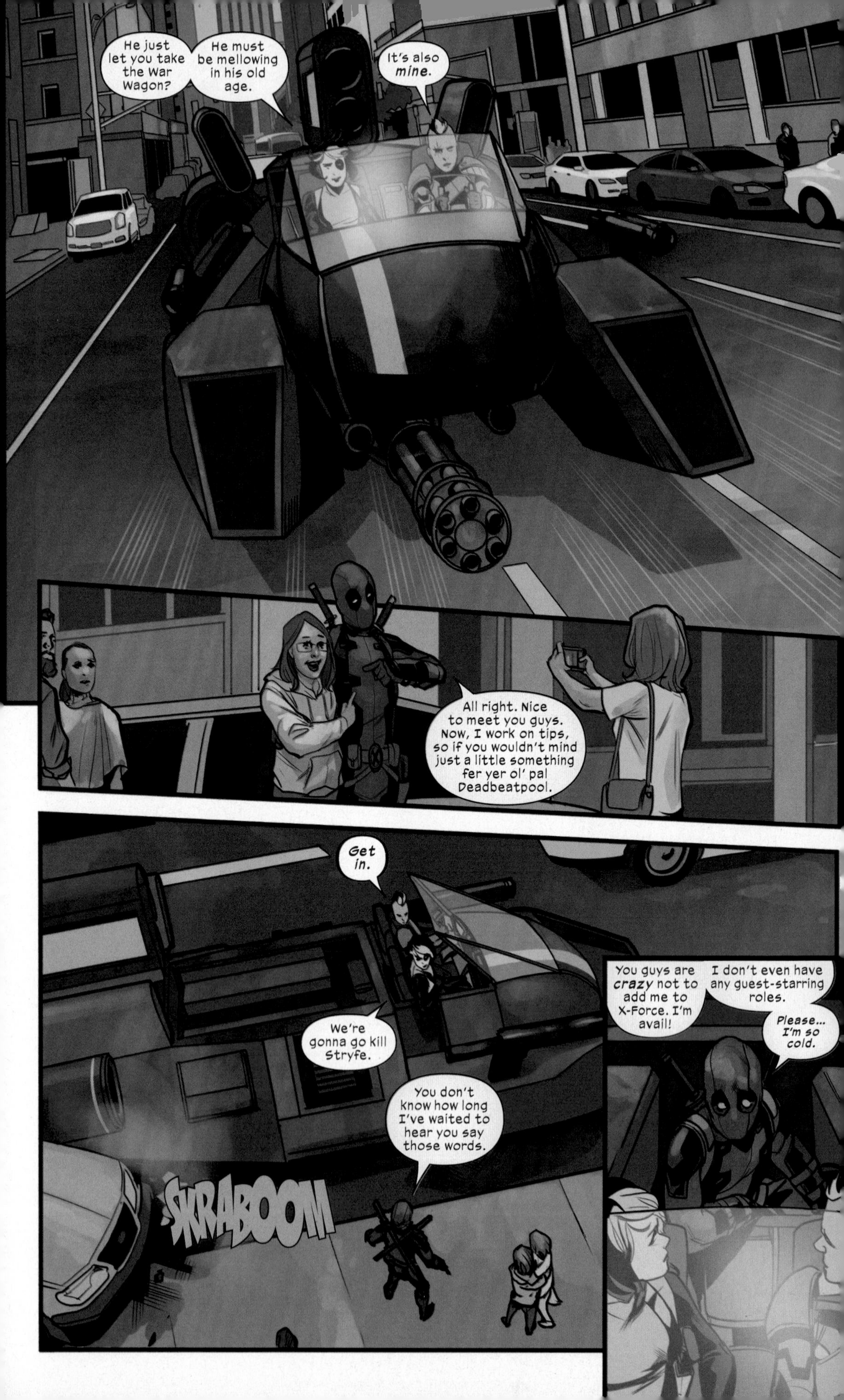
He just let you take the War Wagon?
He must be mellowing in his old age.
It's also *mine*.
All right. Nice to meet you guys. Now, I work on tips, so if you wouldn't mind just a little something fer yer ol' pal Deadbeatpool.
Get in.
We're gonna go kill Stryfe.
You don't know how long I've waited to hear you say those words.
SKRABOOM
You guys are *crazy* not to add me to X-Force. I'm avail!
I don't even have any guest-starring roles.
Please... I'm so cold.

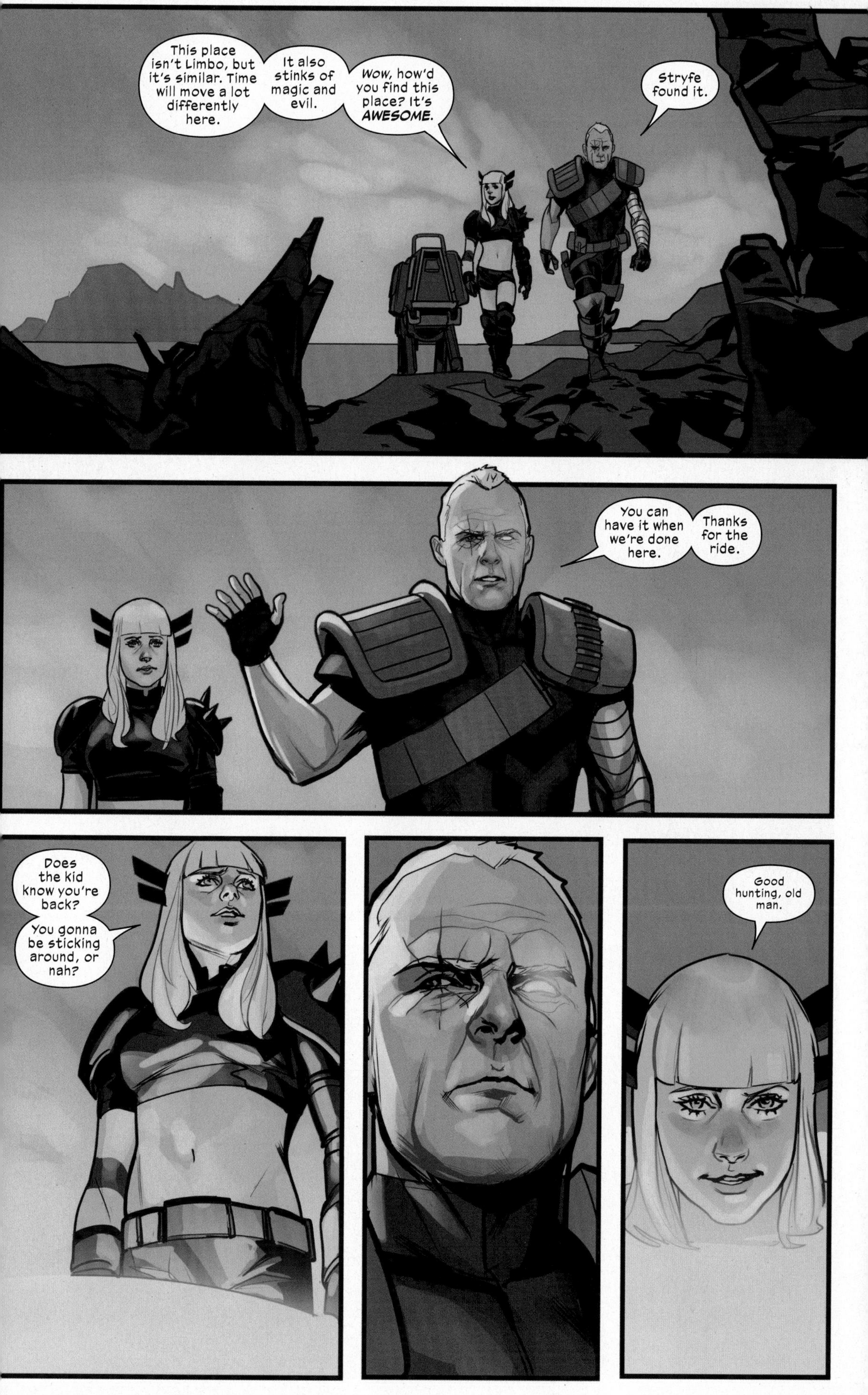

This place isn't Limbo, but it's similar. Time will move a lot differently here.
It also stinks of magic and evil.
Wow, how'd you find this place? It's AWESOME.
Stryfe found it.
You can have it when we're done here.
Thanks for the ride.
Does the kid know you're back?
You gonna be sticking around, or nah?
Good hunting, old man.

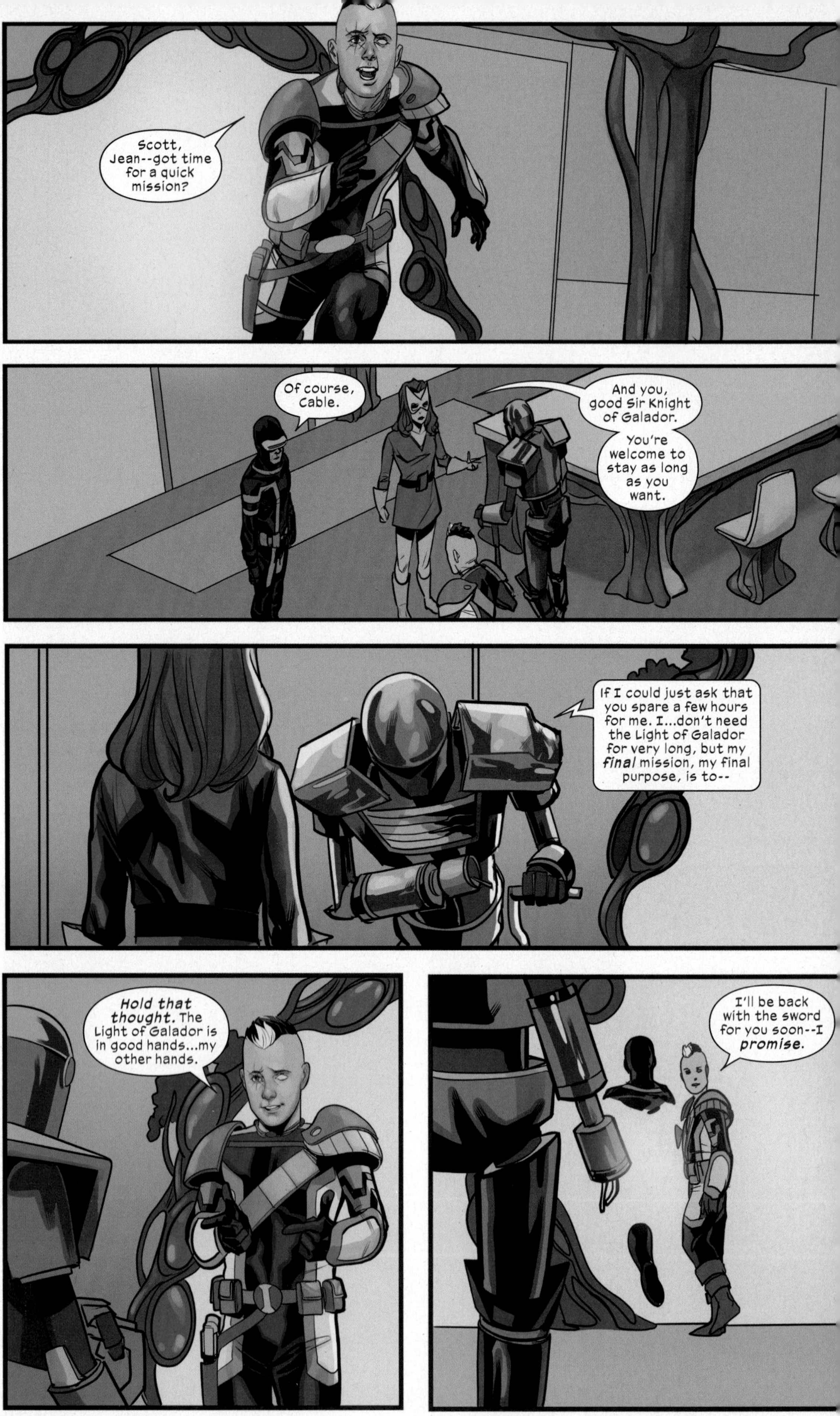
Scott,
Jean--got time for a quick mission?
Of course, Cable.
And you, good Sir Knight of Galador.
You're welcome to stay as long as you want.
If I could just ask that you spare a few hours for me. I...don't need the Light of Galador for very long, but my *final* mission, my final purpose, is to--
Hold that thought. The Light of Galador is in good hands...my other hands.
I'll be back with the sword for you soon--I *promise*.

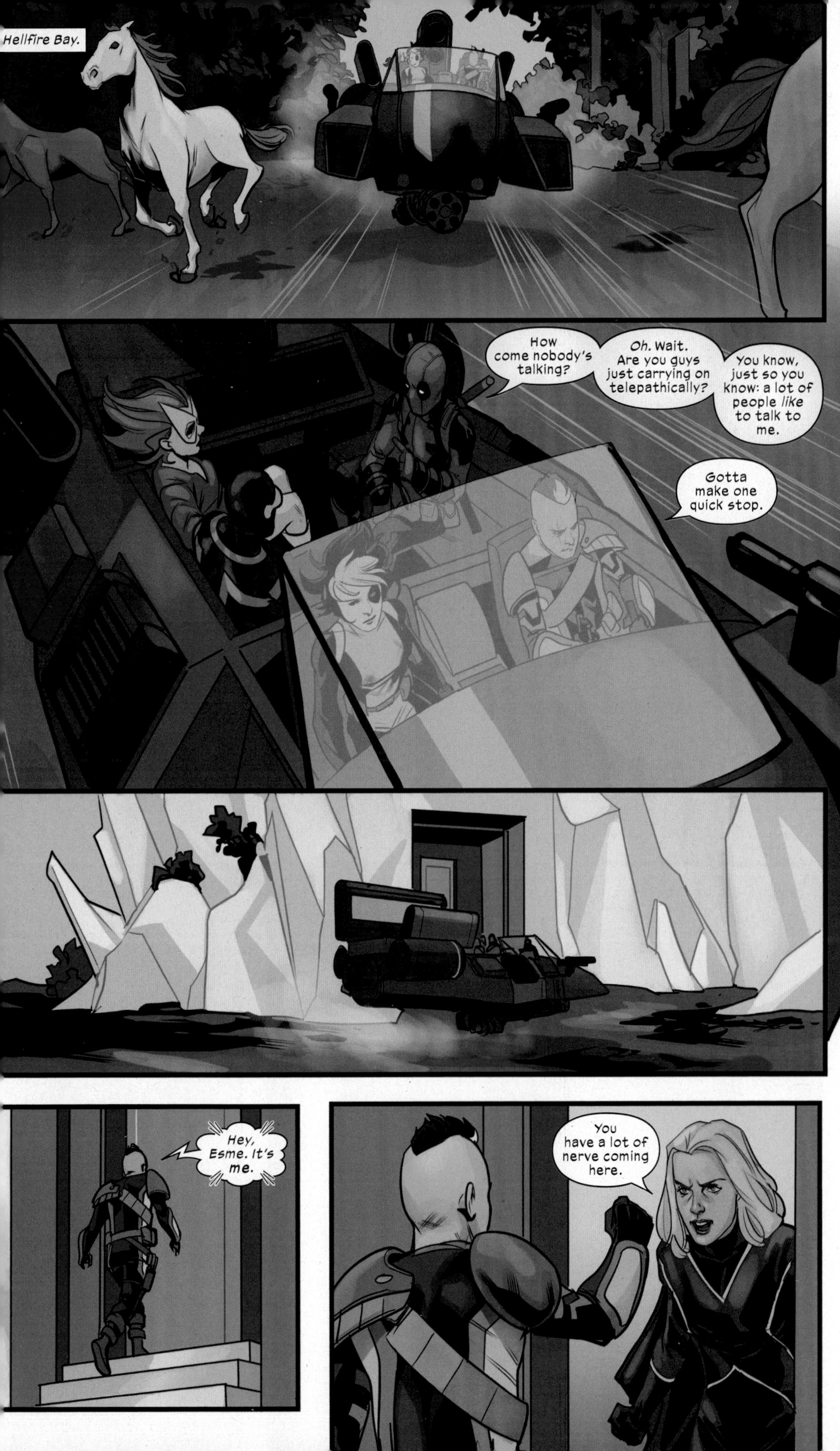
Hellfire Bay.
How come nobody's talking?
Oh. Wait. Are you guys just carrying on telepathically?
You know, just so you know: a lot of people *like* to talk to me.
Gotta make one quick stop.
Hey, Esme. It's me.
You have a lot of nerve coming here.

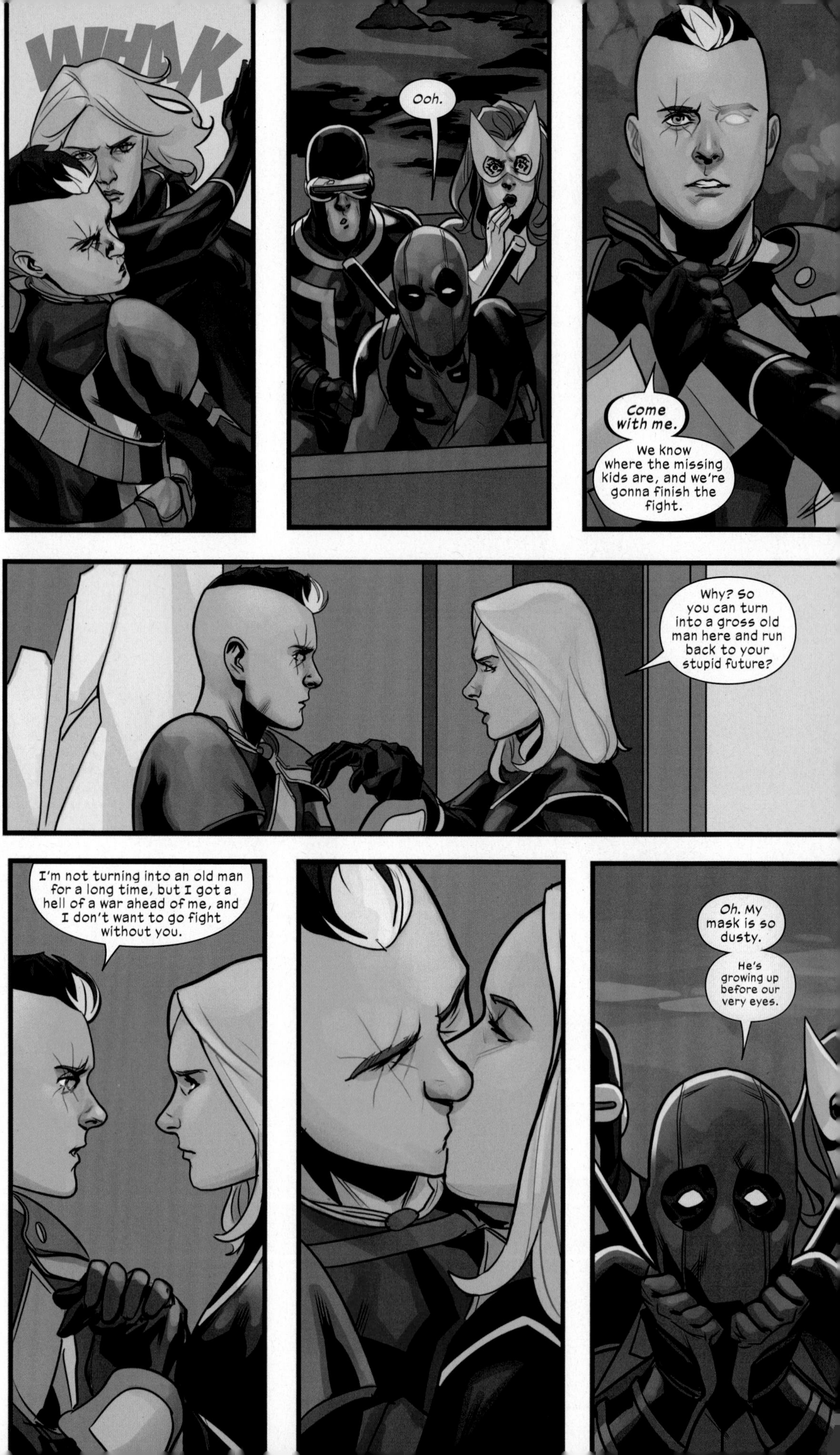
WHAK
Ooh.
Come with me.
We know where the missing kids are, and we're gonna finish the fight.
Why? So you can turn into a gross old man here and run back to your stupid future?
I'm not turning into an old man for a long time, but I got a hell of a war ahead of me, and I don't want to go fight without you.
Oh. My mask is so dusty.
He's growing up before our very eyes.

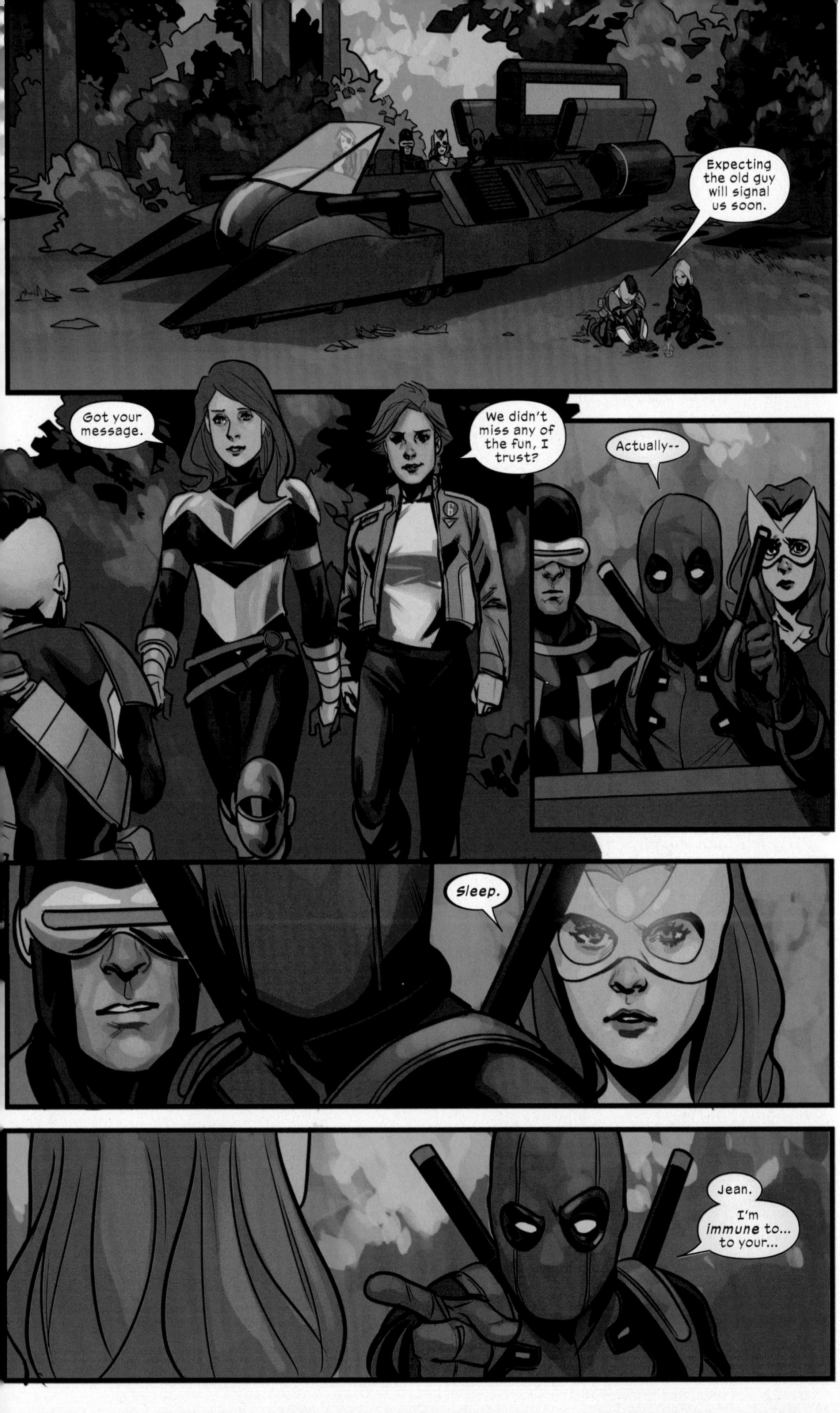
Expecting the old guy will signal us soon.
Got your message.
We didn't miss any of the fun, I trust?
Actually--
Sleep.
Jean.
I'm immune to... to your...

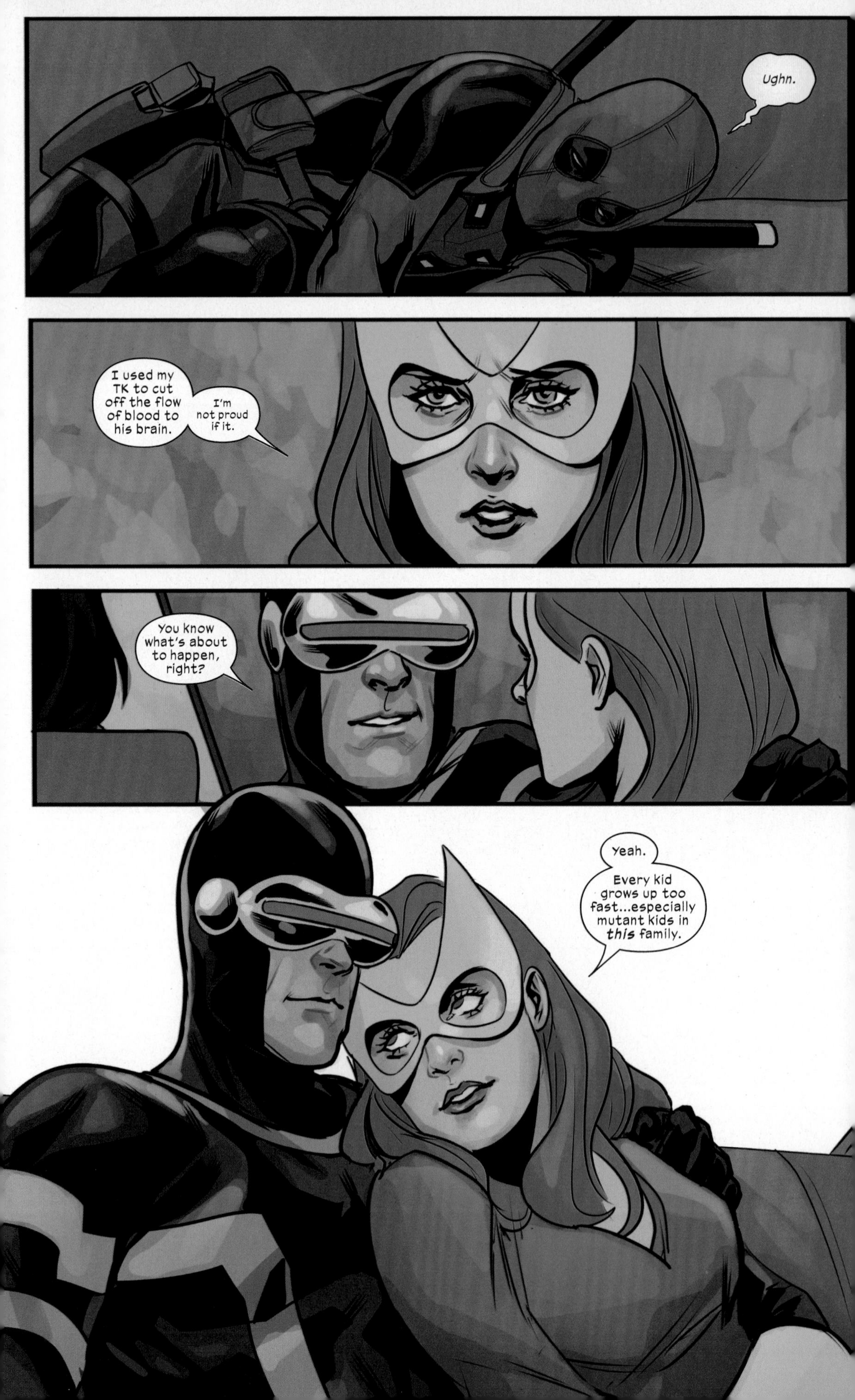
Ughn.
I used my TK to cut off the flow of blood to his brain.
I'm not proud if it.
You know what's about to happen, right?
Yeah.
Every kid grows up too fast...especially mutant kids in *this* family.

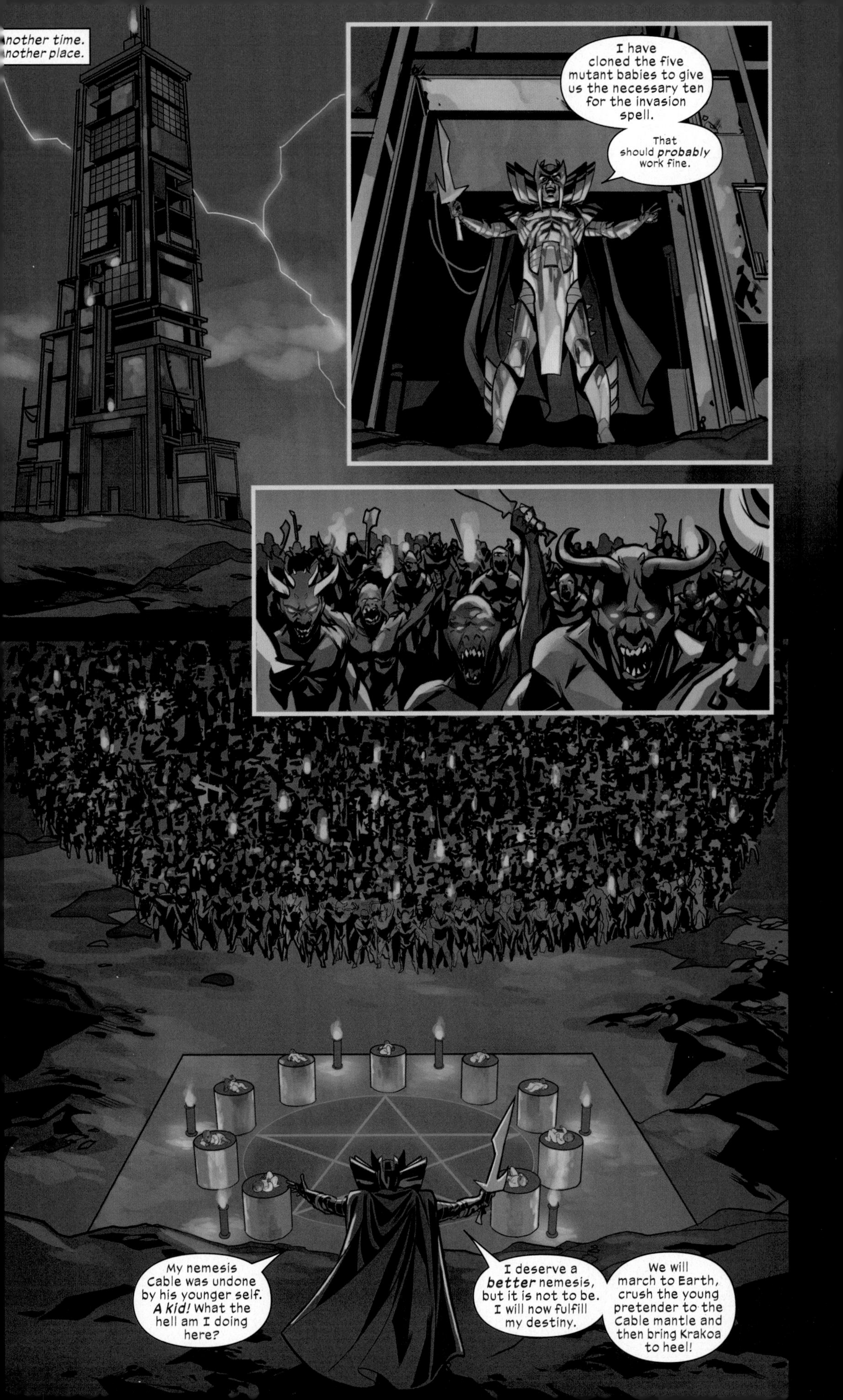
nother time.
nother place.
I have cloned the five mutant babies to give us the necessary ten for the invasion spell.
That should *probably* work fine.
My nemesis Cable was undone by his younger self. *A kid!* What the hell am I doing here?
I deserve a *better* nemesis, but it is not to be. I will now fulfill my destiny.
We will march to Earth, crush the young pretender to the Cable mantle and then bring Krakoa to heel!

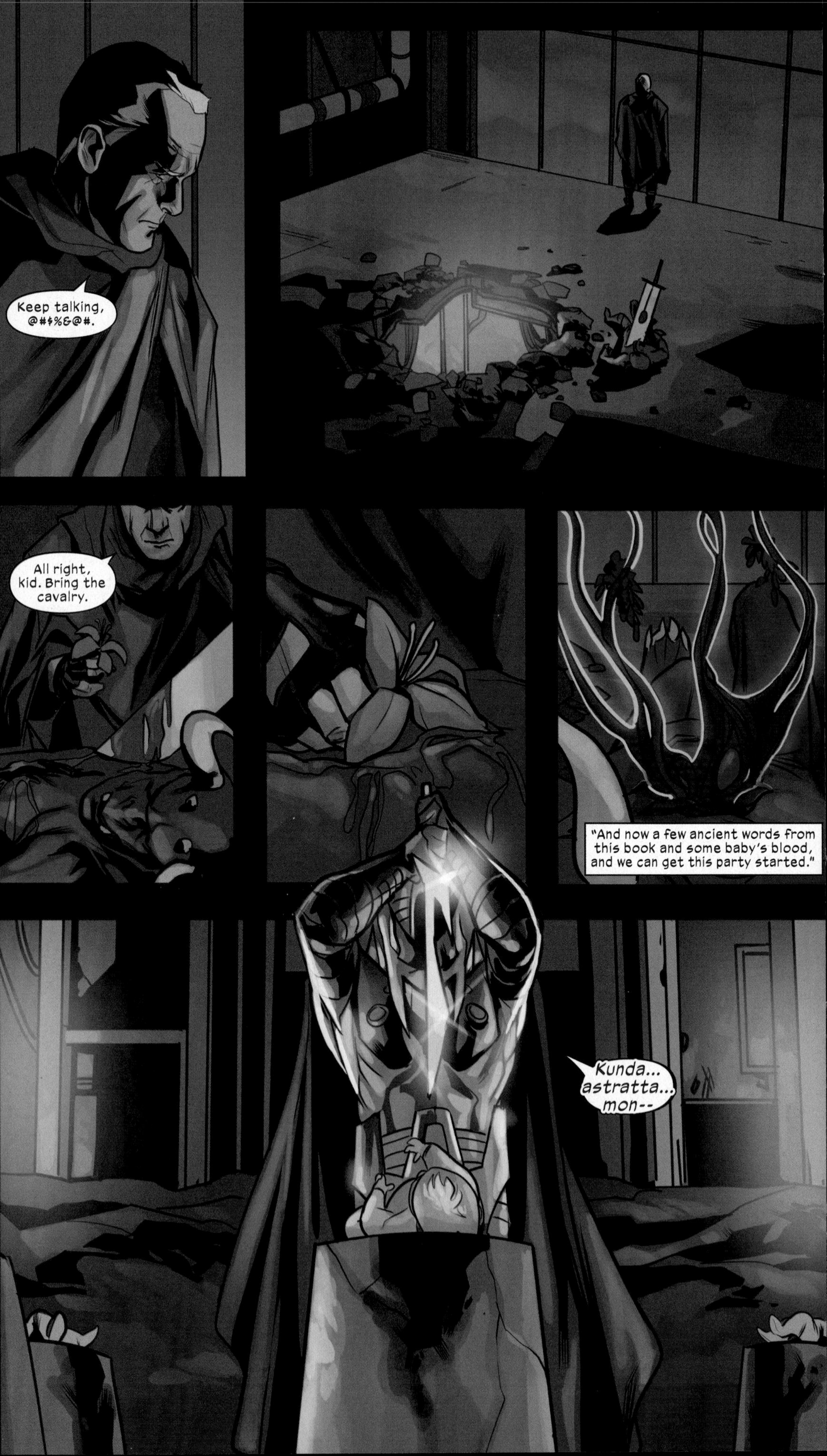
Keep talking, @#$%&@#.
All right, kid. Bring the cavalry.
"And now a few ancient words from this book and some baby's blood, and we can get this party started."
Kunda... astratta... mon--

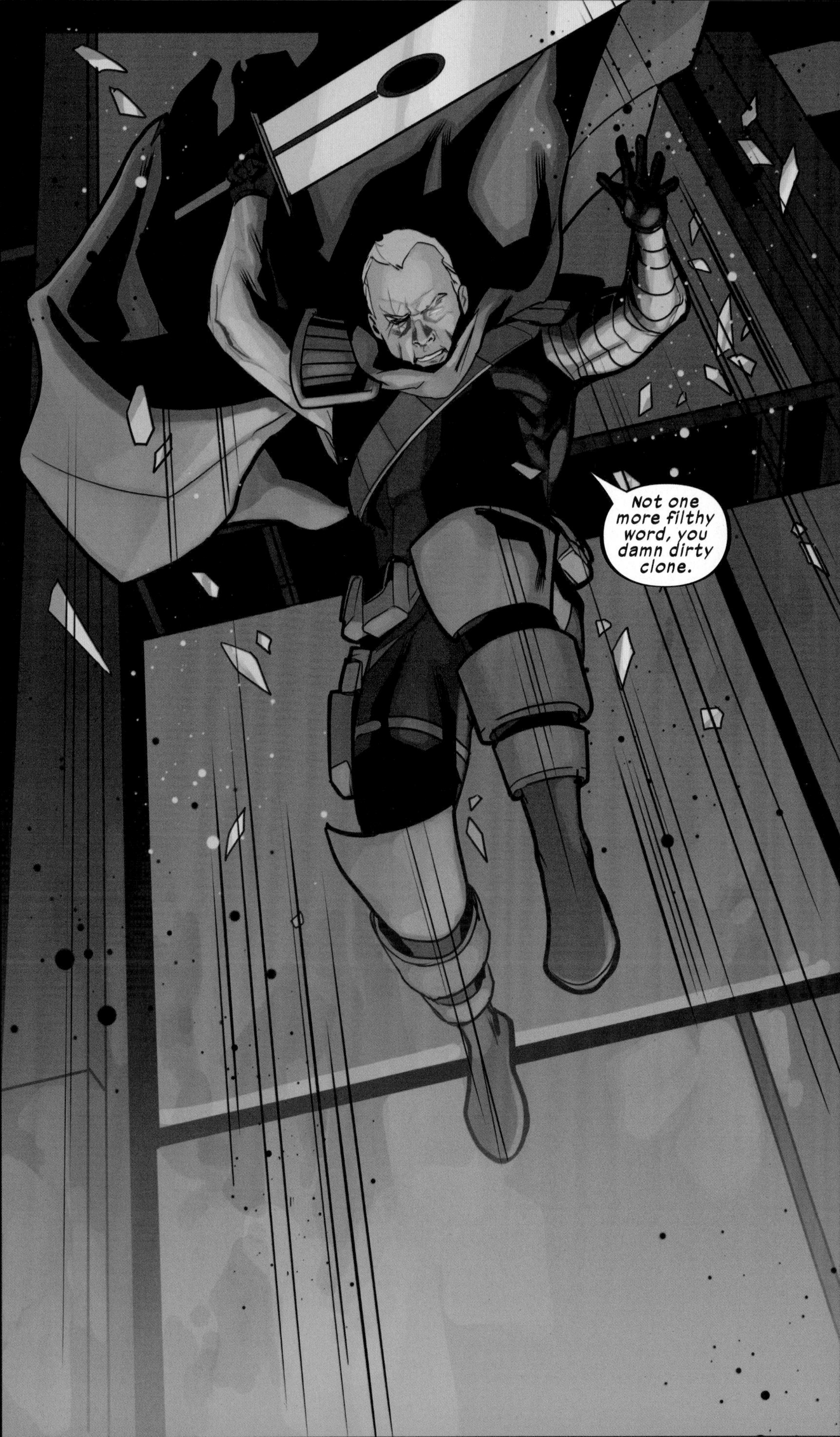
Not one more filthy word, you damn dirty clone.

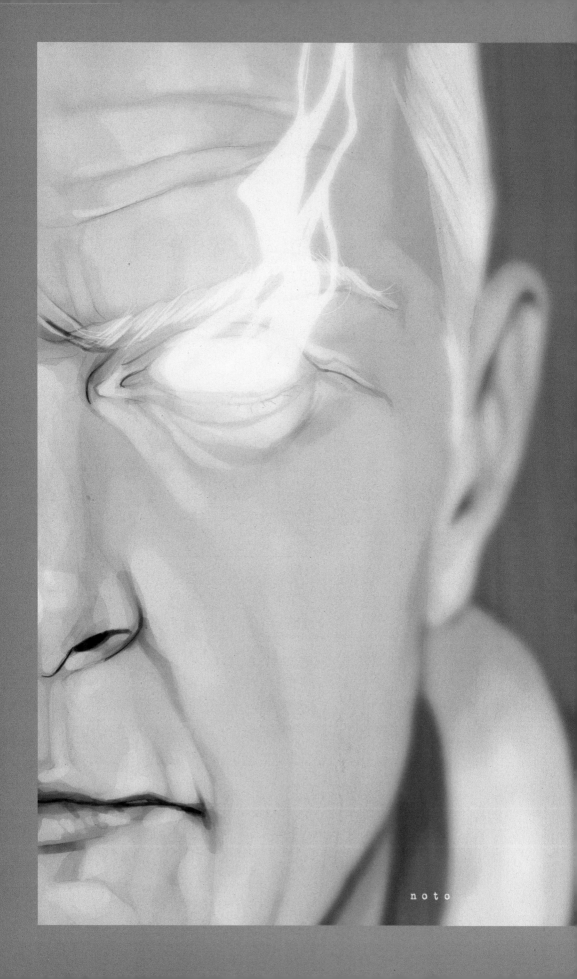

noto

Shakespeare in the Zark

[ca__[0.12]
[ble_[0.12]

Cable...*you're relieved of your duty.*

-- CABLE

[ca__[0.XX]
[ble_[0.XX]

[ca__[0.12].....]
[ble_[0.12].....]

[Cable_alpha.]

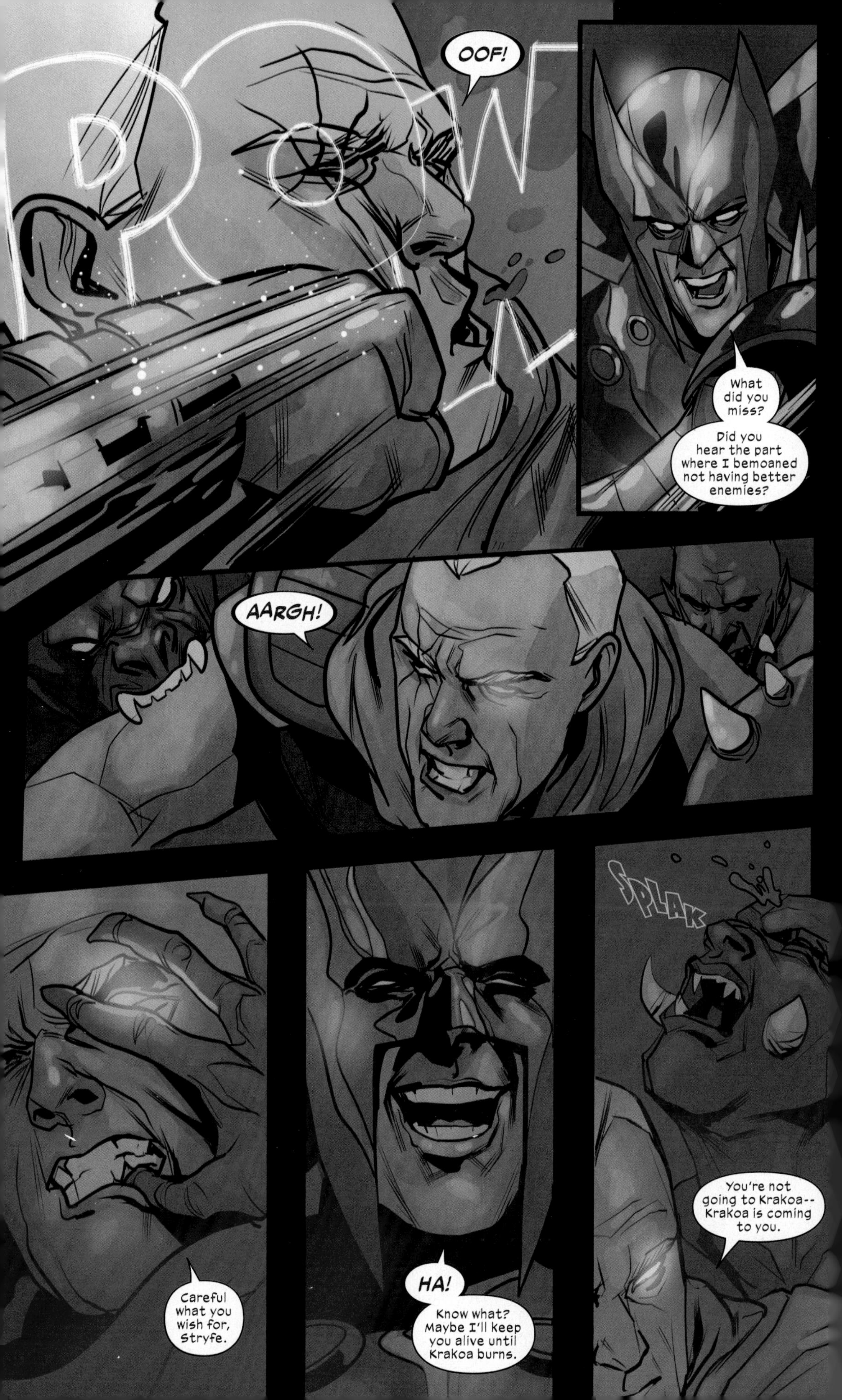
POW
OOF!
What did you miss?
Did you hear the part where I bemoaned not having better enemies?
AARGH!
Careful what you wish for, Stryfe.
HA!
Know what? Maybe I'll keep you alive until Krakoa burns.
SPLAK
You're not going to Krakoa-- Krakoa is coming to you.

Let the old bastard go.

Heeeey! Now I'll get to kill you both!

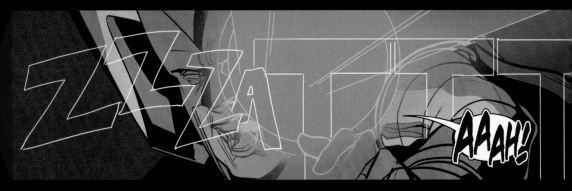

ZZZZATTTTT

AAAH!

Call it. Jam Stryfe, and get the babies away from him.

Nice. I'll handle the babies.

Aw! I guess the old man and the kid thought they needed a little help.

Or a lot of help.

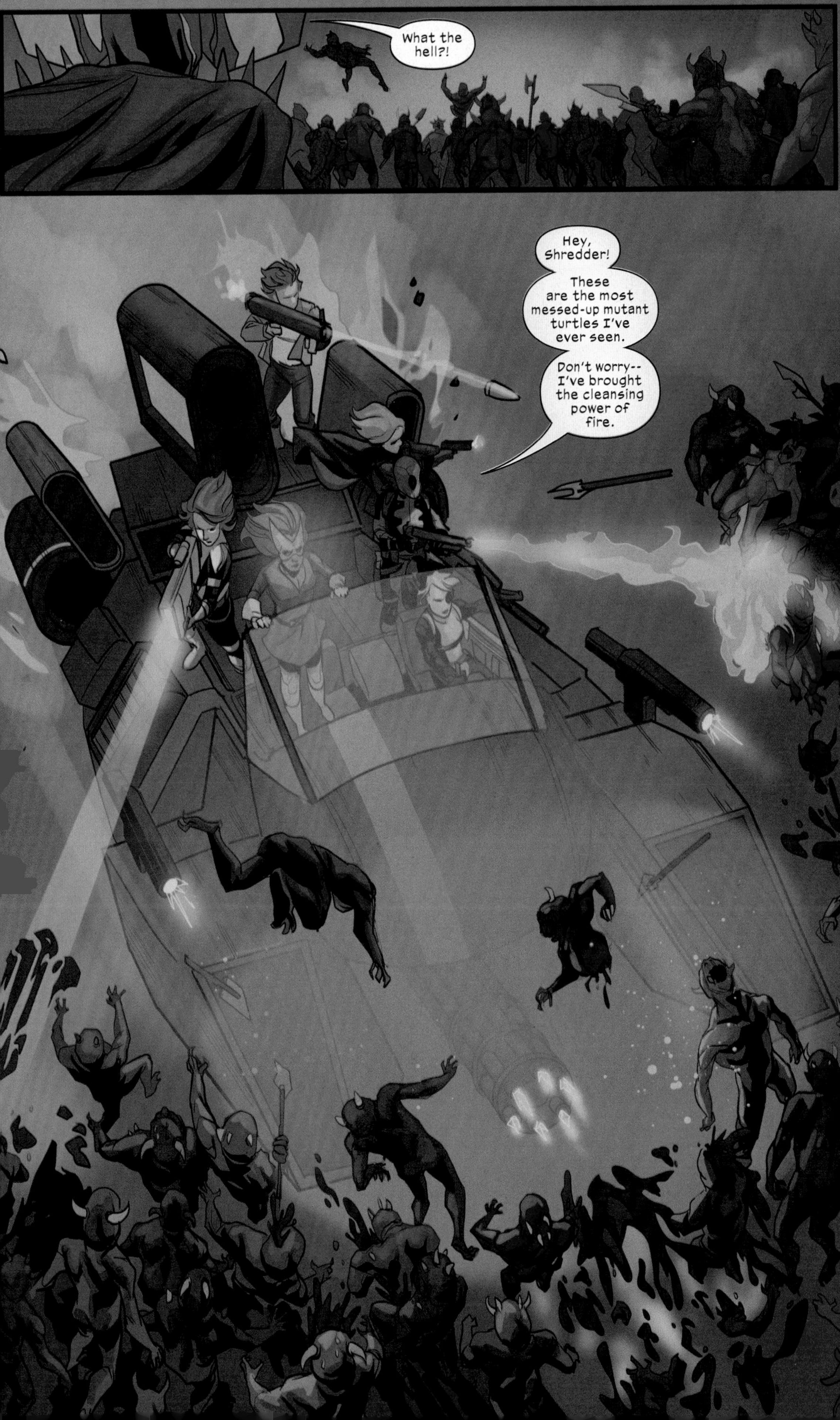

What the hell?!
Hey, Shredder!
These are the most messed-up mutant turtles I've ever seen.
Don't worry--I've brought the cleansing power of fire.

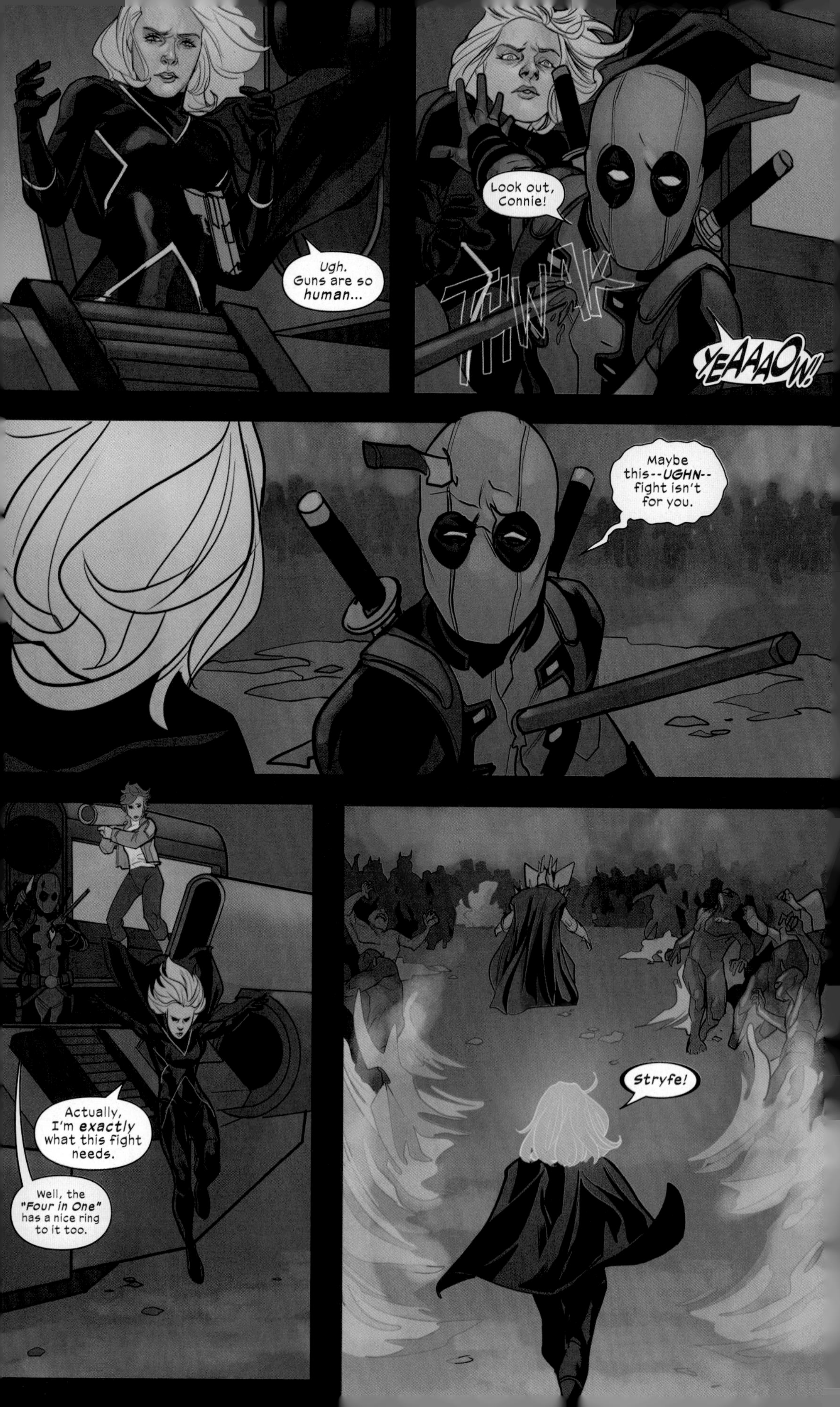
Ugh. Guns are so *human*...
Look out, Connie!
THWAK
YEAAAOW!
Maybe this--*UGHN*--fight isn't for you.
Actually, I'm *exactly* what this fight needs.
Well, the *"Four in One"* has a nice ring to it too.
Stryfe!

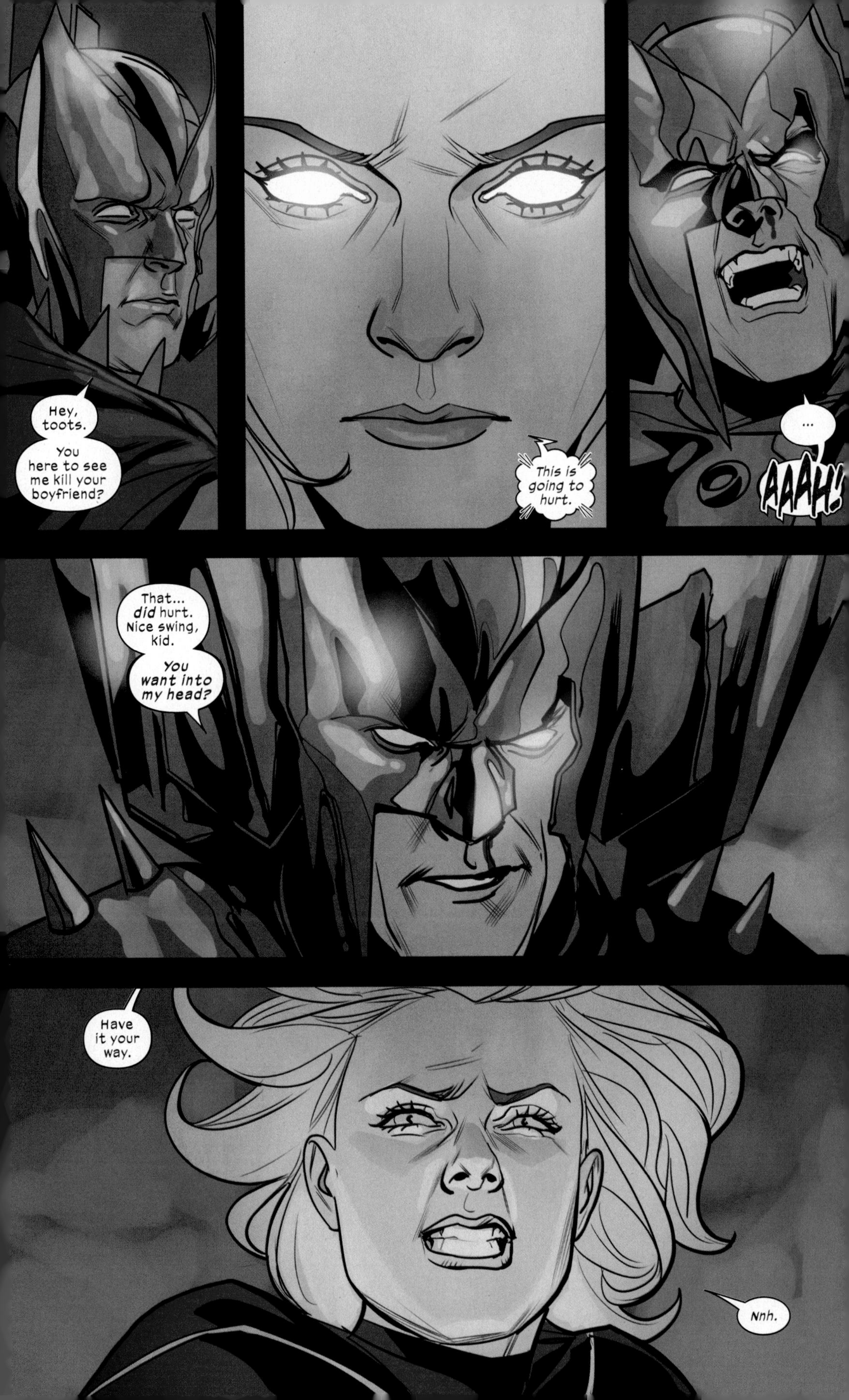
Hey, toots.
You here to see me kill your boyfriend?
This is going to hurt.
...
AAAH!
That... did hurt. Nice swing, kid.
You want into my head?
Have it your way.
Nnh.

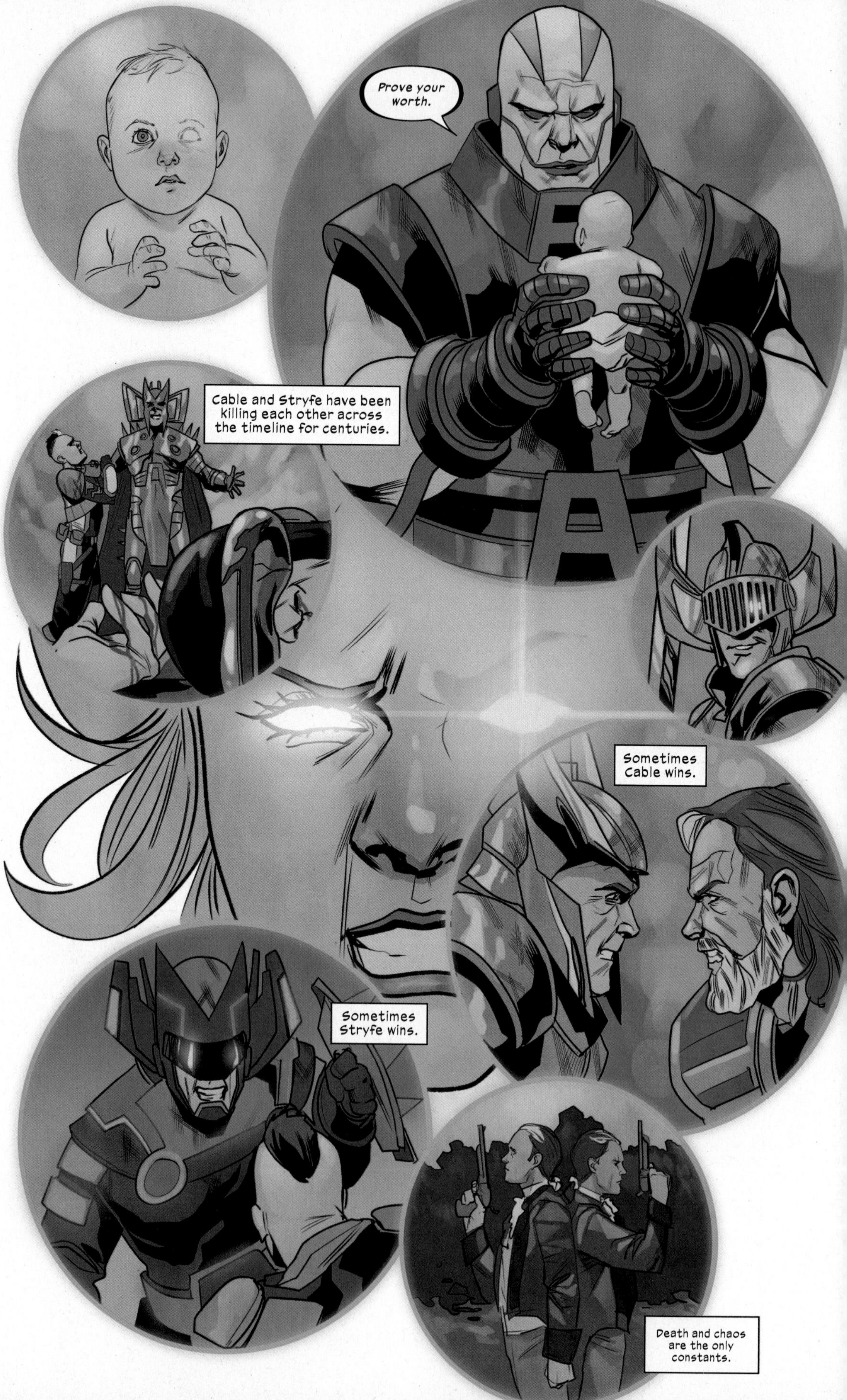

Prove your worth.
Cable and Stryfe have been killing each other across the timeline for centuries.
Sometimes Cable wins.
Sometimes Stryfe wins.
Death and chaos are the only constants.

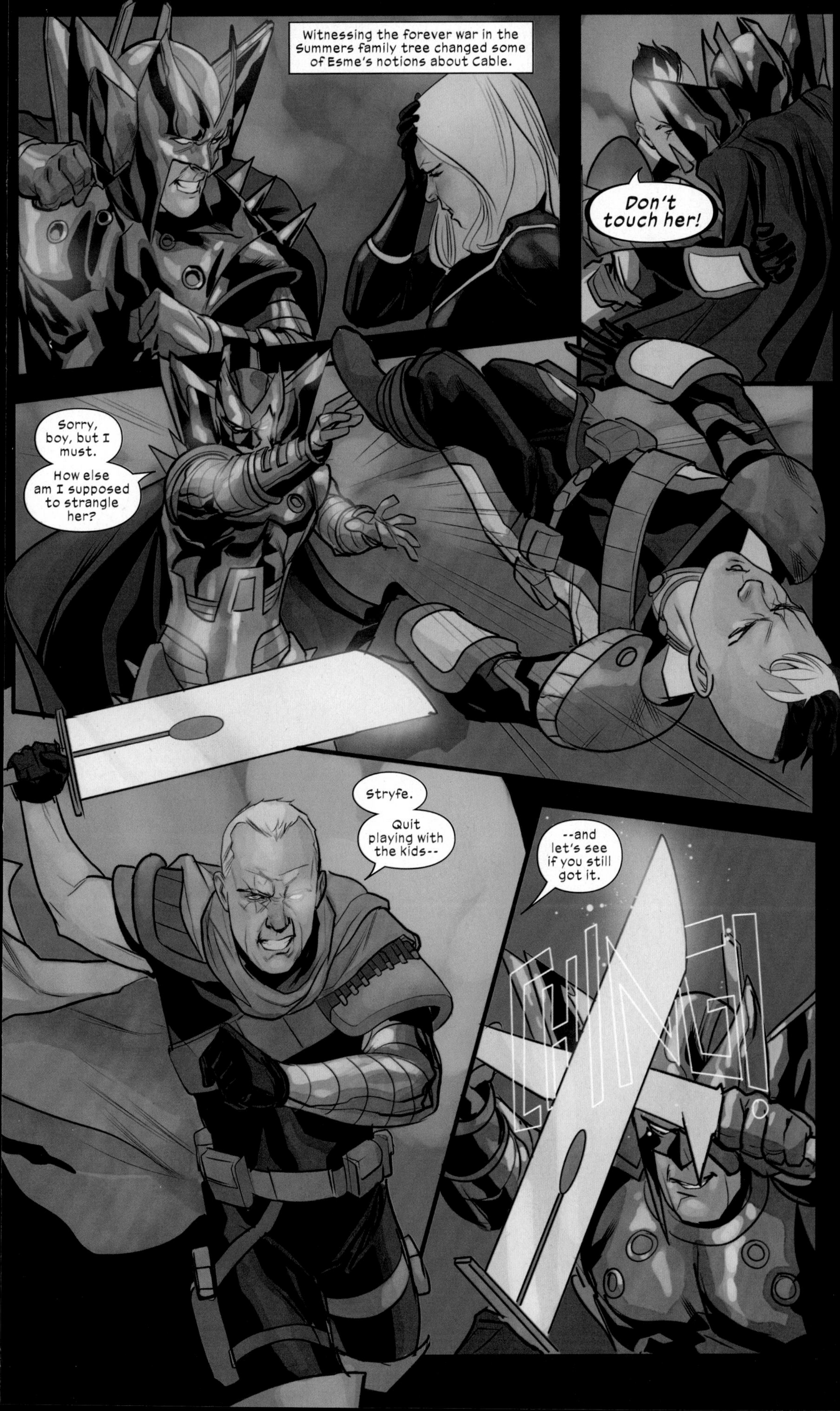

Witnessing the forever war in the Summers family tree changed some of Esme's notions about Cable.
Don't touch her!
Sorry, boy, but I must.
How else am I supposed to strangle her?
Stryfe.
Quit playing with the kids--
--and let's see if you still got it.
CHING!

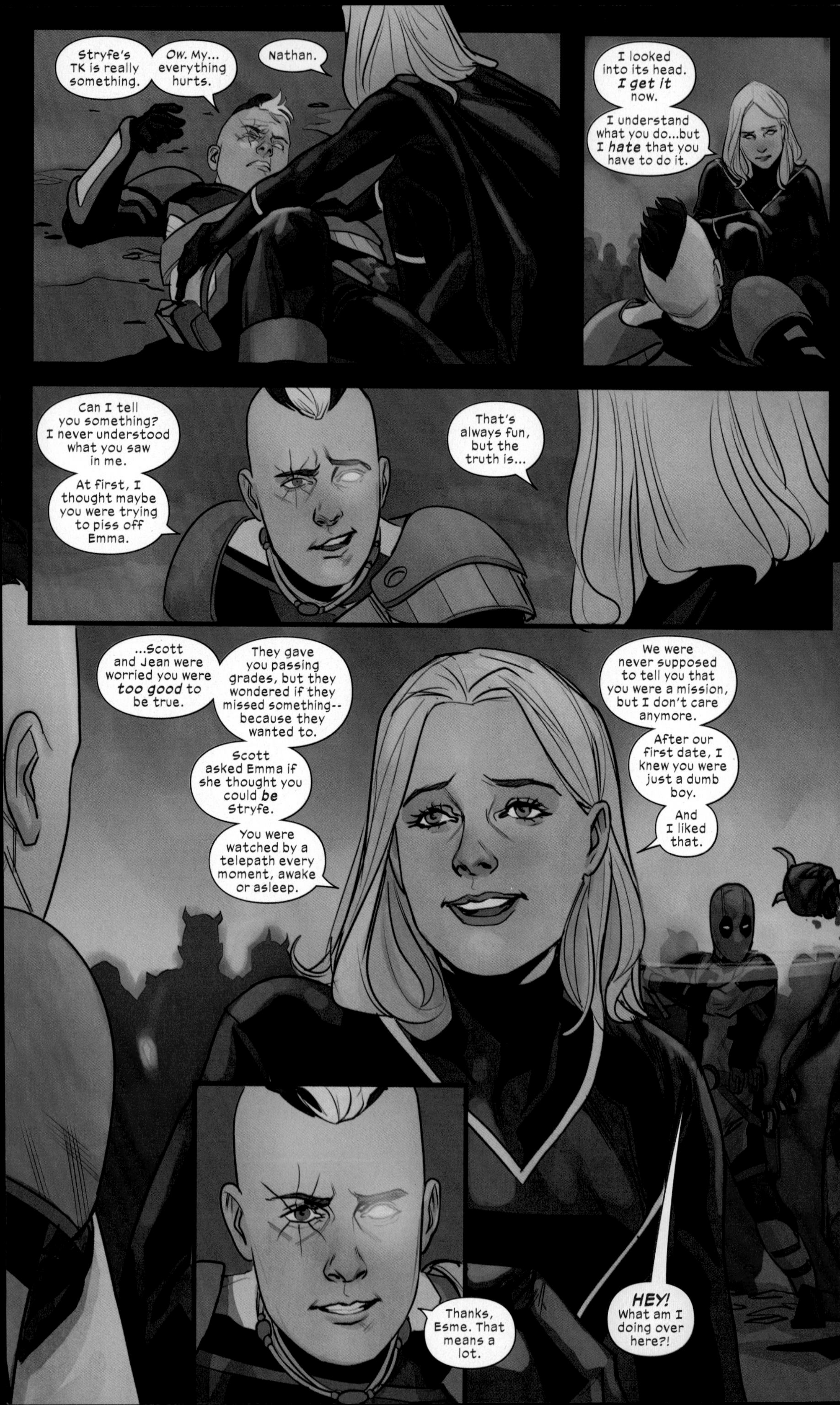

Stryfe's TK is really something.
Ow. My... everything hurts.
Nathan.
I looked into its head. I get it now.
I understand what you do...but I hate that you have to do it.
Can I tell you something? I never understood what you saw in me.
At first, I thought maybe you were trying to piss off Emma.
That's always fun, but the truth is...
...Scott and Jean were worried you were too good to be true.
They gave you passing grades, but they wondered if they missed something--because they wanted to.
Scott asked Emma if she thought you could be Stryfe.
You were watched by a telepath every moment, awake or asleep.
We were never supposed to tell you that you were a mission, but I don't care anymore.
After our first date, I knew you were just a dumb boy.
And I liked that.
Thanks, Esme. That means a lot.
HEY! What am I doing over here?!

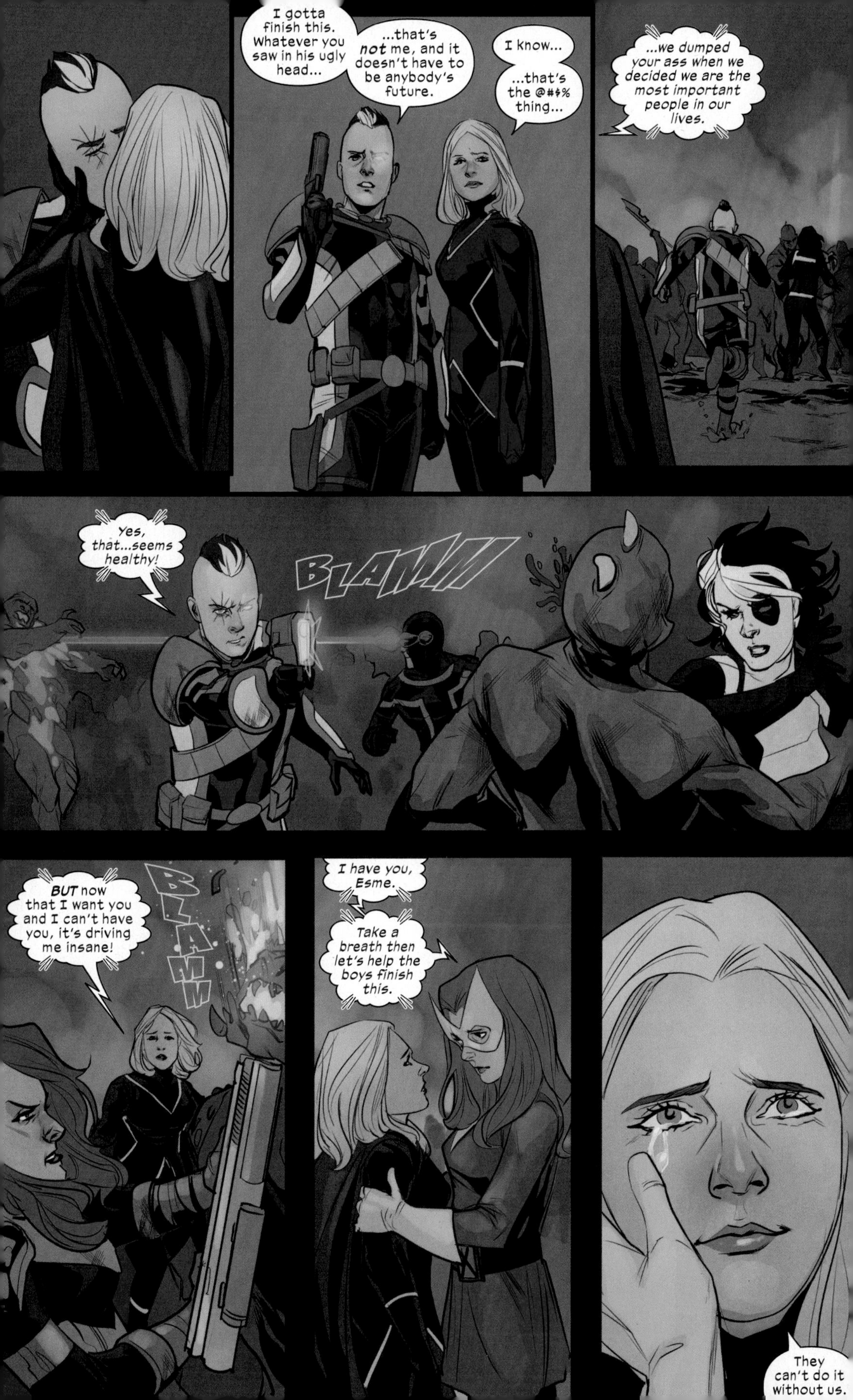

I gotta finish this. Whatever you saw in his ugly head...
...that's **not** me, and it doesn't have to be anybody's future.
I know...
...that's the @#$% thing...
...we dumped your ass when we decided we are the most important people in our lives.
Yes, that...seems healthy!
BLAMM
BUT now that I want you and I can't have you, it's driving me insane!
BLAMM
I have you, Esme.
Take a breath then let's help the boys finish this.
They can't do it without us.

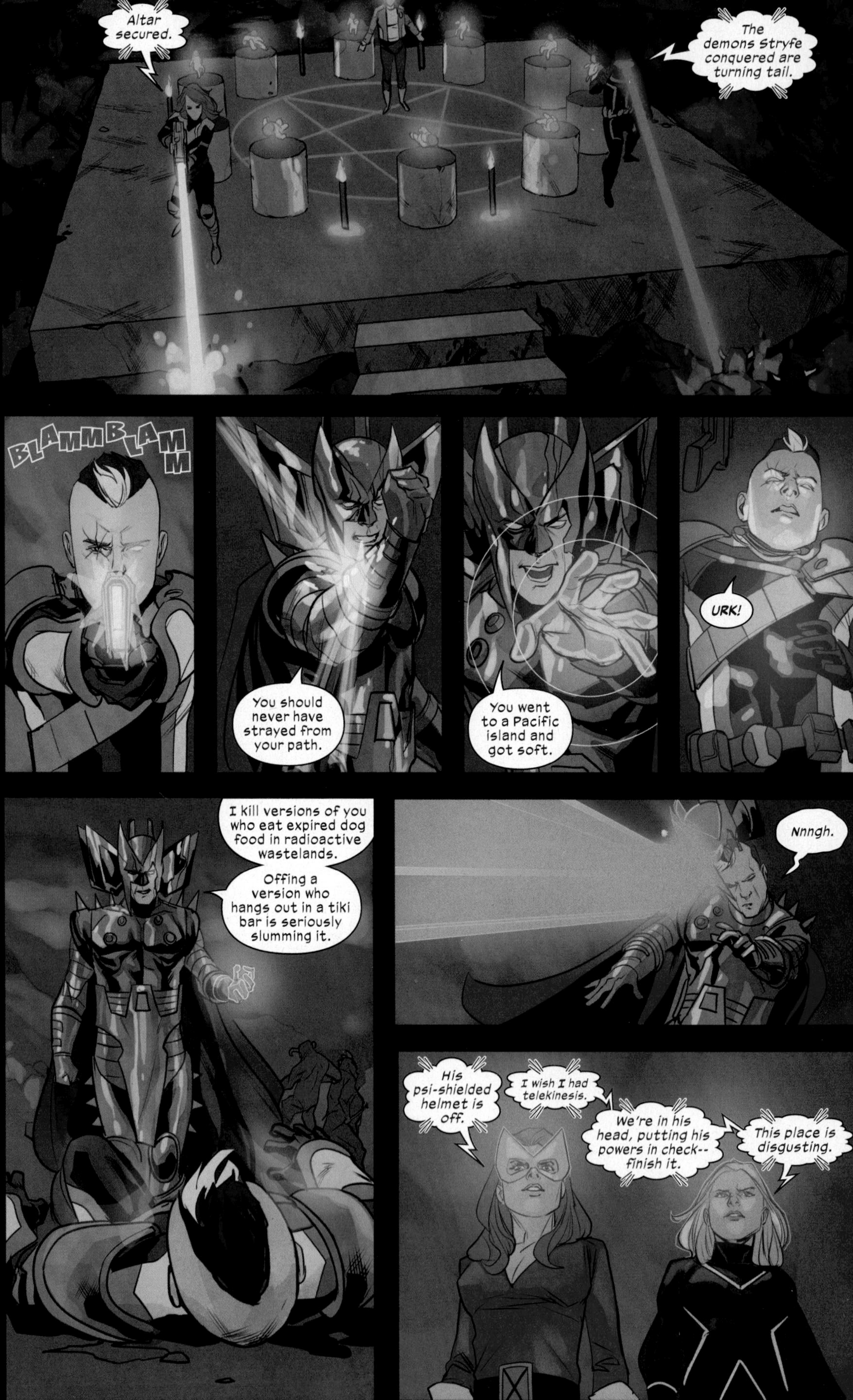
Altar secured.
The demons Stryfe conquered are turning tail.
BLAMMBLAMM
You should never have strayed from your path.
You went to a Pacific island and got soft.
URK!
I kill versions of you who eat expired dog food in radioactive wastelands.
Offing a version who hangs out in a tiki bar is seriously slumming it.
Nnngh.
His psi-shielded helmet is off.
I wish I had telekinesis.
We're in his head, putting his powers in check-- finish it.
This place is disgusting.

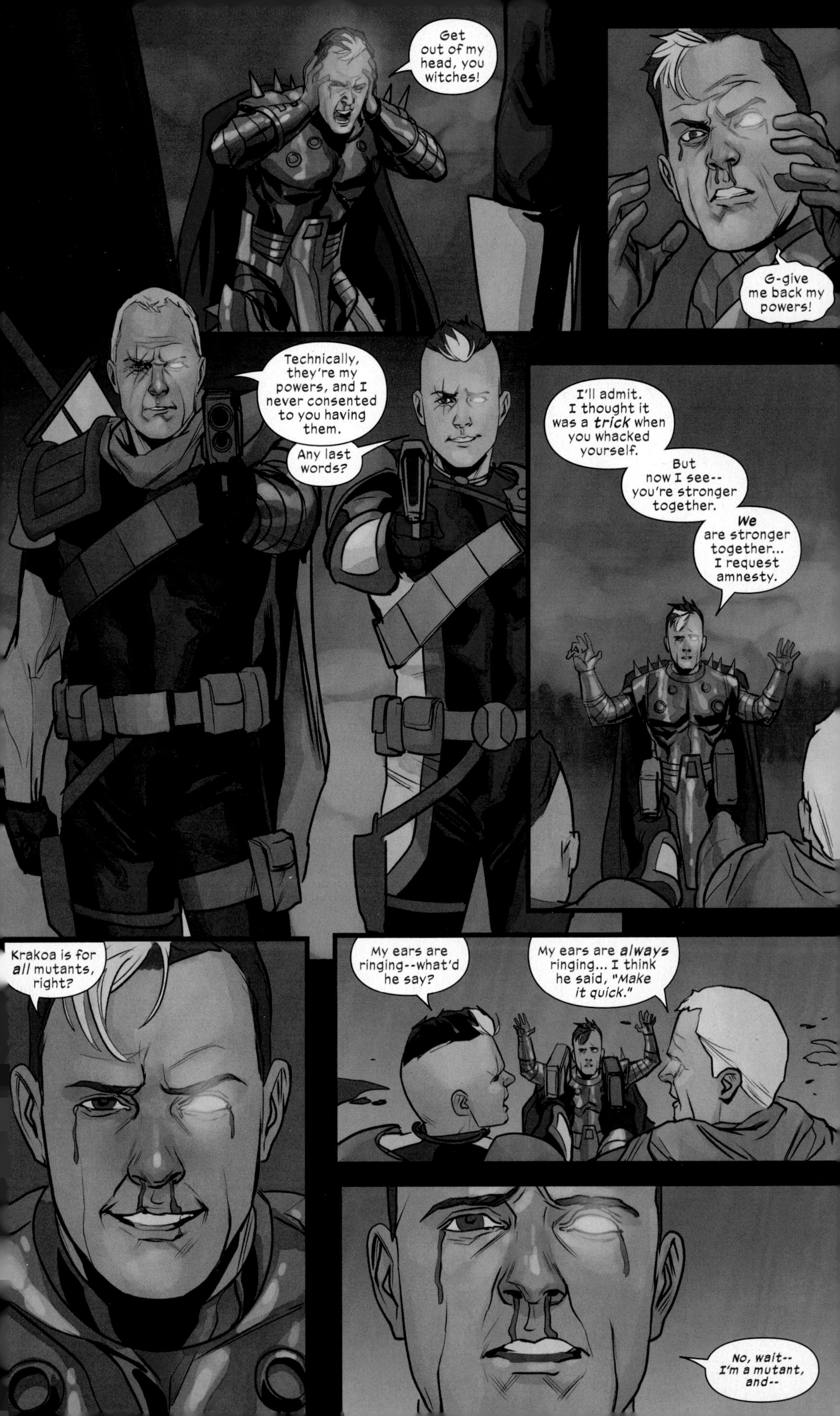

Get out of my head, you witches!
G-give me back my powers!
Technically, they're my powers, and I never consented to you having them.
Any last words?
I'll admit. I thought it was a *trick* when you whacked yourself.
But now I see-- you're stronger together.
We are stronger together... I request amnesty.
Krakoa is for *all* mutants, right?
My ears are ringing--what'd he say?
My ears are *always* ringing... I think he said, *"Make it quick."*
No, wait-- I'm a mutant, and--

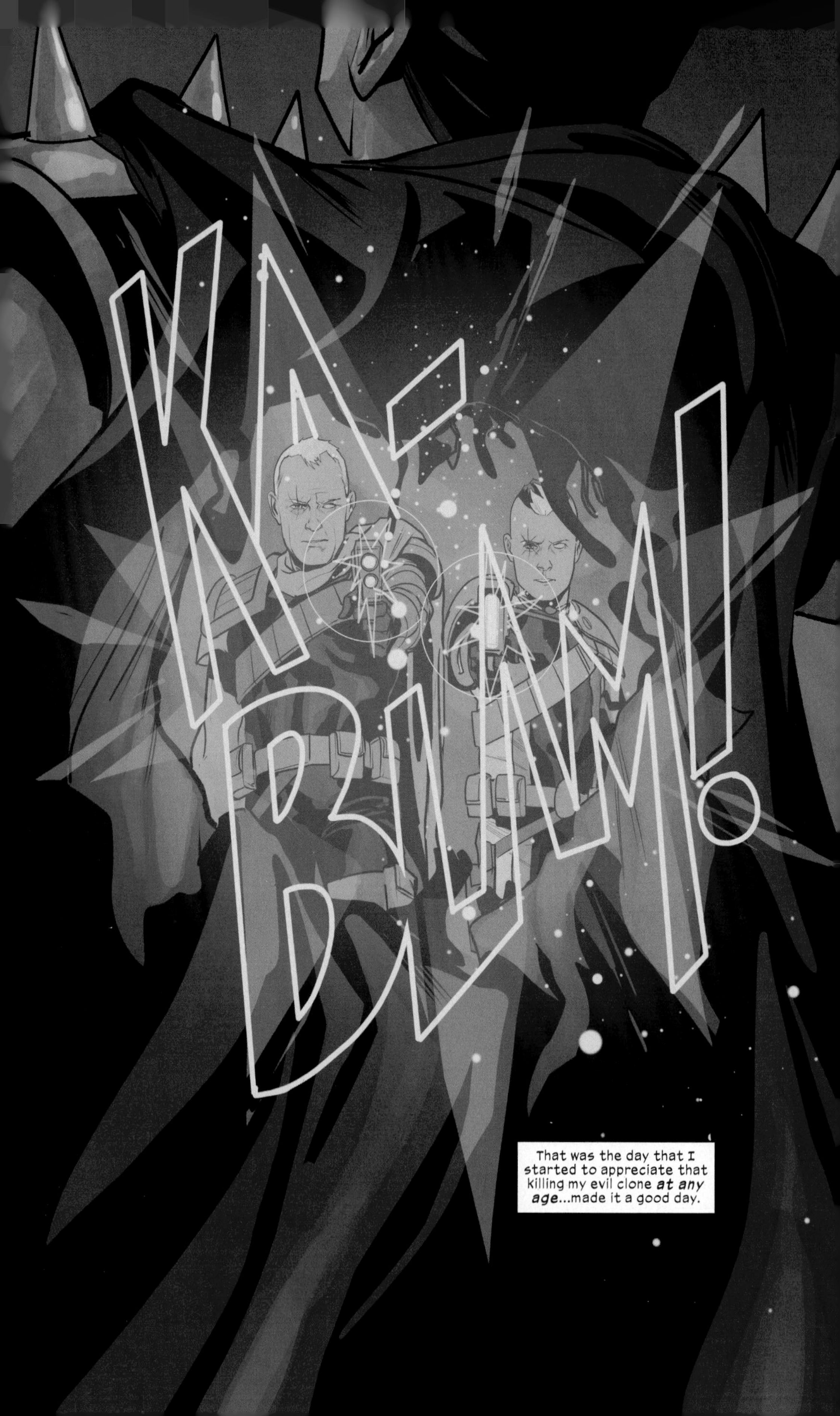
KA-BLAM!
That was the day that I started to appreciate that killing my evil clone *at any age*...made it a good day.

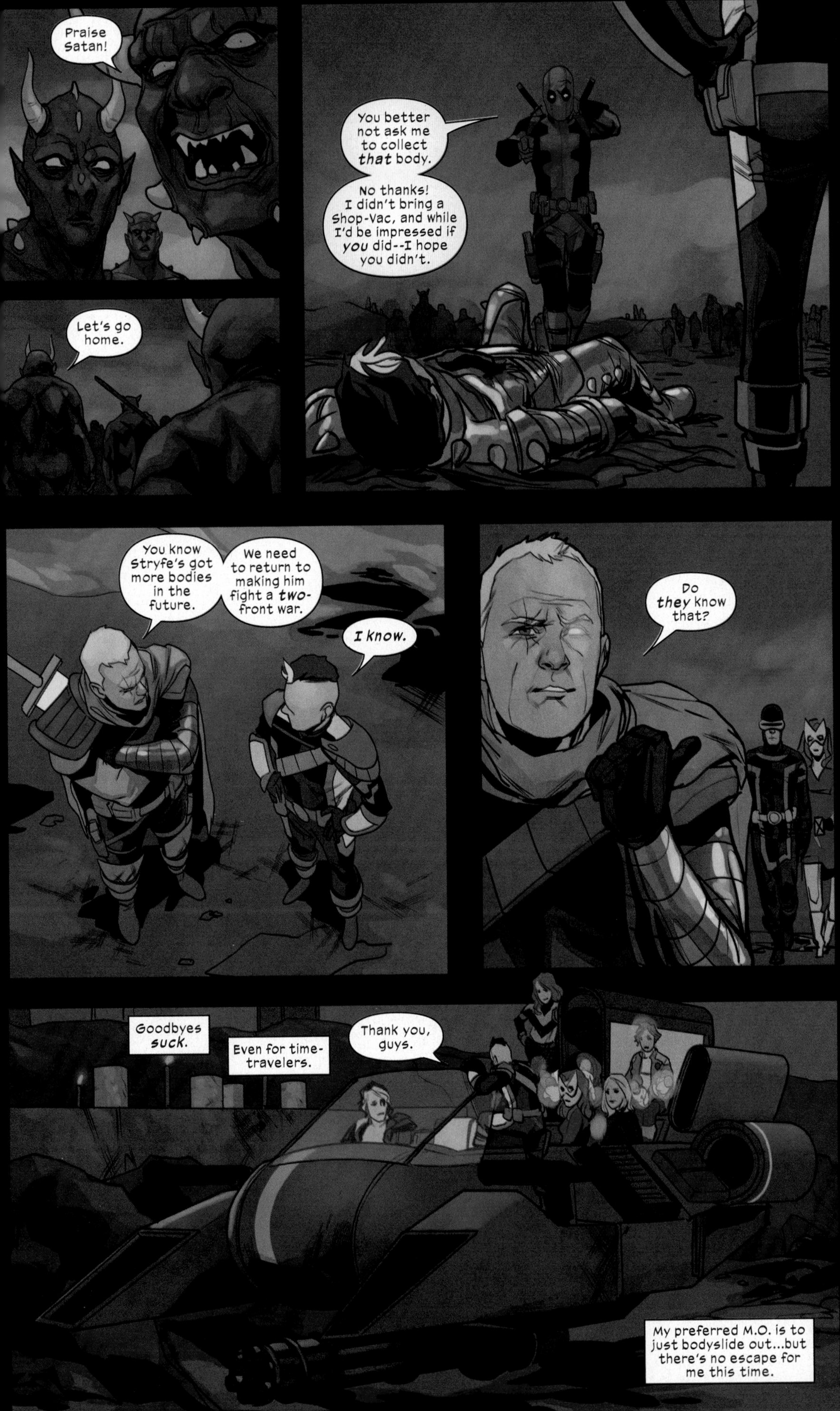

Praise Satan!
Let's go home.
You better not ask me to collect *that* body.
No thanks! I didn't bring a Shop-Vac, and while I'd be impressed if *you* did--I hope you didn't.
You know Stryfe's got more bodies in the future.
We need to return to making him fight a *two*-front war.
I know.
Do *they* know that?
Goodbyes *suck*.
Even for time-travelers.
Thank you, guys.
My preferred M.O. is to just bodyslide out...but there's no escape for me this time.

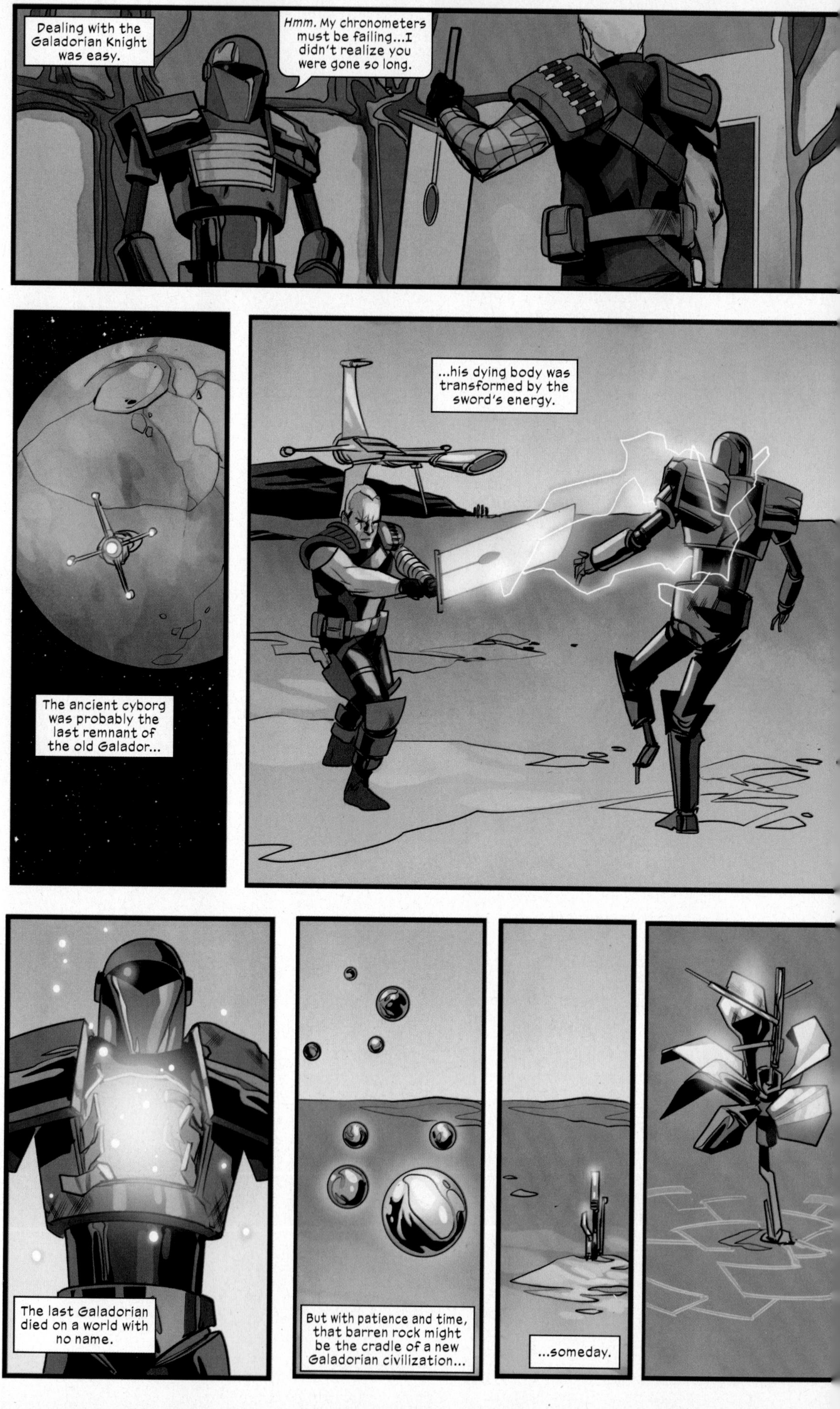
Dealing with the Galadorian Knight was easy.
Hmm. My chronometers must be failing...I didn't realize you were gone so long.
The ancient cyborg was probably the last remnant of the old Galador...
...his dying body was transformed by the sword's energy.
The last Galadorian died on a world with no name.
But with patience and time, that barren rock might be the cradle of a new Galadorian civilization...
...someday.

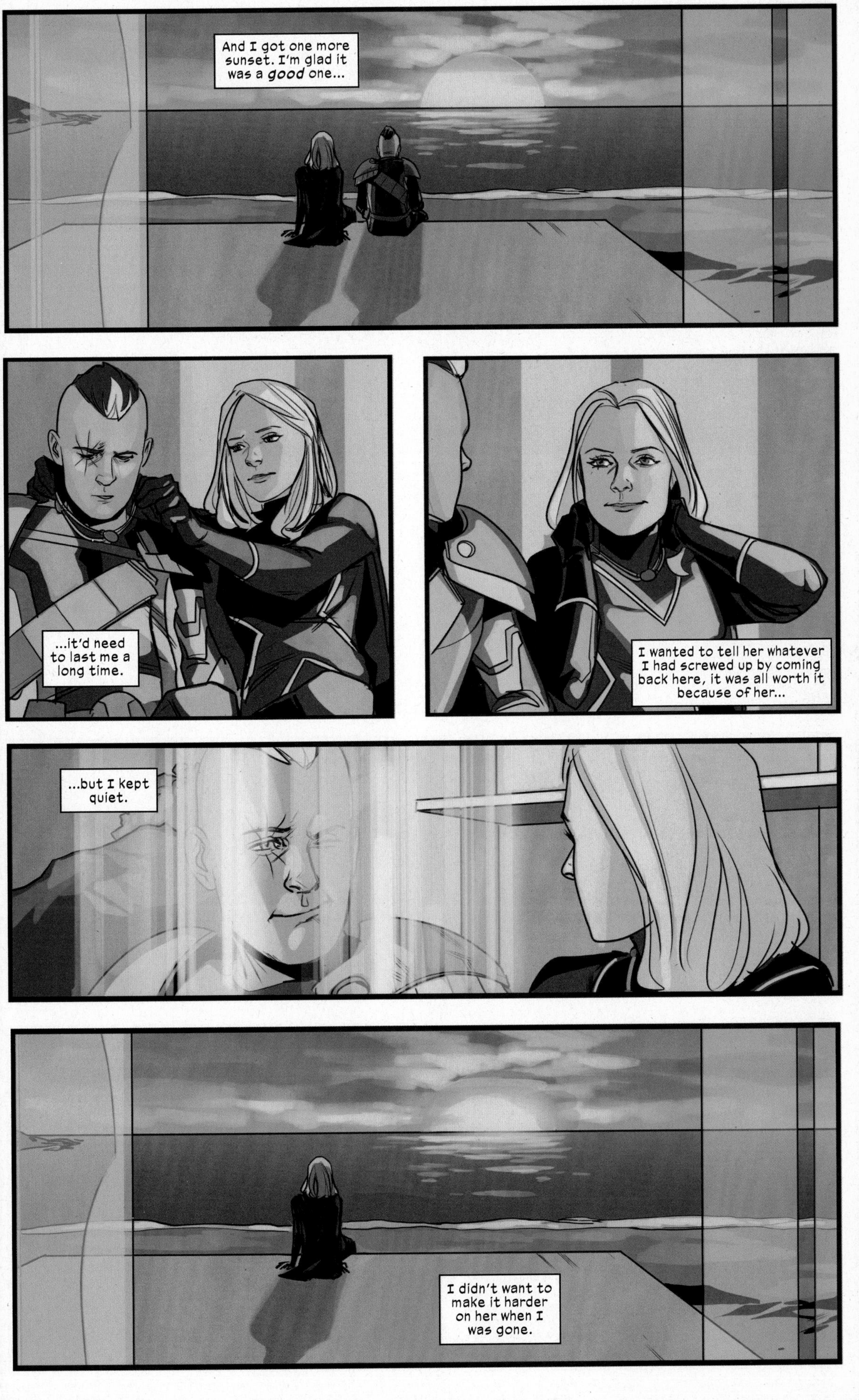

And I got one more sunset. I'm glad it was a *good* one...
...it'd need to last me a long time.
I wanted to tell her whatever I had screwed up by coming back here, it was all worth it because of her...
...but I kept quiet.
I didn't want to make it harder on her when I was gone.

It was harder at home on the Moon.

You know when to find me if you need me.

What do we do to win?

Whatever it takes.

You make me proud at any age.

Go give 'em hell.

Thanks.

Bodyslide by one.

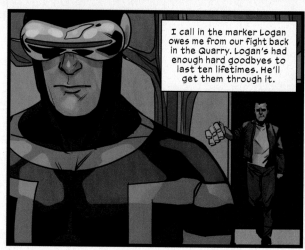

I call in the marker Logan owes me from our fight back in the Quarry. Logan's had enough hard goodbyes to last ten lifetimes. He'll get them through it.

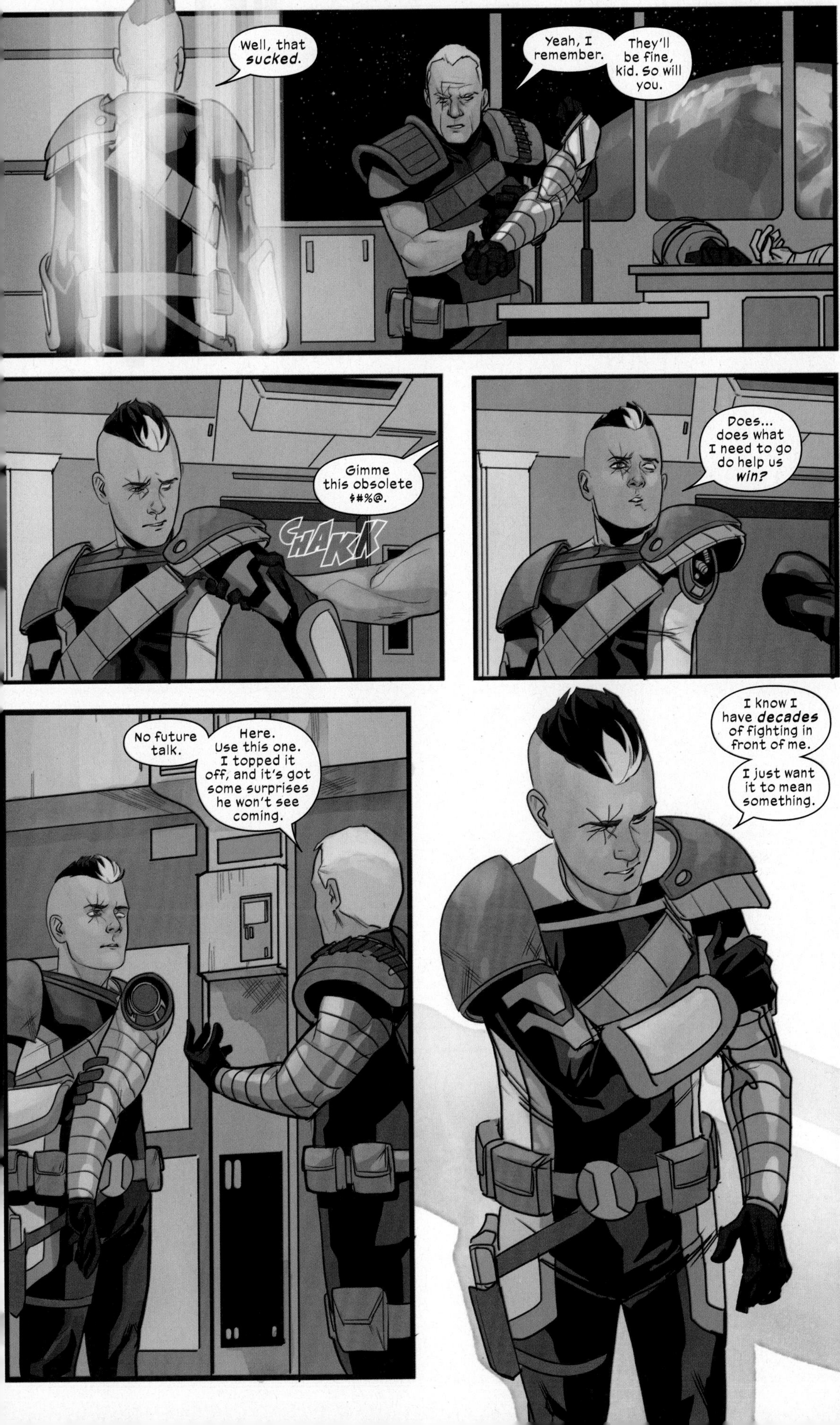
Well, that sucked.
Yeah, I remember.
They'll be fine, kid. So will you.
Gimme this obsolete $#%@.
CHAKK
Does... does what I need to go do help us win?
No future talk.
Here. Use this one. I topped it off, and it's got some surprises he won't see coming.
I know I have decades of fighting in front of me.
I just want it to mean something.

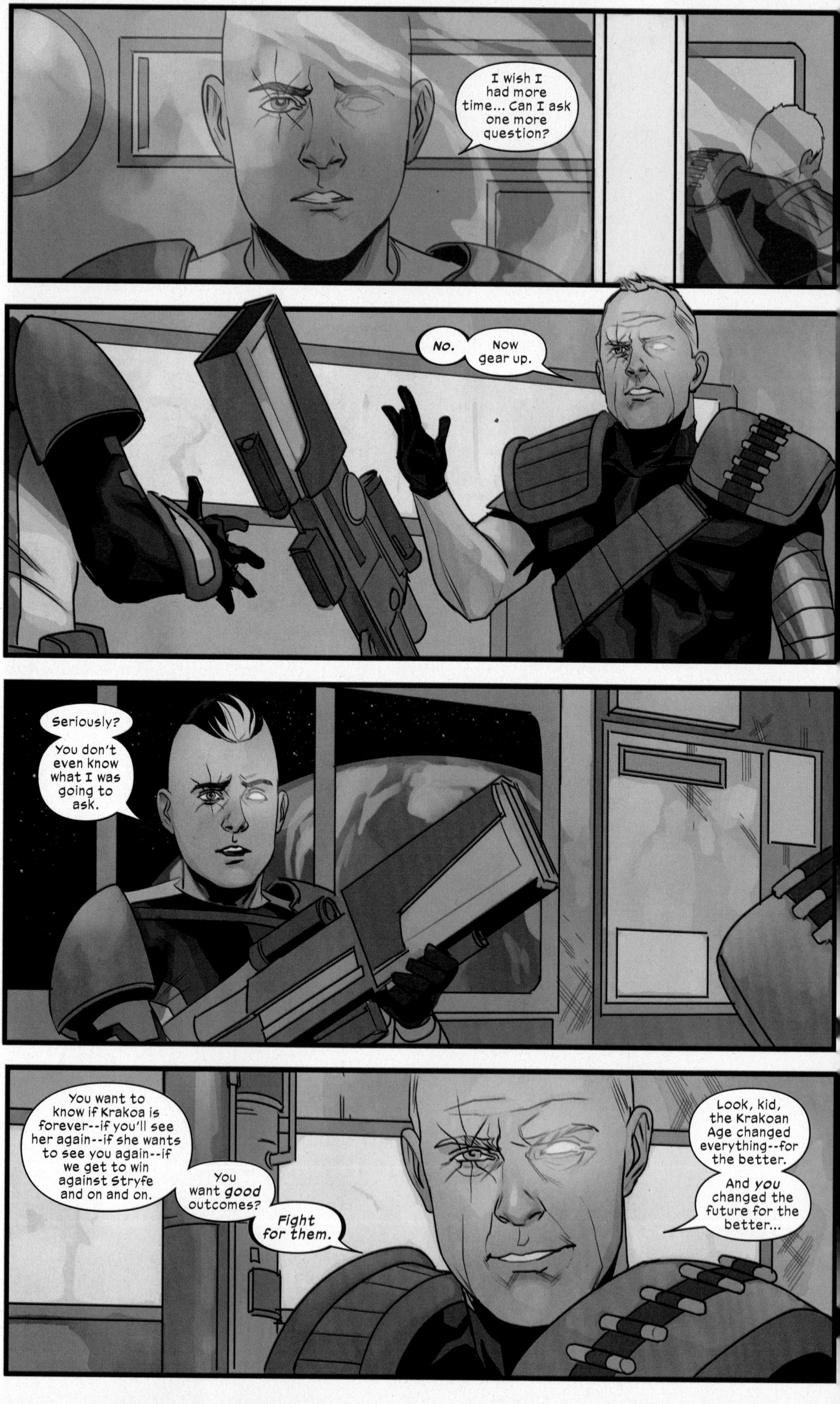
I wish I had more time... Can I ask one more question?
No.
Now gear up.
Seriously?
You don't even know what I was going to ask.
You want to know if Krakoa is forever--if you'll see her again--if she wants to see you again--if we get to win against Stryfe and on and on.
You want *good* outcomes?
Fight for them.
Look, kid, the Krakoan Age changed everything--for the better.
And *you* changed the future for the better...

"...we all have more, but now we have more to *lose* if we slip up."

Stupid little @#$%.

Go easy on that kid, old man.

He's got a soft spot in my heart.

Have fun dying.

I always do.

See you on the other side.

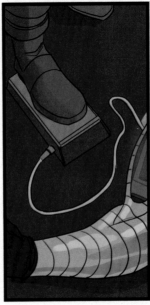

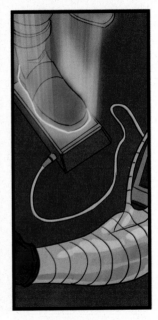

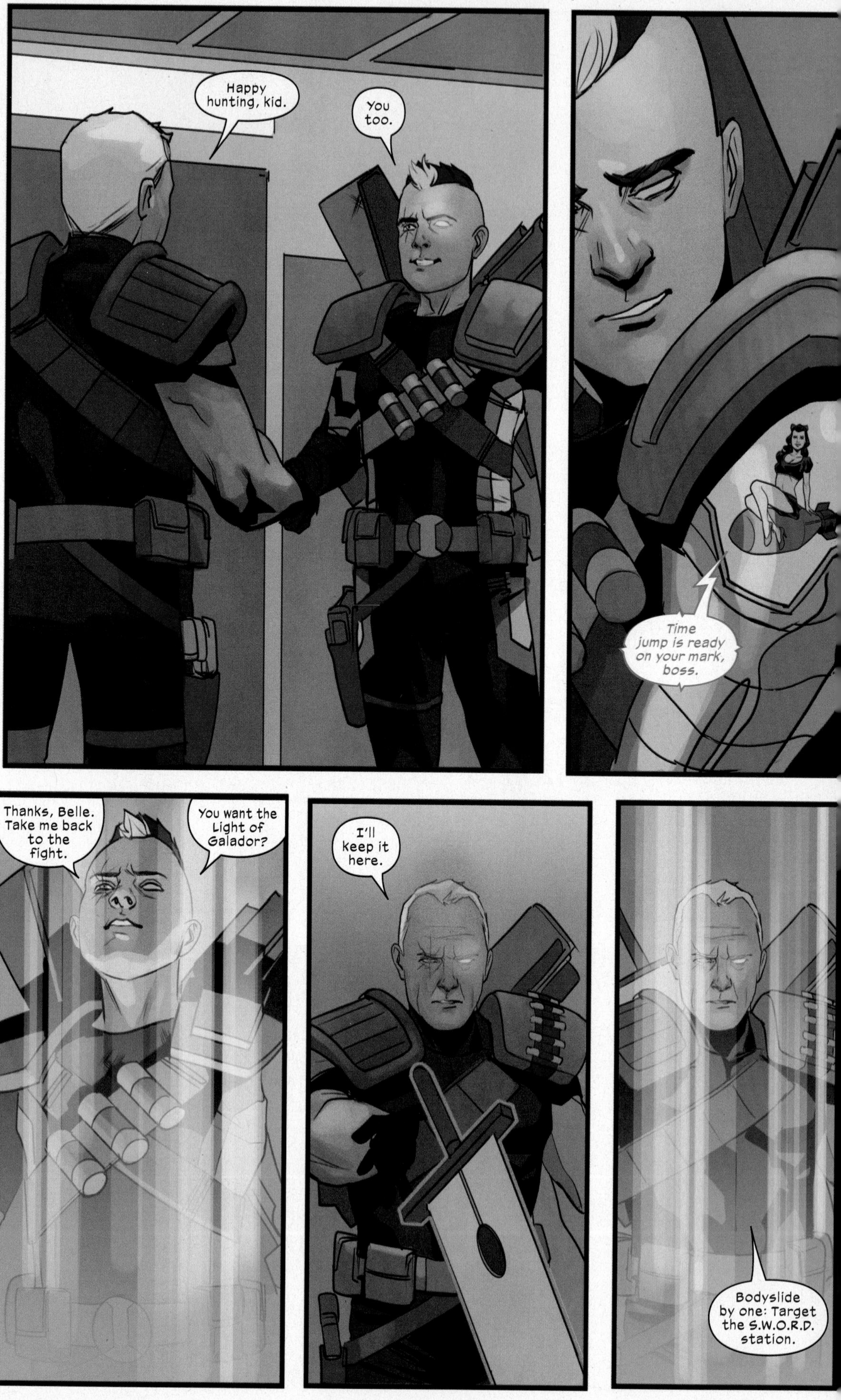
Happy hunting, kid.
You too.
Time jump is ready on your mark, boss.
Thanks, Belle. Take me back to the fight.
You want the Light of Galador?
I'll keep it here.
Bodyslide by one: Target the S.W.O.R.D. station.

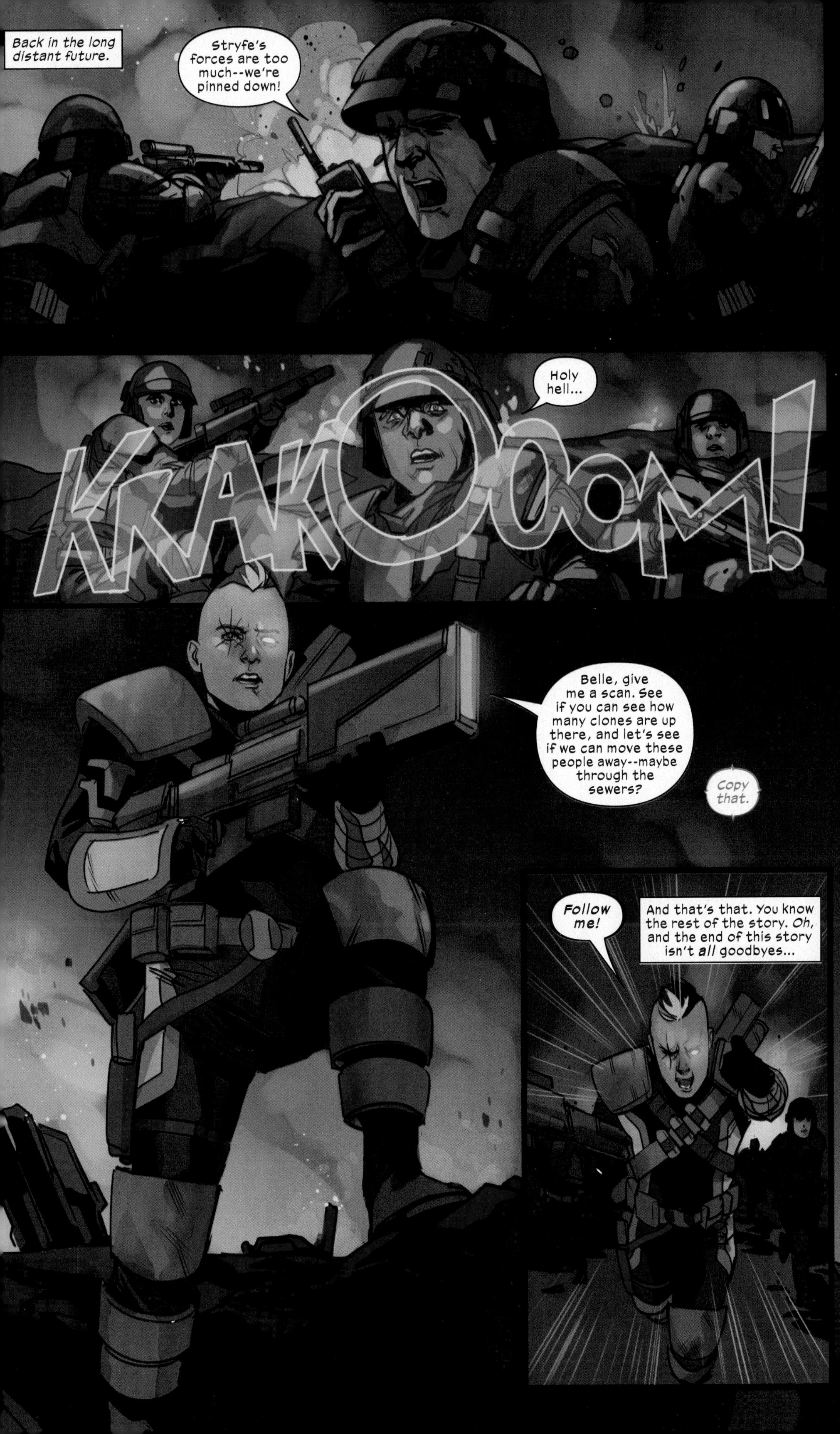
Back in the long distant future.
Stryfe's forces are too much--we're pinned down!
Holy hell...
KRAKOOOOM!
Belle, give me a scan. See if you can see how many clones are up there, and let's see if we can move these people away--maybe through the sewers?
Copy that.
Follow me!
And that's that. You know the rest of the story. Oh, and the end of this story isn't all goodbyes...

The five mutant families were reunited with their kidnapped children. And their new twins.

It was awful losing the baby for as long as we did...

...but I don't mind the sudden addition. They'll be able to keep each other company.

They'll always have each other.

Strange things seem to happen to mutant families.

Sometimes your one baby gets kidnapped and two of them return to you...

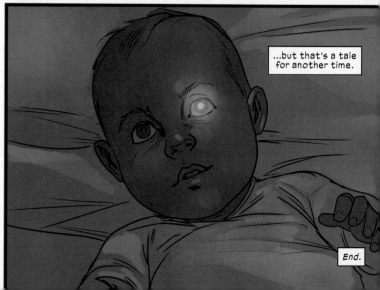

...but that's a tale for another time.

End.

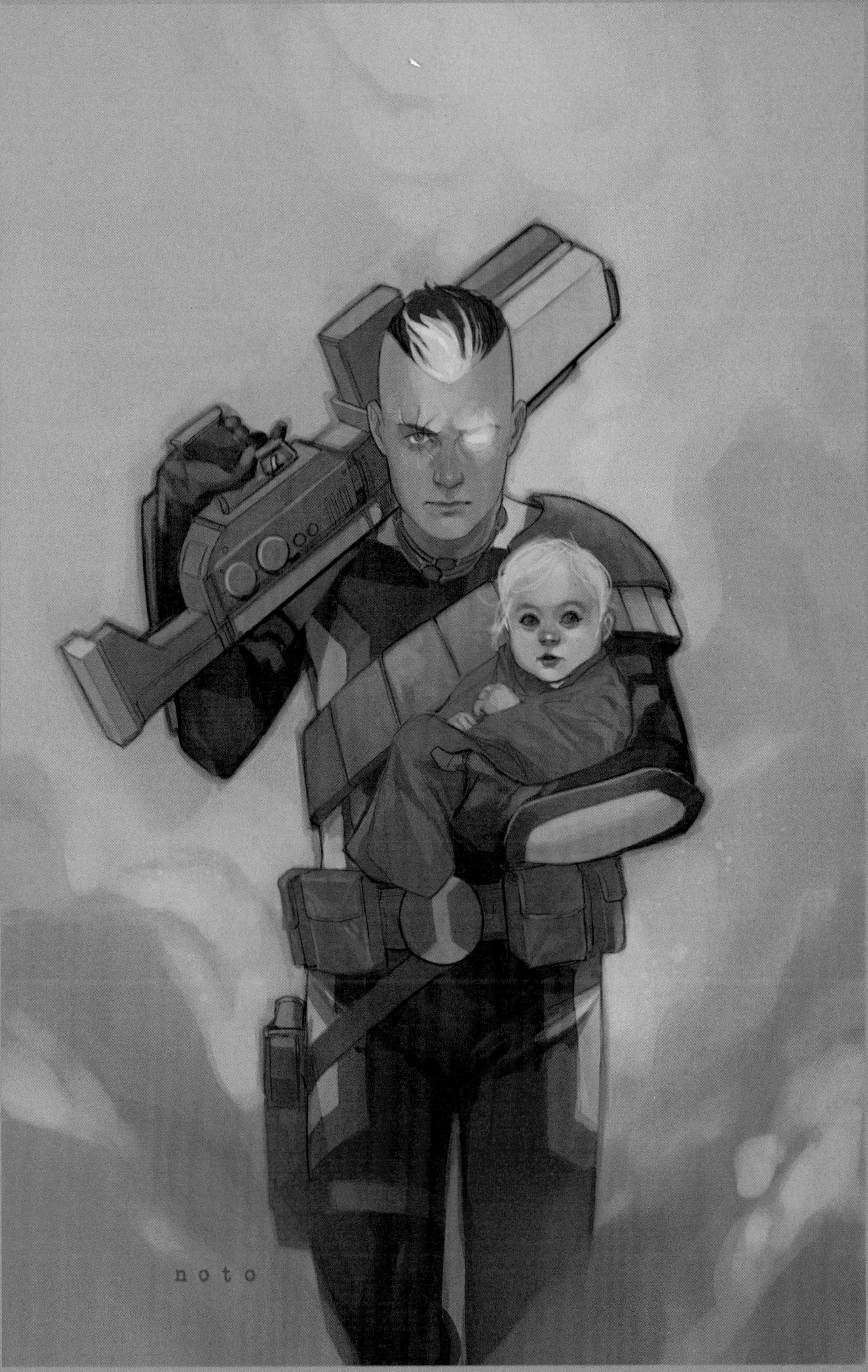
noto

Cable #7 by Phil Noto

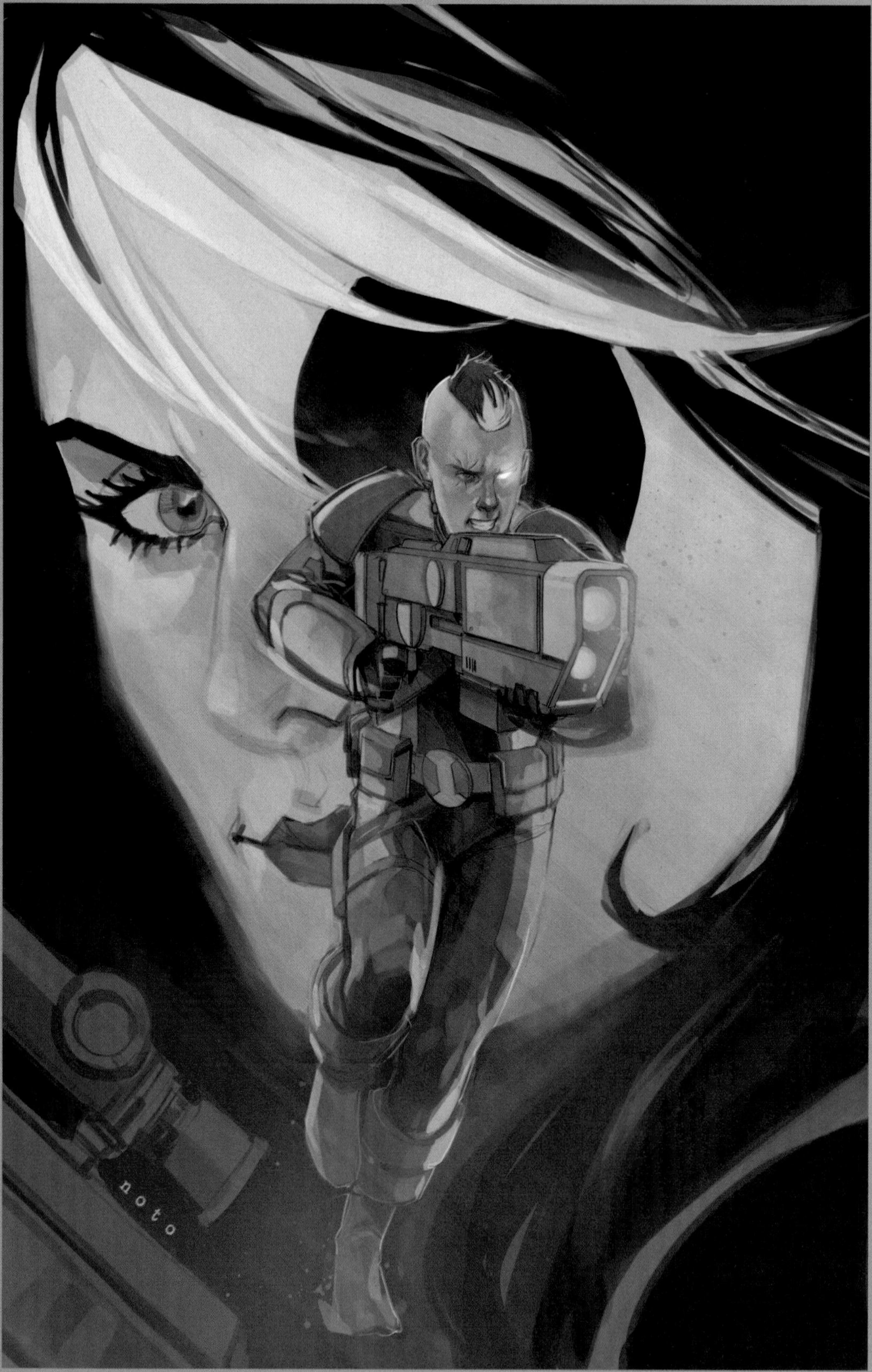
noto

Cable #8 by Phil Noto

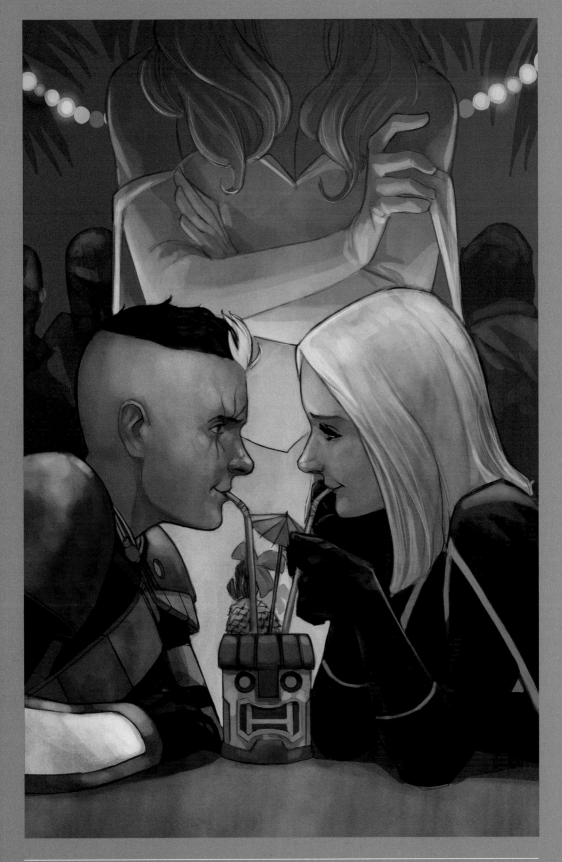

Cable #9   by Phil Noto

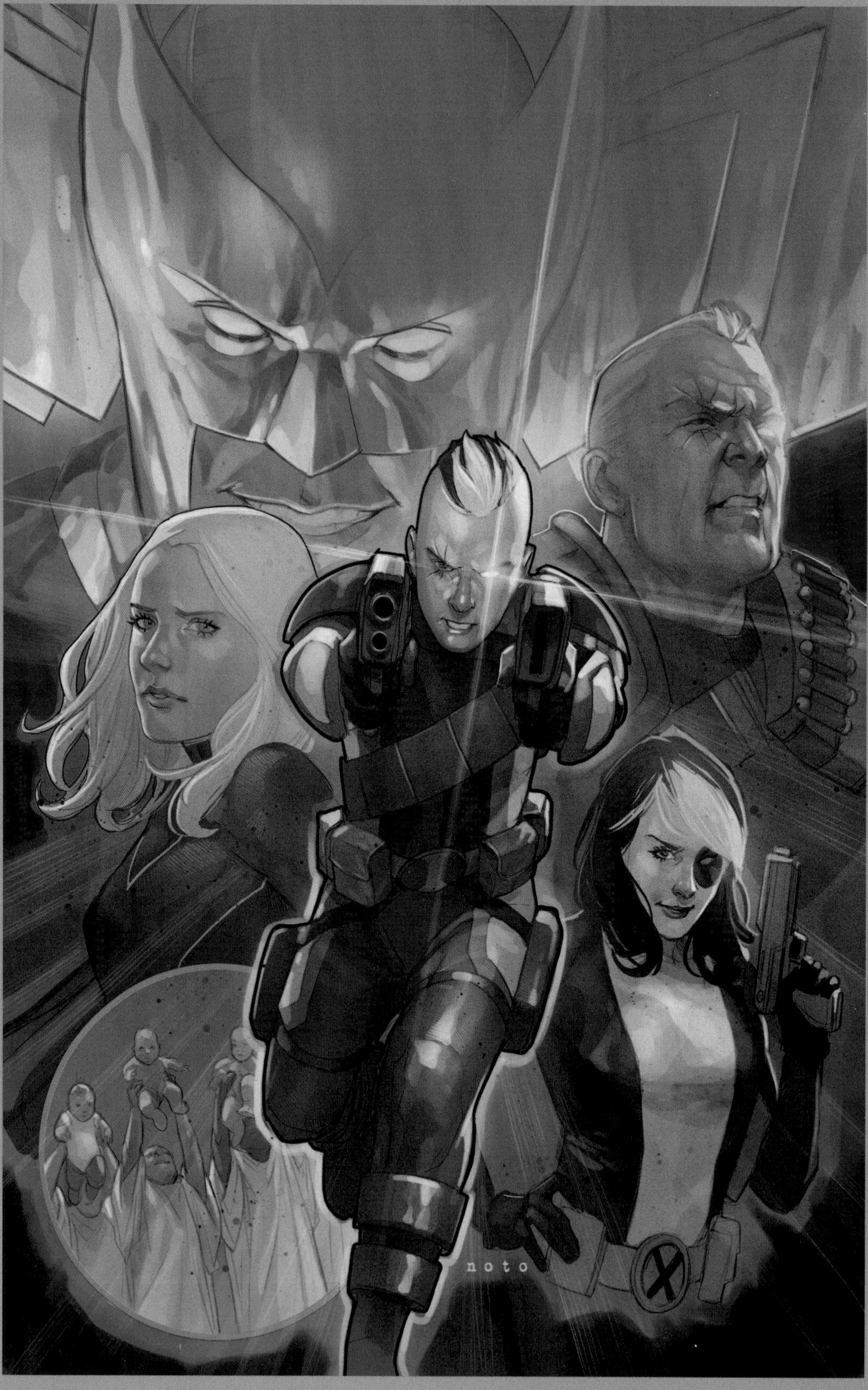
noto

Cable #10 by Phil Noto

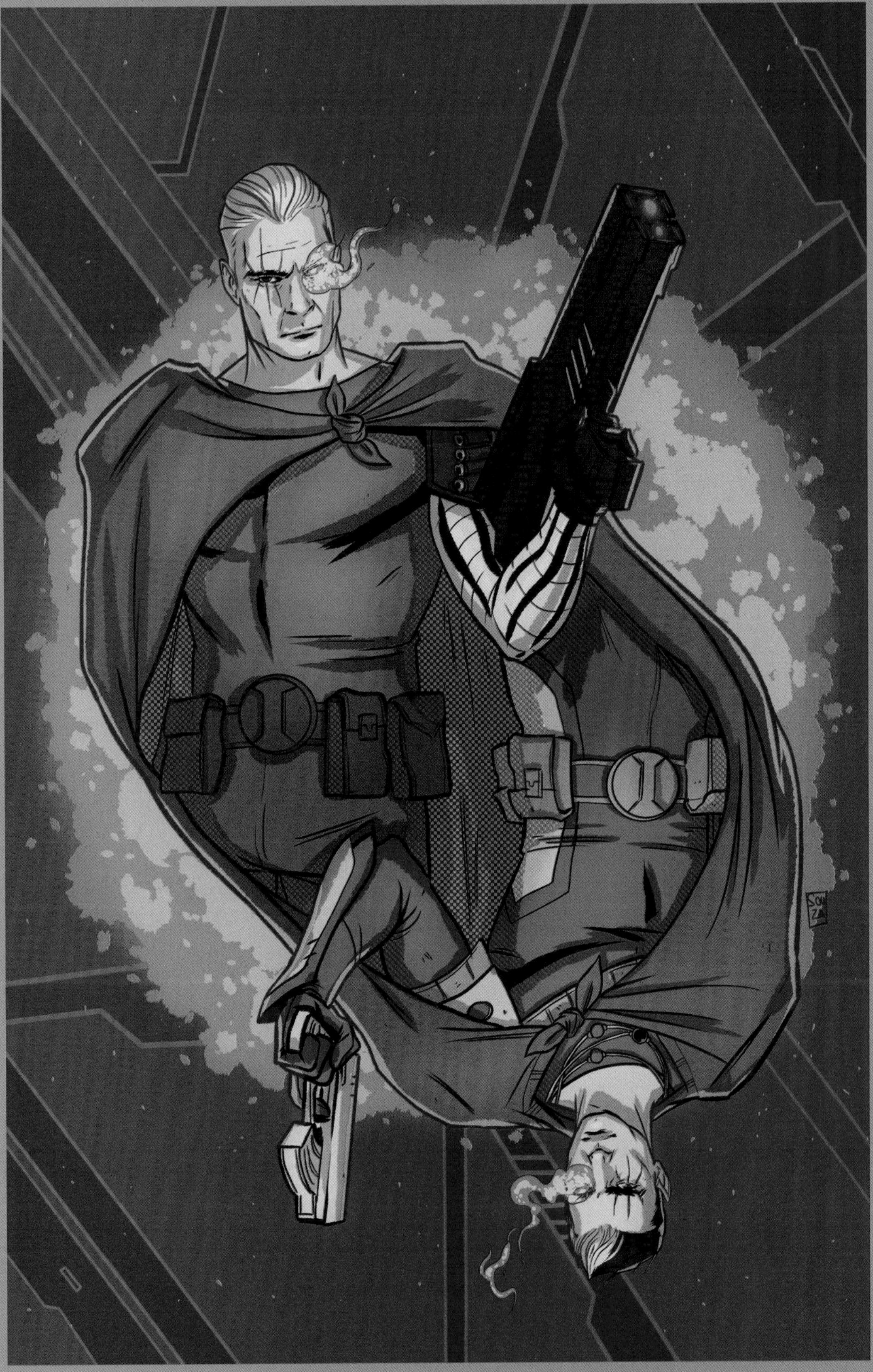

Cable #12 Variant by Ernanda Souza

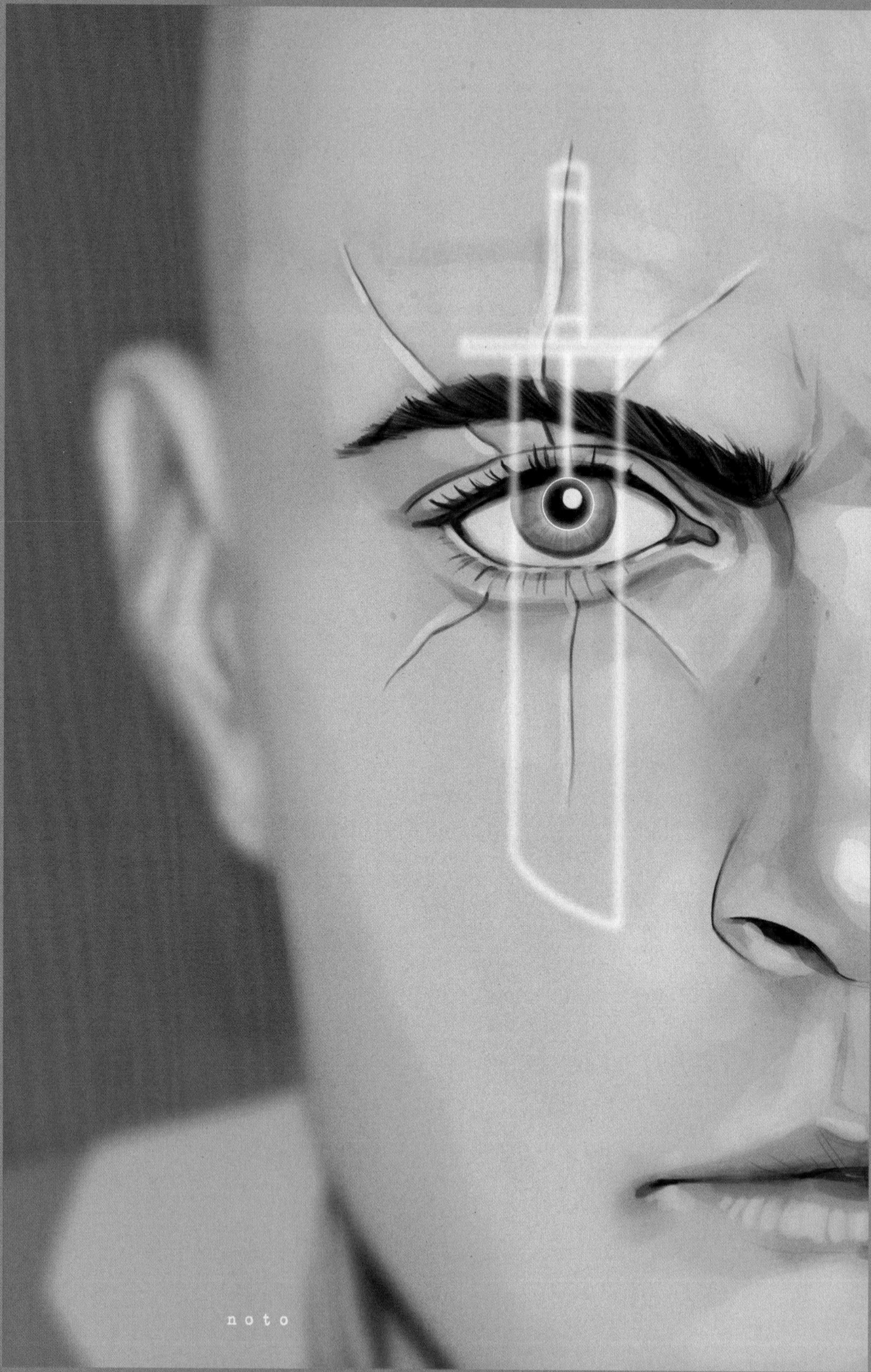
noto

Cable #11 by Phil Noto

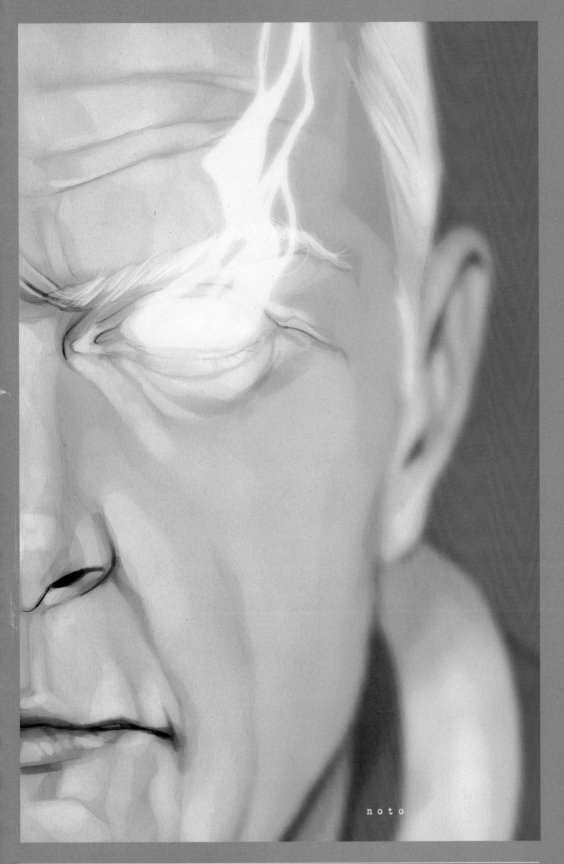

noto

Cable #12   by Phil Noto